COMMON SENSE
POLICE SUPERVISION

ABOUT THE AUTHOR

GERALD W. GARNER, a 40-year veteran of law enforcement, is Chief of the Greeley, Colorado Police Department. Specializing in law enforcement leadership, police-press relations and officer survival, he has written six books and over 200 magazine articles. He instructs widely and has served as a guest lecturer for the FBI National Academy, the International Association of Chiefs of Police, the Western Institute for Police Administration and the National Park Service. He also has extensive experience instructing for police academies and colleges.

Garner holds a Master's Degree in Administration of Justice and is a P.O.S.T. certified law enforcement instructor in Colorado. His undergraduate degree is in Journalism.

During his law enforcement career the author has held various assignments including patrol officer, patrol sergeant, detective sergeant, crime prevention specialist, SWAT hostage negotiator, public information officer, watch commander and division chief. Greeley, a city of 90,000 people, is the second jurisdiction in which he has served as law enforcement chief executive.

Fourth Edition

COMMON SENSE POLICE SUPERVISION

Practical Tips for the First-Line Leader

By

GERALD W. GARNER

Chief
Greeley Police Department
Greeley, Colorado

CHARLES C THOMAS • PUBLISHER, LTD.
Springfield • Illinois • U.S.A.

Published and Distributed Throughout the World by

CHARLES C THOMAS • PUBLISHER, LTD.
2600 South First Street
Springfield, Illinois 62794-9265

© 2008 by CHARLES C THOMAS • PUBLISHER, LTD.

ISBN 978-0-398-07833-1 (hard)
ISBN 978-0-398-07834-8 (paper)

Library of Congress Catalog Card Number: 2008026861

First Edition, 1981
Second Edition, 1995
Third Edition, 2003
Fourth Edition, 2008

With THOMAS BOOKS *careful attention is given to all details of manufacturing
and design. It is the Publisher's desire to present books that are satisfactory as to their
physical qualities and artistic possibilities and appropriate for their particular use.*
THOMAS BOOKS *will be true to those laws of quality that assure a good name
and good will.*

Printed in the United States of America
MM-R-3

Library of Congress Cataloging in Publication Data

Garner, Gerald W.
    Common sense police supervision : practical tips for the first-line leader /
by Gerald W. Garner. – 4th ed.
        p. cm.
    Includes index.
    ISBN 978-0-398-97833-1 (hard)–ISBN 078-0-398-07834-8 (pbk.)
    1. Police–Supervisor of. 1. Title.

HV7936.S8G37 2008
363.2'2–dc22   2008026861

*To
Kathy*

PREFACE

The supervision of law enforcement personnel is unlike any other endeavor on Earth. It is not easy. The work is saddled with great challenges, but it can produce tremendous rewards.

A great deal has been written and spoken about law enforcement supervision and leadership. Some of it has been quite helpful. At other times, theory has smothered practicality. Considerable psychobabble and "modern management" gibberish has been uttered on the topic. Neither is very useful to the working law enforcement leader.

This book aims to stimulate the veteran, novice, or would-be police supervisor to utilize his or her most powerful tool in carrying out the duties of an effective leader. That tool is COMMON SENSE. Made up of life experience, good judgment, prudence, and a well-developed ability for solid reasoning and logical decision making, common sense will guide the intelligent individual in finding effective solutions to most of the problems he or she will encounter while leading police personnel.

The first edition of *Common Sense Police Supervision* presented the basics needed by the successful police supervisor. The second edition bolstered them and added chapters for the leader facing the twin challenges of leading his troops into the era of community-oriented policing while keeping them safe on the street. The third edition updated the leadership guidelines and added two more chapters. One chapter furnished the law enforcement leader with the know-how he will need when called upon to represent his agency in front of the news media. The second offered him guidance in leading his people to provide exceptional customer service in a day when true service is increasingly rare. This edition furnishes more real-life examples pertaining to leadership issues and adds yet another chapter, this one aimed at helping the leader plan his future in a law enforcement organization.

This book will not enable its reader to speak glibly in the latest, pop management catch phrases and buzz words. What it DOES offer is solid, practical leadership advice developed from the experiences and observations of real police supervisors.

While this text emphasizes the extreme importance of the police sergeant, its contents will be of equal value to anyone in a position of leadership in a law enforcement agency. Although the narrative most often uses the male gender, it should be obvious to all that the choice is for ease of reading only. Women long ago established that they are the equal of their male counterparts as effective law enforcement leaders. In the future they should be better represented in law enforcement's leadership ranks.

It is the author's sincere belief that the current or wannabe supervisor who follows the dictates of his or her ethics, conscience and common sense cannot help but serve law enforcement as a highly capable leader. It is towards that potential for excellence that these efforts are directed.

G.W.G.

INTRODUCTION

It is impossible to learn too much about how to be an effective leader. A great leader never stops learning. He or she does it for the right reason: to help others by helping guide the people, policies, and operations of a modern law enforcement organization. But there is a more "selfish" yet equally legitimate reason for learning to excel as a leader. In a world in which seemingly everyone is willing to sue everybody else for just about anything under the sun, the responsible police supervisor will see to it that he protects his organization, his people, and himself by doing things the right way for the right reasons at all times. Equally important, he will ensure that those he leads do the same. He will assure that any lawsuit ever targeted on him and his agency alleging "failure to supervise" does not accurately describe the way in which he leads his law enforcement employees.

This book emphasizes the real value of common sense in good leadership practices. The first two chapters examine just what supervision means and seek to show the hopeful leader what he or she needs to know and do to make the leap from front-line officer to first-line supervisor.

Chapter Three discusses supervisory ethics and professional responsibilities while Chapter Four explores the key qualities of true leadership. Chapter Five looks at the police leader's tasks as educator and trainer and offers some helpful hints for succeeding as an instructor. Chapter Six examines the supervisor's vital job as an evaluator of employee performance and gives tips on how to do it well. Pitfalls awaiting the careless job performance appraiser are exposed, too.

Chapter Seven scrutinizes the leader's role as a disciplinarian in the correction process while Chapter Eight covers his or her work as a planner in areas ranging from special operations to personnel deployment to personal goal setting. Meanwhile, Chapter Nine targets the very important communication function and furnishes concrete suggestions for improving both oral and written communication skills. Barriers to effective communication are identified. Chapter Ten supplies problem-solving advice to aid the police leader as an effective counselor to subordinates experiencing a variety of difficulties.

Chapter Eleven sees the law enforcement leader as a manager of human and material resources who can visualize the integral parts of the organizational "Big Picture." Chapter Twelve delves into the difficult job of the complaint or grievance processor. The proper handling of allegations of police misconduct is detailed. Chapter Thirteen takes a candid look at some special problems such as organizational survival for the ethical police leader.

Chapter Fourteen analyzes the first-line leader's pivotal role in today's community-oriented style of policing. Chapter Fifteen reminds the police leader of his or her responsibilities as a teacher, inspector, advocate and role model for officer safety.

The last three chapters are presented in a slightly different format than the rest of the book. Chapter Sixteen gives the first-line leader the skills he will need when he is given the task of serving as his agency's on-scene spokesperson in front of the ladies and gentlemen of the news media. Chapter Seventeen serves as a resource the leader can rely upon when he educates his subordinates on the intricacies of providing exceptional customer service, a commodity too often missing in both public and private sectors today. Chapter Eighteen is intended to help the police leader in planning his career and his future.

In addition, each chapter concludes with a brief "Points to Remember" section that provides a quickly-read and easily remembered checklist of the chapter's salient points. This feature should prove especially useful for today's in-a-hurry reader.

Not a single law enforcement organization in the country has too many competent leaders. It is time to get on with the task of creating more.

CONTENTS

COMMON SENSE
POLICE SUPERVISION

Chapter One

WHAT IS SUPERVISION?

"He takes care of you."
"He helps you."
"He looks out for your interests."

"He picks on you."
"He gets on your case."
"He's a pain in the neck (or worse)!"

The two separate categories of descriptions would appear to describe two very different individuals. The first set would be good descriptors for Santa Claus or the Tooth Fairy. The second group might better be used to describe Darth Vader or some other character from a bad dream.

Yet, all six of these descriptive comments have been and could be attributable to employees describing a person quite important to their workaday lives: their supervisor. At one time or another, more than a few members of the national work force have felt many or most of these emotions for the man or woman they know as "boss."

In reality, of course, what constitutes a supervisor and the manner in which he supervises is a bit too complex for such simplistic explanations, however sincerely they might be felt.

What, precisely, is a supervisor? What is it the supervisor is supposed to do? Many attempts have been made in an effort to answer that question.

Over the past decade much has been said and written about supervision and supervisors. Some of it has even been put forward by people who *know* something about their subject matter. Such contributions have been valuable to those charged with leadership responsibilities in virtually every field of human endeavor. Many of these hints on how to supervise effectively are equally applicable to both men and women in all types of occupations.

At the same time, however, each field of work has its own peculiarities; it only follows that there must be corresponding adjustments in the supervision function. Law enforcement, by the very nature of the work performed and the special nature of its performers, certainly involves some aspects of supervision not found in other fields of endeavor. This chapter will examine some of these peculiarities and their meanings for supervisors and the supervised.

THEORY AND COMMON SENSE

When one speaks of theories, he is of necessity talking about a particular concept or view of something that generally involves a set of guiding rules or principles. The theorist is most likely proposing an explanation for something in terms of propositions or suggestions of fact. If the theorist happens to be living in the ancient world and is attempting to explain thunder, for example, he may speak in terms of angry gods, riled godly sensibilities, and a need to humble a human race gotten out of line. If, instead, he is a modern management theorist attempting to reason out what it is that motivates people to do work, he may talk of personal needs, drives, and interrelationships.

All of this is well and good. The practical supervisor's most common complaint with the theorist, however, is that he sometimes fails to relate his neatly constructed postulates to the everyday world of work with its attendant everyday crises. The working supervisor may not be a student of formal theories himself. He may be a very pragmatic individual who daily sees the effects of what the theorists are trying to talk about–as seen in his workers and the work they do. He may not be able to label their behavior as neatly as the theorist could do. The important thing for him is that the behavior is real.

Unfortunately, what the formal theorists are trying to say to help the practicing supervisor may be lost or overlooked in the demanding practicalities of the everyday push to get the job done. At the same time, the working supervisor, regardless of his field, does have something going for him that many theorists may heed far too little in their well-intentioned efforts. That very real something is frequently referred to as *common sense.*

In defining common sense, dictionaries use such phrases as "normal intelligence" and "practical sense." Common sense includes considerably more. Common sense also entails the practical application of good judgment, prudence, and an aptitude for calm and logical reasoning. It is the total of formal learning added to life experience. Yet its total is more than formal education and life added up. Common sense might be what the bright if "uncivilized" individual with no formal training whatever might apply when faced with a new situation or problem.

The police officer must, of necessity, possess a large ration of common sense. It sees him through the field situation or crisis that no training manual or departmental procedure deals with directly. By applying good common sense to procedures or techniques which he *has* been taught this very practical officer frequently can solve the unique problem at hand.

It is not reasonable to expect that a supervisor can survive and prosper with only good common sense and nothing else any more than it is reasonable to assume that the patrol officer can successfully do his job with no formal training and only his ample common sense to guide his actions. With common sense *and* some training in practical skills and a bit of theory, the contemporary supervisor can do his best as a leader.

Theory of supervision can be picked up from a myriad of books and professional journal articles. It will remain this book's aim to show the supervisor the great potential contained within the intelligent application of his own common sense to a variety of supervisory tasks.

SUPERVISION IN GENERAL

Not unlike the term *common sense,* the word "supervision" invites some fairly standard responses in any attempt at definition. One often sees references to "the overseeing of the actions or performances of others." Another not unreasonable phrase notes that supervision is "the act of directing and controlling the talents and actions of others in carrying out certain goals and objectives." With the exception of "overseeing," a term that seems to reek of bullwhips, the given definitions for supervision are quite acceptable for present purposes. Supervision must, in fact, deal with workers and their actions, abilities, and work products. In the case of the police employee, that work product will be delivered in the form of police service.

It is perhaps enough to say that the supervisor of any sort of work will find himself involved in certain, universal functions and responsibilities of leadership. First of all, he will be expected to lead. Unfortunately, it is possible to direct and control others (although with very little success) without setting the right example that a good leader provides. In this manner, the ineffective supervisor can temporarily get away with espousing the old "do as I say, not as I do" philosophy. His shortcomings are, however, destined to catch up with him.

The true leader knows that he cannot afford such a morally lazy approach to supervision. He does not ask anything of his subordinates that he is incapable of living up to or accomplishing himself.

A "follow me" philosophy can cover a wide range of activities and expectations. A patrol supervisor, for example, could hardly exhort his officers to maintain a high degree of physical fitness while he nurtures a fat gut himself. Likewise, his exhortations to avoid anything short of absolute integrity would look a little pale as long as he is personally accepting payoffs from the precinct's biggest bookmaker. The true leader does not operate that way.

The supervisor also will be responsible for the continuing training of his charges. Whether he is working in an ice-cream factory or a police detective bureau, the supervisor will shoulder the responsibility for preparing his people for their roles. Some of this preparation may come from written materials; other parts of it may spring from a "hands on" practice session. Still more may be furnished via computer programs, lectures, discussions, and demonstrations. It will be the job of the supervisor to tailor and guide this imparting of knowledge and skills to all of his employees.

As an educator and trainer, the supervisor in just about any line of work will have to stay abreast of the latest approaches and devices for the transmittal of new knowledge to others. As a teacher himself, he will have to develop his own abilities to attract and hold the attention of his students while he endeavors to impart his subject matter.

The supervisor will be a planner. Whether he is plotting how many chickens he will need when his caterers feed the family reunion or how many officers he will have to have for his patrol team to handle the ball-game crowd, he will be a planner. The supervisor's planning duties will range from relatively uncomplicated daily decision making to special projects and assignments for his boss. Whether he is scheduling the deployment of a patrol team or laboring over the chief's annual report, the police supervisor will need the skills of a planner.

The supervisor in any field will be a disciplinarian, too. The correction of improper conduct by his subordinates will be an important responsibility that he will not treat lightly. In his disciplinary function, the supervisor will not be working in an entirely negative area. His disciplinary efforts will be addressed more to changed behavior and improved performance than to outright punishment. He will be attempting to change for the better his peoples' actions. He will not be attempting to change the people themselves.

The responsibility to discipline fairly and wisely will sometimes be an uncomfortable burden for the leader to bear. Nonetheless, his decisions and actions as a disciplinarian will impact heavily upon the effectiveness of his subordinates as individuals and the organization as a whole. The duty to discipline, he will find, is a task he can never afford to avoid by "kicking it upstairs" or by blaming unpopular decisions on others. His unique position as part labor, part management demands that he be heard by his boss as the best judge of what is fair and proper discipline for one of his subordinates in a given situation.

Whatever his business or profession, the supervisor will be a counselor, confidant, and nonjudgmental listener. He will be a sympathetic ear for troubled employees. Where it is within his power to do so, he will attempt to help them solve their difficulties, job related and otherwise. While he will not be their solution, he will try to help them to find one. Where the problem lies outside of his area of expertise or authority, he will attempt to find a source that can provide the needed aid for his employee.

As a counselor, the supervisor will be patient. He will learn via experience when a subordinate may not want any specific action from him, but merely to be heard. This venting of frustrations and gripes will be recognized as healthful and necessary by the empathetic supervisor. He will listen.

As a counselor, the supervisor also will talk. He will give careful advice, knowing that a misunderstood or mistaken recommendation could boomerang on the troubled employee. The experienced supervisor will know when not to talk, too. He will recognize the appropriate confidences given him by his employees as things to be guarded and never misused.

The supervisor will support his charges when they need a boost. He also will have courage enough to tell them when they are wrong. Friendship will not prevent him from cutting off improper or dangerous conduct. A true friend should do no less.

Whether he is drafting an order for making truck tires or writing a news release for a police department's community relations program, the good supervisor will excel in the concise use of words as tools. He will put clarity and accuracy into his own communications, whether written or oral. He will expect the same of his subordinates and help them learn to achieve this goal. His allied role of teacher will come into play here.

As a communicator, the supervisor will gain understanding of just how the exchange of thoughts, ideas, and information occurs. He will begin to see how dangerous blocks to good communication can occur and will learn to remedy such breakdowns.

The supervisor will be an arbitrator and complaint processor for diverse persons, groups, and interests. If he is a supervisor in a department store, he will no doubt hear from the customers about how they were insulted by his clerks. He will hear from his clerks about how they were abused by the customers. Then, he may hear from the clerks' union about how the clerks were mistreated by customers and company alike.

If the supervisor happens to be a police sergeant, he will listen to complaints from citizens about how they were mistreated by his officers. He will hear gripes from the officers concerning the abuse directed at them by the populace and the police department. Then, he may find himself caught up in a grievance proceeding brought about by the police employees' association against the agency and its supervisors, including him!

Quite obviously, the supervisor can be no stranger to complaints and problems without and within the organization. His leadership role will expose him to various inquiries and complaints from above and below. His role as "somebody in authority" will target him for distressed customers and citizens. His position as one who disciplines, evaluates, and controls subordinates will identify him as a contact and an occasional opponent for employees' associations and unions. Dissatisfied, confused, and unhappy people will, of necessity, be a part of the supervisor's work world.

The supervisor will be a performance evaluator. He will rate and grade the actions and work products of his subordinates, just as his own efforts are rated by others in turn. He will assess performance in order to secure changes in work activities, attitudes, and results that will benefit employee, employer, and the customer being served. He will identify weaknesses and recommend additional training or changes in operational procedures, where indicated. He will reward superior performance and take corrective action in problem areas.

As an evaluator, the supervisor will be impartial, thorough, and accurate. He will report facts, not assumptions. He will communicate clearly his evaluation findings to both the employee being evaluated and his own reviewing superiors. He will be prepared to back his findings with specific proofs, not general innuendos.

The supervisor will be a manager, too. When called upon to do so, he will be capable of helping formulate his employer's policies as well as specific operational guidelines. He will be able to work smoothly with persons from other parts of the organization and with officials from other firms or agencies.

The supervisor carrying out his managerial functions will meet the public and present an accurate image of his organization, whether that organization manufactures "whatnots" or provides police services.

The supervisor will help fulfill his managerial responsibilities by grooming himself to handle his own superior's job. The supervisor at the small janitorial service may learn the ropes for doing the pay vouchers when his boss is away. The police patrol sergeant may learn the role of watch commander to cover his lieutenant's time off.

Regardless of what specific tasks may be required of the manager in a given line of work, the line supervisor in that field of endeavor prepares himself to handle them for the boss today and, perhaps, to do them for himself tomorrow. He also learns the general responsibilities of the general management role, no matter what sort of specialized work may be involved. He learns to direct, control, and communicate well.

None of these manager's tasks will be new to a good supervisor. He will just be performing them on a little higher plane of responsibility, authority, and accountability. Here his decisions and actions may have an even wider range of influence on the overall organization than his similar activities and decision making as a line supervisor.

All of these functions, and others, will constitute the obligations and rewards of the competent supervisor's job. They remain generally applicable across a wide spectrum of human work activities.

Now, a look at a more specific area of supervisory concerns is in order.

POLICE SUPERVISION IN PARTICULAR

The police supervisor serves more than one master and has more than a few functions. He serves both the individual (his subordinate) and his organization (the police agency). He must show loyalty, fairness, and genuine concern for both.

As for his functions, the police supervisor carries out most of the same duties expected of a supervisor in any area of work: he relays, explains, and obtains compliance with the orders and policies of the agency's managers. He serves as an instructor in his work group. He transmits, where necessary, the worries and problems of the work group to a level of the police organization where they can be acted upon. He evaluates performance of members of the work group, with emphasis upon helping the individual and the organization to reach full potential. He rewards, corrects, and disciplines members of the work group in accordance with their actions.

In such functions the police sergeant or his equivalent is very little different from supervisors elsewhere. Yet, there are some very real differences between what he does and the tasks of the bakery supervisor or road crew boss. It is perhaps that contrast that sets law enforcement apart from all other areas of endeavor. Some of those differences bear further examination for what they may tell about the person who would be a police leader, as well as about the people he leads.

First of all, the "average" police officer's attitude towards his job presents something of a contrast over that of the so-called average worker from other fields. This mythical average policeman may see himself as part of a cause—an idea almost dead in those who work for pay in modern times. As outdated as it may sound, many a police officer truly does see himself as a part of the thin blue line separating the innocent from the carnivores of the world. In this belief, he may not be all that far from correct.

As an element of that cause many police officers profess a strong affection for justice—or the idea that right should prevail over wrong. Indeed, some of these officers will admit that such a belief figured prominently in their decision to seek police work as a career. These same officers may confess a real desire to help out in what they see as a struggle to overcome injustices against those least prepared to defend themselves.

Where it does exist, such a feeling for being a part of a cause can make the police officer easier to supervise than, for example, a bricklayer who may see little in the way of a cause in his tedious physical labor. The wise supervisor will use this high interest in the job in successfully motivating his employees. In this kind of motivation, benefits will accrue to both worker and employer. The worker will obtain satisfaction from doing the job that he personally recognizes as very important. The employer will find reward in a worker who needs little added incentive to do a good job at whatever he undertakes.

At the same time, the police supervisor may discover the pitfalls incumbent in being the leader of a group of workers laboring in a cause. He may find that the police officer who feels so strongly may be terribly unhappy if caught in a menial law enforcement job which he does not feel contributes significantly to that cause. The rookie officer who dreams of chasing murderers but ends up on parking violation duty will be more than a little bit disappointed. He rapidly may become a supervisory problem.

The police officer who feels too strong a zeal for justice and right may also pose a special problem for the police leader. Again, it is one less likely to be found in other fields of work. The officer who decides to mete out illegal "curbside justice" because he has given up on getting justice from the courts provides a huge problem for the supervisor, his agency, and the public at large. Such an officer might be able to convince himself that since no court will ever really punish the brute who broke his own child's arms, the officer must ensure the delivery of that "justice" by breaking a bone or two belonging to the arrested offender. In such a case, the supervisor obviously must act promptly to prevent or interrupt such felonious behavior.

Belief in a cause can definitely have either good or bad influence upon its believer. Whatever the ultimate effect, it will bring about a job interest level not often found elsewhere. It may enable one of its believers to carry on when a difficult task would otherwise be given up as hopeless. It also can bring about real unhappiness when the believer does not feel his employer (or perhaps his supervisor) is doing enough to further the attainment of always unreachable perfection. It will be up to the supervisor to help keep the really committed employee involved in the organization in an active and constructive way.

Perhaps closely allied with the belief in a cause among American police officers is their often expressed need to feel that they are accomplishing something worthwhile for their considerable efforts. An officer who feels this need quite strongly may become a real challenge to his supervisor if he feels his current duty assignment accomplishes little worthy of note. The police supervisor likely will find it necessary to show such an employee the real contributions of his work to the larger team effort, even if those contributions are not high profile ones.

Unfortunately, such a demonstration may not be an easily arranged one. The officer assigned to a relatively limiting job, such as processing report forms or staffing a remote security post, may find the supervisor's explanation of his importance to be unconvincing. Showing this employee some tangible accomplishments for his extended efforts may tax the abilities of the most imaginative police supervisor. The effort remains worthwhile all the same.

True enough, workers in other fields frequently report a similar need for a sense of accomplishment in their work. Police work and police supervision are thereby not unique in their focus on this need. The need for a sense of accomplishment nonetheless remains strong and wide spread enough in the police endeavor to warrant its being considered as a factor of some importance setting apart the police supervisor's tasks from those of work leaders in other areas.

Official concern for his subordinates' personal behavior, off duty as well as on the job, clearly sets the law enforcement supervisor apart from his peers in other fields. In few other jobs is the employee's personal conduct so important and so closely examined from within and without the employing organization. The police officer soon learns that he really does not have exactly the same rights and privileges as do his non-police friends. In reality, he may have less.

He finds that the badge of office he carries sets him just a little bit apart, perhaps as some sort of example of what an honest and responsible citizen should be in contemporary society. The badge can become heavy. Perhaps this is just and is to be expected as a consequence of the oath he took upon entering the police field. Still, he cannot get roaring drunk like his neighbor, indulge in gambling like his barber, or drive his sports car too fast like the guy down the street. He is serving as a very visible example. He has to do what is right.

The police supervisor will sometimes find himself prying into matters that his counterpart in the civilian world would never dream of invading. The electrician's supervisor probably could care less if his employees take illicit drugs on their own time. The supervisor of the house painter may not care at all if his man gets jailed for drunk driving on his day off. If he can make it back to work on time after he is released, everything probably will be alright.

The police supervisor, meanwhile, cannot afford the luxury of not caring about his subordinates' dubious pursuits. The public expects a very high standard of moral and ethical conduct from those who would enforce these same laws on others. It is left up to the police supervisor to see to it that the public is not disappointed. It is also up to him to at all times serve as a positive role model for correct and moral behavior, on duty and off. No lesser standard is acceptable for the police leader.

The police sergeant's intervention in personal misconduct will not often be welcomed by the misbehaving employee. Cooperation may well be lacking. Real hostilities may result from a "it's none of your business" response on the part of the subordinate. The employee himself may recognize the oddity of his boss interfering where bosses in other lines of work would not tread. His resentment may be intense.

Yet, despite the supervisor's own discomfort and a real desire to be "anywhere but here," he must take clear and decisive action where necessary. His responsibility to maintain official concern for his employees' behavior and character will not be a burden easily shouldered. All the same, it remains one that will have to be faced on a continuing basis.

Motivational problems can occur in many forms and places for the unwary police supervisor. Outside of the desires of many police officers to be part of a just cause and to accomplish something real, sometimes little outside motivation to do a good job may be evident. Again, unlike his cohorts in other lines of work, the police leader will have to help furnish mental rewards for the officer who gets few thanks from a public that may understand very little about his job.

The very nature of a police officer's work may make his job just slightly "unclean" to some citizens, even if that work does retain something of an air of excitement and adventure about it. The officer may be called upon to tell an exciting or humorous war story among his civilian acquaintances and, at the same time, be avoided for closer friendships because people are somehow a little nervous with a cop around. Perhaps none of this discrimination really exists, but it is enough that it is real in the police officer's mind. The supervisor may thus have to suggest substitute job rewards not to be found elsewhere for some of his employees.

The supervisor may be able to do nothing about the fact that a subordinate of his has relatives who are unhappy that he is a cop. He should be able to do something, however, to show the same subordinate that there are plenty of other people who *are* proud of his chosen profession and his part in it. His advice to his uncomfortable subordinate may include the reminder that, on occasion, the approval and acceptance of his on-the-job companions must replace kudos from the world at large. This may not be the most pleasant of admissions, but on occasion it may be a very accurate one. Once again, the supervisor's task is not easy but quite necessary.

What has come to be called the "police personality" also may pose a problem for the police sergeant that is virtually unknown to supervisory peers in other lines of work. Without debating the existence of a police personality (or lack of same), one can note several attitude traits evident in the majority of police officers. It is not too difficult to see that many officers are slightly self-conscious about the authority and responsibility loaded upon them. Likewise, many are constructively suspicious, mildly cynical, and maybe somewhat egotistical. At the same time, they are often courageous, patient, and caring about others. They are independent creatures; and they are proud.

Police officers are also a great many other things in their total personality makeup. Not every one of these characteristics is good for the officer or those around him. The police officer of several years experience is often increasingly cynical or distrusting in his approach to life. Over time, he may develop and voice an "us vs. them" attitude regarding the world he lives and works in, and he may even become embittered.

The supervisor working closely with such potentially troubled people must be extremely sensitive to human problems and concerns. He may serve as counselor, confidant, and disciplinarian all at the same time. Few supervisory positions outside of law enforcement require such attentiveness for employee reactions and changing attitudes that may be symptoms of trouble brewing. Few supervisors elsewhere have so great an opportunity to defuse an unpleasant or even dangerous attitude problem before it becomes deeply ingrained in the personality of its bearer.

Because he is the proud and independent creature that he is, the police officer having difficulties with his mental outlook may resist the supervisor's "interference." If the officer in question is already somewhat cynical in outlook, he may doubt the supervisor's sincerity in wanting to help him. Even if he does choose to accept the leader's advice to talk about his difficulties, he may remain inwardly suspicious of the supervisor's motives. He may erect barriers around what he is really thinking and feeling.

The problems faced by the police supervisor are certainly not unique. Other high stress occupations produce some of the same difficulties. Supervisors of air traffic controllers, critical care medical personnel, and high-readiness military units can attest to the very real nature of these problems. They can quite readily compare stress notes with the police leader.

Still, no single category of human endeavor demands greater reliance upon the consistent common sense and good judgment of the line supervisor than does professional law enforcement in modern day America. Because of the critical demands of this job, the police supervisor remains a very special individual. A survey of some of his duties and obligations might suffice to illustrate just how really "special" he must be.

SOME SPECIFIC TASKS

Today's police supervisor must be adept in many arts and sciences. The police leader's job description certainly will vary somewhat from one jurisdiction to another and even within the range of the various assignments within a single police agency. Yet, whether he is a patrol sergeant, intelligence unit supervisor, or investigations agent-in-charge, the primary supervisor will find at least portions of his job description unchanged across the nation.

With some allowances for the additional requirements of specialty assignments, it can be said that the American police sergeant guides, monitors, and evaluates the performance of subordinates on a scheduled patrol shift, in a detective or intelligence unit, or in a specialized work group such as evidence processing or training. He may direct non-sworn clerks, secretaries, or technicians performing auxiliary or support duties for the sworn force. It is not at all unusual to find a sworn supervisor directing a communications section staffed by civilian employees.

The sergeant himself carries out his responsibilities under the direction of a superior command officer, often a lieutenant or commander. He operates according to accepted work practices and departmental policies, rules, and regulations. He is charged with the responsibility of translating those broad guidelines into on-the-job compliance by his own subordinates.

In carrying out his obligations to management, subordinates and the public he serves, the police sergeant may become personally involved in hazardous and strenuous field activities. It would be unreasonable to expect the patrol sergeant to direct the search of a building containing an armed felon without sharing the realities of the scene with his officers.

The supervisor directs and guides his troops through a number of specific job-related tasks. To carry out his functions of direction and guidance, he executes a host of specific activities. The patrol sergeant, for example, inspects the equipment and appearance of his subordinates. He provides them with current information on pertinent orders and procedures. He assigns them specific tasks, and places them in specific geographic beats or sectors. He also relays and clarifies written communications from higher up in the chain of command. In addition, he reviews and evaluates his people as they perform in the field, furnishes praise where deserved and constructive criticism where merited. He checks his officers' written reports of all kinds and clarifies and corrects them where indicated. He gives advice and encouragement where and when necessary. He gives legal interpretations and solves procedural conflicts. He is available to lend a strong arm or back where physical assistance is required.

The sergeant assigned to the uniformed or patrol division of his department patrols his assigned area of the jurisdiction to watch for problems that may require police intervention. He spends as much time in the field as possible in order to observe his people in action and responds to the scene of unusual or complex situations to provide leadership and advice for his officers. He also may provide the same services for other officers in the absence of their own supervisor.

The investigations or detective sergeant has his own, unique set of supervisory tasks, in addition to some of the same ones faced by his patrol counterpart. The detective sergeant reviews incoming cases for completeness and proper format and assigns them to his detectives. He reviews the resultant investigative work and written reports of his subordinates. He confers with them concerning problems with their cases and related work. He keeps his own boss advised of the progress of unusual cases and their attendant difficulties and ramifications.

The investigations supervisor assists his detectives on major crime scenes, aids them in examining the site for useful evidence, assists them in the location and identification of victims and witnesses in major cases, and supports his team by helping them secure whatever resources they need to do their jobs well.

The detective supervisor guides his officers in preparing case information for presentation to the prosecutor and may review complex cases with his detectives and the prosecuting attorney. He also may attend courtroom sessions to help guide the prosecution's efforts while simultaneously evaluating the courtroom demeanor and testimony of his subordinates.

The police supervisor also may perform his leadership duties in the role of a specialist. He may supervise officers in carrying out evidence processing, logistics, or other supportive activities; he may work as a police community relations specialist heading up a crime prevention unit; he may perform special assignments for the agency's top managers as an administrative aide in charge of a technical or clerical staff; he may train new recruits, or organize in-service schools for experienced officers.

The supervisor might direct the operations of his department's internal affairs investigative unit, looking into all allegations of employee misconduct. He might even chair a committee assigned the task of rewriting the agency's rules and regulations.

He probably will do much more, as well.

The question, *"What is supervision?"* cannot be adequately answered with a short, trite definition. It cannot be satisfied by reference to a few choice buzz words or catch phrases from a management or supervision course. A comprehensive answer to the question requires that the questioner examine the functions of leadership in all their various facets. Then, to really understand the particular and peculiar aspects of police supervision as opposed to supervision in general, he must know still more. He must take a look at the frequently unique challenges of the law enforcement supervisor's existence.

SUMMARY

Supervision means a lot of things to a lot of people. If he is to supervise effectively, a police leader will have to serve as a trainer, planner, disciplinarian, counselor, listener, confidant, communicator, performance evaluator and a number of other things. He will be a manager, too, and move ideas and information up and down the chain of command.

The police supervisor will find his work more challenging than will most first-line leaders outside of law enforcement. The police leader already knows that this profession is something different and apart, and so are the people who labor in it. The police supervisor will find many of his subordinates espousing a strong sense of justice and belief in a just cause. Those are assets the supervisor very likely shares with his people and can build upon to the benefit of his agency and the citizens they all serve.

Supervision in law enforcement is indeed, in many ways, different. It requires a special sort of individual to do it well. The following chapters will detail HOW it is done.

POINTS TO REMEMBER

- Effective supervision requires common sense and practical skills.
- First of all, the supervisor is expected to lead.
- The first-line supervisor is the single, most important figure in the work lives of front-line employees.
- The effective supervisor's attitude towards his job varies from that of the first-line employee.
- The supervisor's most important role is that of a positive role model.
- Many of the challenges a police supervisor faces are not unique

to the law enforcement profession.
- Law enforcement supervision is much more about practical application than theory.

Chapter Two

PREPARATION FOR THE ROLE
OF POLICE SUPERVISOR

It has been said that there is no more difficult nor radical a change in a police officer's entire career than that which occurs when he or she makes the jump from line worker to line supervisor. Most often, the change means giving up the job classification of patrol officer for that of patrol sergeant. Less frequently, it means surrendering the title of detective or investigator and replacing it with the label of detective sergeant.

The big change involves more than just titles and labels. It encompasses much more than a little fatter paycheck and a greatly altered job description. It goes far beyond a change in the insignias worn on the police uniform.

The police officer aspiring to the job of police supervisor is looking at a host of changes in the way he must think and perform both on and off the job. Such a change will not be attempted by the prudent officer without some sweeping and thorough preparation for the brand new role. This chapter will examine that preparation in its several facets.

PSYCHOLOGICAL PREPARATION

The officer who is pondering the decision as to whether or not he truly wants to be a supervisor should do his thinking with deliberate care. This is not a decision to be arrived at lightly. The officer exchanging a subordinate's duties for those of the team or unit leader will find a set of new responsibilities, duties, expectations, problems, and rewards awaiting him. The change will impact upon his very lifestyle, although just how much will depend on the specific nature of his agency, assignment, and personality.

With the potential for sometimes radical change in so many areas, the officer contemplating the shift to supervision should very carefully examine his reasons for wanting to make the big move. It is important that he do so for the right reasons. It would be a mistake, for instance, to seek the supervisory post for financial reasons alone. While virtually all American police agencies offer at least some kind of increase in monetary benefits for the promoted employee, the amount of salary increase can vary widely.

Regardless of which police agency the officer may be working for, the salary allocated to the new sergeant over the top grade patrol officer is probably not all that great. When the prospective new leader considers the added responsibilities, hours, and concerns of the police supervisor, the increase in his paycheck's size may seem even smaller. Money alone, then, is probably not the best of reasons for wanting a promotion.

How about peer pressure? Imagine this scene for a moment: The officer has been with the department for several years. A couple of his buddies have been moved up from the most recent promotional list. He is almost forty years old now, and many of his friends, on the job and off, are asking about his plans for the future.

The officer's old answers about really liking what he is doing do not seem to hold the sincerity that they once did. He is now just a little bit uncomfortable to say that he is proud of what he is doing as a street cop. He hates admitting that he enjoys what he is doing. He should be showing more devotion to himself and his loved ones, it seems, by striving to improve upon his station in life. The old ruts of the patrol officer's duties, disregarding the fact that he may feel great pride and accomplishment in doing them, are painful reminders that he is not "a success." He must join his upwardly moving compatriots. He must get promoted.

Peer pressure can be the strongest of motivations, for better or worse. Here it is for worse. The experienced police officer is putting his judgment, common sense, and personal life goals aside for what he thinks *others* expect him to do. Although his courage in facing the dangerous felon may know no bounds, his moral courage to stick with a decision that is right for himself is lacking. He may elect to risk unhappiness and potential failure in a new and really unwanted position simply to satisfy the perceived expectations of others.

Peer pressure alone is clearly not a valid reason for seeking promotion. Other pressures may mount, as well.

Closely allied to the job pressure exerted by fellow officers is that emanating from the police employee's family and friends. The spouse who indicates through words and attitude that he/she feels that it is about time for some career advancement for his or her partner may be affecting their future together greatly. Once again, the officer made to feel that he is somehow less than successful because he does not wear chevrons or bars may feel forced into seeking a promotion he neither wants nor feels prepared to seek.

Should this employee succeed in attaining a promotion sought for such a reason, he may find himself blaming his mate for each failure and unpleasant moment that the job brings. In such an accusatory atmosphere marital discord will result which may cause further job problems. The resultant cycle of failure and reaction to failure can be a terminal one for any marriage.

How about some very personal feelings and goals that might be served by a promotion to supervisor? Fine, provided that they include the right kind of emotions and personal objectives. The officer who seeks advancement because of pride in his agency and in his own abilities should be encouraged in his endeavor. The officer who wants to move up because he knows he has some unique abilities to lead and direct, which he feels will greatly benefit the agency's operations and image while simultaneously polishing his own reputation, should be cheered on, too. Likewise, the competent, capable man or woman who seeks the job of supervisor as a first logical step in a planned lifetime career in an agency should not be obstructed in this effort. All of these people can do much good for their subordinates, their employers, the community, and themselves.

Conversely, the employee whose strongest personal feeling is a desire to gain the rank of supervisor to "get even" with a peer who offended him at some time in the past is on the wrong track in seeking promotion. He probably will find his own bitterness to be a poor companion in the isolation he will surely feel in a position gained through such motivation.

The employee who competes for promotion to fulfill a desire to somehow feel "better than thou" over his old peers also will find few real rewards in a new set of stripes. Any such display is practically sure to bring hostility from subordinates and criticism from one's fellow supervisors. The man or woman who attempts to supervise while looking down on subordinates will end up being looked down upon by those same morally superior underlings.

This book has discussed many of the specific responsibilities and expectations placed upon the police supervisor. Any officer considering whether or not to seek a supervisory position should first review the preceding pages and ask himself honestly if the listed demands and requirements would make him hopelessly uncomfortable as a new supervisor.

The ethics of a good supervisor should cause the potential candidate no problems. If he is an honest and interested police officer, he operates under a similar set of professional and personal guidelines already. Yet questions arise about his added responsibilities as a recognized and official leader. Will serving as a constant role model and perpetual good example make him terribly self-conscious, perhaps very uncomfortably so? Does he have the patience required of a good supervisor? If not, can he develop it?

Is the potential supervisor willing to spend a considerable amount of time off the job working on his techniques and knowledge of police matters? Will he be willing to keep up with the latest law enforcement readings in both professional journals and general interest media? Will he use some of his own time, if necessary, to stay physically fit? Will such added tasks detract from family relationships or personal plans too much?

Is the would-be supervisor comfortable in the instructor's role? The skills of instruction can be taught in a class or even self-taught. However, the ability to be functionally at ease in front of a gathering of people comes a little harder. Is the potential leader willing to work for the acquisition of such a trait?

How about the supervisor's vital task of evaluating his subordinates? Again, the skills of effective evaluation can be taught. But is the man or woman who was perhaps only recently a member of a close-knit fraternity of working peace officers now ready to tactfully convey to former peers their weaknesses as well as strengths in job performance? The process of personnel review and evaluation must be carried out continuously in the successful police organization. Again, however, not everyone is mentally and emotionally suited to carrying forward a function that may make him or her at least temporarily unpopular with former co-workers.

To do the job of personnel evaluation properly, the supervisor must above all else be frank and sincere. The new supervisor quickly learns that even the best-intentioned constructive criticism can still sting a relationship and cool a friendship, at least for a time.

If the supervisor-to-be finds himself uncomfortable as an evaluator, he may find the role of disciplinarian an intolerable one. The line supervisor should be very closely involved in the disciplinary process at both the determination and assessment levels. It is inexcusable for him to lay the blame for an unpopular disciplinary action on "the brass." While he may fight valiantly in a losing cause against discipline he feels to be disproportionate or otherwise out of line with the offense, once the decision is made the supervisor must fully support it. To do otherwise would be to participate in the destruction of the agency itself.

Discipline is a process in which the line supervisor must demonstrate participation and support. The individual who cannot show ownership in a corrective action or decision in which he has been involved has no place in the supervisory ranks.

Planning, too, must occupy some of the police leader's time. Whether it involves spending ten minutes planning the day's personnel deployment or occupies hours of off-duty time on a special research project, planning remains an inescapable part of the supervisor's life. The supervisor who conserves and plans his minutes wisely can minimize the time that planning keeps him from the chores and pursuits he enjoys more. All the same, he still must count on spending some less than-thrilling moments eyeballing a computer screen or thumbing through volumes in a library.

If the officer determines that even a moderate amount of time devoted to planning and related pursuits is a major discomfiture, then a career decision that excludes supervision from his immediate future would be a wise choice. Any other course of action would be to submit himself to unnecessary misery.

The ability to communicate freely and openly as a supervisor is also vital. The officer who has great difficulty expressing himself in a written form acceptable in both content and format will have serious obstacles to overcome as a supervisor. If he is unwilling to devote a lot of time to learning to write in a clear, concise, and accurate manner, police supervision probably will bring him more pain than pleasure.

Along the same lines, the officer who remains ill at ease in front of groups or uncomfortable as the center of subordinates' attention on occasion may find some real difficulties in addressing a roll call briefing session. Many people simply do not like to talk in such a setting, which is perfectly fine. At the same time, such an allergy could be quite fatal to a lasting supervisory career. Fortunately, the malady is generally treatable.

As with most other skills required of a good supervisor, communication abilities can be learned and cultivated through instruction and repeated application of good techniques. Also like many other supervisory skills, mastering them requires of the student the contribution of much time and considerable effort. The police officer unwilling to give of both should not set his cap for the police leader's job.

Then there is the supervisor's role as a grievance processor for unhappy citizens and disgruntled employees. The potential supervisor who cannot fathom that one of his employees could ever do wrong has no place as an impartial fact finder for complaints of police misconduct. Just as certainly, a man or woman likely to take off on a witch hunt for a prejudged-guilty employee should never be a supervisor, either.

Even more is expected of the supervisor while he is wearing his grievance processor hat. He must do more than be fair and thorough in his inquiry into a complaint situation. He must always broadcast a clear-cut impression of fairness and competency in his dealings with citizenry and police employees alike. The officer who is not yet ready to create such an honest impression is not ready for a position of leadership.

Employee grievances against the agency and its supervisors also require an extreme amount of supervisory patience, fairness, and integrity. It is the supervisor's duty to convey his subordinate's complaint to those in higher authority whenever it cannot be satisfactorily addressed at the first-line supervisor level. He must convey the complaint accurately and without coloration of his own making, regardless of the reaction it might be expected to elicit from the person it is relayed to by the supervisor.

Just as much supervisory courage is required to relay a reply to a grievance to the concerned employee. Again the facts must be reported accurately, regardless of the anticipated reaction. Real supervisory courage is required to avoid compromising or betraying either the subordinate or the manager. The would-be supervisor should thoughtfully and honestly examine himself in determining his own quotient of moral courage for supervisory mediation duties. If he finds himself lacking, he is not yet ready for the grievance processor's job.

Finally, the key role of personal counselor for troubled subordinates must be anticipated by the aspirant to leadership ranks. Some very good police officers readily admit that they are reasonably comfortable and generally effective in counseling their citizen clients. They defuse various disputes, talk down potential suicides, and cajole violent offenders into meek submission. When it comes to tackling the equally vexing problems of police officers, however, these same officers admit to a strong desire to be anywhere else, but fast. Once again, such a feeling is not out of the ordinary and it is certainly nothing to be ashamed of. Also once again, however, it is not a feeling or an attitude that the police supervisor can allow to dictate his actions. Becoming involved in the difficulties of subordinates, sometimes at a very sensitive level, is a necessary part of the supervisor's role as counselor and source of help in difficult situations.

Very few people take any pleasure in hearing of the personal difficulties of their friends and fellow employees. Police supervisors are no exception to this rule. At the same time, a ready ear with a patient listener attached to it is a right that the subordinate must be able to rely on in stormy times, job related or otherwise. Likewise, the troubled employee should be able to expect some advice from his supervisor in at least making a start towards a solution of those troubles, even though they may not be entirely (or perhaps even remotely) job connected.

A disinterested, bored, inhumane supervisor is of no use to the worried employee or the police organization. If the budding supervisor feels that he would be unreceptive in the occasional role of substitute "older brother," confidant, or even kind parent/confessor to his subordinates, perhaps he should reconsider his aim on the supervisory post.

Skills such as counseling and active listening can be taught where there is a sincere desire to learn. The desire to share and work on the pains and problems of a subordinate cannot be taught so easily, if at all.

So, there can be many very real reasons for not rushing into that promotional exam. They can best be summarized by reminding the officer considering an attempt at promotion that life is far too short to spend a lot of time unhappy, nervous, and disappointed in a job not really meant for him. Mistakenly to commit oneself to such an undertaking cannot help but harm family, friends, subordinates, the police agency, and self.

Fortunately, there are also a good many right reasons for seeking the job of the police supervisor. It is widely recognized and acknowledged that promotion in just about any job brings with it improvements in pay, fringe benefits, social position, prestige, and overall working conditions. This is all well and good. There is certainly nothing wrong with the intelligent individual who seeks to make his life a little more comfortable with some improvements in his social status and his finances. This is quite normal.

At the same time, there are some other very good motives behind actively seeking the promotion to supervisor that deserve some attention. Not a few supervisors cite as a big plus the opportunity to participate much more closely in determining the future course of their unit or the agency itself. No matter how much a given police organization claims to further the goal of participatory management, it remains a fact of organizational life that one's chances to impact significantly on the agency and its operations increase steadily as one rises in the rank structure of that agency. The sergeant or line supervisor, by the necessity of his very practical outlook on operations and procedures, can be an extremely valuable person in the agency's critical planning process. To the officer wishing to set his mark on the agency employing him, supervision is definitely the place to be.

Other new supervisors have identified the opportunity to be a part of an important cause as a good reason for attaining the supervisory rank. Although the loyal police officer probably has already listed such a reason for being in police work in the first place, the supervisor may find that he has an even greater role in carrying out the community service functions of his department. His leadership role is vital if the police team is to achieve its goals and objectives in that cause. Once more, the desire to be a participant in a cause of is an excellent reason for being a police leader.

Another answer often heard from the police officer questioned about why he is on the job is the sincere response, "because I want to help people." Here once more the supervisor may find that he has an increased ability to do good as a consequence of his new position. He likely will continue to have at least some opportunity to aid the citizen in distress directly on a one-to-one basis. In addition, he will now have an important added chance to benefit and aid a very special group of people: the police employees who are his subordinates.

As an instructor, leader, helper, and sometimes disciplinarian, the new supervisor has a great opportunity to aid his fellow peace officers in meeting the daily challenges of working in a complex and trying world. Surely no endeavor pursued with an equal degree of fervor could bring a greater sense of satisfaction and accomplishment.

Having completed a personal inventory of his own attitudes, ideas, and perceptions of the supervisor's role, the candidate for promotion has now finished his initial psychological preparation for the "Big Move." Assuming that his department employs some kind of competition to decide who gets promoted to supervisor, the prospective competitor must now set about preparing himself for the action ahead.

WHAT'S TO KNOW?

In an era in which being the biggest and meanest and gruffest are no longer accepted as the mandated criteria for promotion, the candidate for the supervisory slot must demonstrate that he has acquired wide-ranging job skills. In addition, he must show an aptitude for learning yet other tasks. Finally, he must also display a manner or demeanor expected of the professional police officer and competent leader.

How, then, should the candidate prepare for a police promotional examination that may be written, oral, or a combination of the two? Every agency will have its own peculiarities in the examination process. However, sound preparation in some specific fields of study will better enable the candidate to successfully handle written or oral queries into some time-honored exam topics.

There are some valuable sources of worthwhile information that every student of the promotional process should have near at hand before beginning his studies. Sources of special value would normally include the following books: state criminal statutes, local ordinances and codes, pertinent traffic statutes, agency rules and regulations, text on current case law, and a text on supervisory principles.

These volumes are a minimum library for the serious promotional student. Other sources will need to be consulted. For example, if the candidate is trying for a detective sergeant's post, then texts on modern case investigation techniques, scientific evidence collection and processing, and similar material on specialized skills would have to be added to the list. The candidate shooting for the job of traffic unit supervisor would be wise to add resources on selective enforcement, accident investigation, and so on.

A working knowledge of the contents of the book list provided here should be at the core of the supervisory candidate's preparations. An examination of the benefits each source should yield follows next.

Criminal Statutes

The officer should review all of the criminal laws that he may expect to work with as a supervisor. Most of his time should be spent on gaining recognition and understanding of which elements must be present for a specific crime to have occurred. He also should spend time comparing similar yet not identical offenses that he might expect to encounter. He might, for instance, make himself well aware of the fine line between first- and second-degree burglary, simple assault and aggravated assault, and so on through the list of common criminal acts.

In other words, the supervisory candidate does not need to memorize every element of each crime in the statute book. He should, however, gain sufficient familiarity with the statutes to recognize quickly which crime, if any, is present in a given field situation. The same holds true whether the situation is a hypothetical one on a promotional exam or a very real and critical one on the street some day.

Local Ordinances and Codes

The pupil preparing for a promotional test should review his jurisdiction's penal laws that he can reasonably expect to meet in his future position of police supervisor. Obviously, he needs to be familiar with laws against criminal behavior that his troops will enforce. He also should gain at least a basic knowledge and understanding of the less familiar laws that he may confront on occasion. For example, many jurisdictions have ordinances giving health and animal control officers rather broad powers to cite offenders in those areas of regulation. Such ordinances usually include provisions allowing the animal control or health inspections officers to arrest anyone opposing their official efforts. Other laws sometimes grant those officers the right to make forced entry onto premises in certain situations.

Inasmuch as the police may be called to assist these other agents of the law in peace-threatening situations, the wise supervisor (and the smart test taker) will be aware in advance of police authority and responsibility in such matters as assistance to another agency. At least a very basic knowledge of some of these less-used ordinances will stand the future supervisor in good stead to handle unusual situations as they arise.

Traffic Statutes

Most promotional exams are going to cover some general areas of traffic law and accident investigation skills, at least at the patrol sergeant test level. Whether he is working with state laws or city and/or county traffic regulations, the adequately prepared test taker will have reviewed the traffic laws in use in his locale.

The promotional student should devote some time to covering the laws governing accident reporting and investigation requirements in his jurisdiction, as this is an area in which problems (hypothetical now and later real) often come up. Time spent with the sometimes complex drunk driving and expressed consent laws also will turn out to be effort wisely expended. While he need not be a technical expert in the field of vehicle accident investigation, the wise promotional candidate will know how to conduct a highly competent accident investigation.

Agency Rules and Regulations

The potential supervisor would do well to be quite familiar with an up-to-date version of his agency's rules and regulations. Some departments may have one book dealing with formalized rules and another document detailing operating procedures for handling everything from booking evidence to ordering supplies of toilet paper. Yet other organizations may produce still another set of documents addressing the issue of department policy.

Whether he is dealing with one big book or several shorter volumes, the officer preparing himself for the promotional exam must know the content and meaning of such written guidelines. When he has questions about unclear or complex passages, he must consult with his own supervisors for a translation. Not least, he must engage in repeated mental practice in which he applies these orders, rules, procedures, and guidelines to a host of hypothetical situations that he might face on a test or real ones that might confront him on the lob. Such mental exercise is test preparation in its most useful form.

Current Case Law

The prospective leader must be conversant with up-to-date court decisions affecting law enforcement operations and tactics. If there is a new holding dealing with searches of impounded vehicles, he must be aware of it and the limitations it places on the police officer. If there are new court-imposed restrictions on custodial body searches, the supervisor must be able to apply the restrictions to his everyday work world.

The student should be more interested in the content of a court decision than in worrying about number and citation. Still, he should be well-versed in legal matters to the extent that he can attach the title of the case to the legal principle it represents, if need be. Otherwise, he could stand to miss some points on a multiple-choice exam. Simultaneously, he should practice applying the court decisions he studies to hypothetical field situations he might meet up with later.

The promotional candidate can alert himself to new court decisions of significance by scanning such professional publications as the *Law Enforcement Bulletin* published monthly by the Federal Bureau of Investigation, U. S. Department of Justice. Other publications are available, including *Police, Police Marksman, Law and Order* and the publication of the International Association of Chiefs of Police, *Police Chief.*

If the officer's agency produces a training bulletin of some kind, it, too, could prove very enlightening as study material. Even keeping up with the daily newspaper can inform the interested officer of changes in the mood of the nation's courts. It also can give him the names of specific cases and some of the rationale behind them.

Text on Supervisory Principles

In many agencies, the promotional candidate must prepare himself to give his questioners the catch phrases and acronyms that have come to be associated with managerial and supervisory classes and textbooks. More important, the sharp candidate will review the concepts and principles applicable to effective supervision. These will be more useful to him than learning "pop management" buzz words to parrot back to the board.

As noted, the list of books, periodicals, and computerized material to be covered by the prospective supervisor could be extremely lengthy. He should begin with the core sources listed and then branch out as his time permits. He should obtain additional sources of knowledge that will strengthen him in known areas of personal weaknesses. (First, of course, he will have to identify what he perceives as weaknesses in an honest self-evaluation. His current supervisor can help him in this regard.)

Extra help also can be sought on subjects and skills to be emphasized on a specific or special promotional assignment. A good police department library, where available, can be of much help here. Lacking such a resource, the officer might examine the offerings at public or college libraries nearby. Any school offering a criminal justice or police science program is almost sure to have a decent selection of reading materials on law enforcement subjects. Books on general business supervision topics should not be overlooked for their contributions, as well.

TEST-TAKING SKILLS

Police officers are fond of talking about the supervisor who perhaps cannot do his job to their satisfaction but got the position anyway "because he is a good test taker." Actually, there is no good reason why any officer intelligent enough to perform complex law enforcement duties also cannot do a reasonably good job on any exam, written or oral.

There is no magic in the fingers or the pencil of the officer who gets a good promotional score. The good study habits, logical thought processes, and self-pacing test skills employed by most successful test takers are talents that can be mastered by virtually any person of reasonable intelligence. Hopefully, the police officer would fit easily into such a category.

There are some very nonmagical but still very useful things that the police officer can do to score well on a promotional examination. It would be a good idea to look first at some of the cardinal rules of test taking.

Know the Study Material

No amount of scheming is going to help if the test taker does not know the material to be covered on the test. A list of minimal sources to be studied has already been provided and other resources may be added as needed. Steady, patient study has no substitute. Cramming at the last moment generally does not work very well. Neither does cheating!

Nothing is more important than the officer's attitude towards the test-taking exercise. He will need real willpower to make himself set aside the time necessary for thorough study. He will then have to use this same willpower to make himself sit through his budgeted study time when other, more pleasurable pursuits are beckoning.

Read the Instructions; Ask Questions

Too many of the victims of written tests have victimized themselves by failing to read carefully the printed directions at the start of the test. When taking a written exam, it is not a good idea to assume anything. What appears to be a routine "choose the best answer" multiple-choice test may turn out to be an exercise in which the test taker is actually supposed to identify the least correct response. Or the test may be calling for more than one correct response per question. *Read the directions and be sure!*

Whether the promotional test is written or oral, the test taker must ask questions about any uncertainties in instructions or other rules of the proceeding. If the candidate is not advised of the basis for scoring on the exam, he should ask the test administrator. The same holds true if he is not briefed as to scoring procedures at the conclusion of the promotional oral board or assessment center.

In conclusion, assumptions about any test can be dangerous for the test taker. The smart promotional candidate will clear up all uncertainties possible before an examination of any kind gets underway.

Pace Yourself

The promotional exam will almost certainly have an enforced time limit for candidates to work within. The test taker cannot afford to worry actively over the time factor or become a compulsive clock watcher. Either behavior will work against him. At the same time, however, the officer who dawdles away time for any reason will have trouble finishing the test at his best.

The common sense test taker will remain aware of the clock as the written exam proceeds. If he finds that half of his allowed time is gone and he has only completed a quarter of the work, he will act upon the obvious need to pick up the pace somewhat. This is assuming that the test contents are relatively uniform throughout. If, for example, the latter part of the exam switches from "true or false" inquiries to a discussion-type format, the test taker will naturally have to leave some extra time to work on the exam's concluding section. It helps in this regard if, where allowed by the instructions to do so, the candidate scans quickly the entire test to figure out what is involved before he actually begins work.

A common mistake to be avoided is the spending of too much time on a single difficult question. Since the final score will probably be based upon the number of correct responses given, it is to the officer's advantage to answer as many questions as possible in the time permitted. An especially time-consuming problem should be saved for additional attention later when all other questions have been handled.

Naturally, any time remaining at the end of the candidate's work should be gainfully employed in a review of the completed test to be sure that all questions have been answered as desired. The officer should be hesitant to change answers without a good cause. There is some evidence that a test taker's first response is, in many instances, the correct one, particularly on the "true or false" exercise. Ultimately, too much worrying over a difficult question can work against the test taker if the worrying results in the changing of the first answer given.

BOARDS AND ASSESSMENT CENTERS

A special set of guidelines may be applied to the promotional oral board or exam. In this sort of promotional, a panel of several command officers directs questions at the candidate. "Outsiders" such as psychologists or citizen members are sometimes added to the makeup of this board.

The oral board is an especially valuable tool for assessing the knowledge and potential of the would-be police supervisor in that it tests more than his technical knowledge and expertise. His demeanor and poise under fire also can be examined through the board's posed hypothetical situations. If he folds up under stress here, he may do poorly on the job when the real thing comes along, or so the theory goes.

Oral boards or interviews present a number of hypothetical situations to which the promotional candidate is expected to respond with limited time to think about his answers. Fast, accurate decisions are sought by the board members.

In preparation for an oral board the smart promotional candidate will stay current on what is happening in his department, law enforcement in general and the world at large. He will be aware of major controversies and issues concerning the profession and his agency in particular. He also will have some fact-based opinions on how these situations might be best handled. It is not necessary that he have the one "best" answer to every question. There may not be one. But he must be capable of giving voice to some well thought-out opinions that go beyond emotional, knee-jerk reactions.

In preparing for an interview appearance the wise promotional candidate will practice his oral presentation skills in front of a mirror, video camera and recorder and/or a live and critical audience. He will practice talking intelligently about himself, as he very likely will be asked to do that by the board. In his rehearsed presentation he will note his personal and professional accomplishments, placing emphasis upon those things (scheduling, planning, training, counseling, etc.) that a supervisor might be expected to do. He will practice responding to tough, pointed questions about those accomplishments. Once more, a live and critical audience of peers, friends or even family members can be a big help as honest interviewers and critics.

What questions should the promotional candidate anticipate during an interview or oral board process? The queries obviously will vary from one agency and one process to the next. Nevertheless, there are a few "standard" questions that often appear in one form or another. They include:

1. Tell us about your professional and personal background.
2. What are your personal strengths and weaknesses?
3. Why do you want this position?
4. What have been your most important accomplishments at the department?

5. What issues do you see facing the department today?
6. What is your leadership style?
7. Give us some examples of how you handle conflict.
8. Give us some examples of your decision-making skills.
9. Tell us one thing you would do as a supervisor to improve this agency.
10. In closing, what three to five points would you like us to remember about you?

Additionally, the promotional candidate should be aware of the current issues facing the community, the department, and law enforcement in general and be prepared to answer questions regarding them. He also should expect to be given hypothetical situations in which he will be asked to respond as a supervisor. These scenarios could range from tactical problems to employee counseling sessions to meetings with disgruntled citizens. In each case it is vital that the candidate *think and act* as if he were in the position for which he is competing.

Today, many law enforcement agencies are utilizing assessment centers for first-line supervisor promotions. To a lesser extent, assessment centers are being used for promotion to mid-management positions, too. The assessment center gathers information under standardized conditions about an individual's ability to do the job of a police supervisor. It measures such skills as personal communication (oral and written), planning, problem solving, decision-making and human relations. Those selected to sit as assessors are generally experienced police managers who are at least one level above the position being tested. Most often they are not from the same agency as the promotional candidates. The number of assessors will vary. The assessors are themselves first trained and thoroughly briefed by the coordinator or consultant overseeing the overall testing process.

Assessment centers vary somewhat in content but generally contain several exercises, including such stand-bys as role-playing, oral presentations, impromptu speaking, written exercises and tactical tests. There are others, of course. When each candidate has finished all of the exercises, the assessors meet to discuss the strengths and weaknesses of each candidate. They have been keeping notes and scores throughout the exercises to help them do this. They may arrive at a consensus score for each competitor. The candidates are rank-ordered accordingly and their final scores furnished to their agency head or civil service board for a promotional decision.

Several common exercises the promotional candidate might expect to find in an assessment center are described below. They are accompanied by some tips on how to prepare for each.

Role-Playing Exercises. In a scenario involving live actors, the candidate will be the "supervisor" responsible for handling an irate citizen, recalcitrant employee, etc. Assessors will be scoring decision making, interpersonal relations skills, communication abilities and problem solving. In preparation, the police candidate should be able to make a decision and defend it under questioning. He should know his agency's rules, policies and procedures. He must control his emotions and his voice and not allow the actor(s) to provoke him.

Oral Presentation. This exercise measures the candidate's ability to make an effective oral presentation under the stress of being critiqued by an audience of unsmiling assessors. It also may provide the assessors with important data about the candidate's background and career. In preparation, the candidate should outline the things he wants to say about himself and then practice his oral delivery in front of a video camera and recorder or a live audience. Critical opinions should be sought from his listeners. The candidate must be prepared to maintain excellent eye contact with ALL of the assessors, show enthusiasm and keep the presentation within any established time limits.

Impromptu Speaking. The exercise is somewhat similar to the oral presentation except that the candidate is given a surprise topic to talk about intelligently and confidently for a given period of time. Once again he will appear in front of a critical audience of assessors who will judge his demonstrated abilities for organizing, communicating, decision-making and quick thinking under stress. Basic preparations revolve around self-confidence developed through knowledge of department policies and procedures as well as current, "hot" issues. Well-honed public speaking skills also will help create a good impression. College speech courses can prove helpful to the serious candidate.

Written Exercises. Grammar, spelling and construction are tested as parts of the candidate's communication skills. The ability to express logical, organized thoughts on paper is carefully scrutinized. Attention to detail and proofreading is critical here. Preparation calls for practice and more practice in writing memorandums, letters, special reports and the other documents that comprise the supervisor's work life.

Neatness counts, but so does content. Reviewing known, good quality written work done by real supervisors can prove helpful, too. For the would-be supervisor who is seriously lacking in writing ability, a writing or proofreading course at a community college may prove very helpful. Writers get better by writing, so practice is vital.

In-basket exercise. The promotional candidate is presented with anywhere from half a dozen to two dozen tasks of the sort that a supervisor might find in his basket on a really busy day. The papers, messages, and memos he will find there may include notes from his boss requiring that he write a memo or letter, respond to an angry citizen, or look into a personnel issue. He will be given a limited amount of time to write memorandums and letters and otherwise handle or delegate each of the assignments he has been given. He will have to prioritize each one in the order in which he thinks it should be handled. If the designer of the exercise is a particularly evil genius, the candidate will be interrupted by e-mails, telephone calls, and radio transmissions containing new problems. He will be expected to reply with an answer to the question or advice for the caller. He also might be instructed to indicate on the pieces of paper he has been given exactly what he would do with each one.

When his time to work on the exercise has expired, the candidate likely will be required to explain orally to several assessors what he did, why he did it, and in what order. He may be questioned as to why he prioritized his tasks in the order he did. The assessors will be interested in hearing the logic behind his decisions to prioritize and resolve each issue in that manner. He will be graded down if, for instance, he elected to write a thank you letter to a helpful citizen ahead of responding to a telephone call of an injured officer at the hospital. It probably will not be helpful, either, if he attempts to handle every single issue himself as opposed to delegating and referring as appropriate.

A sharp candidate will garner extra credit for looking beyond the surface of a task for any subtle nuances. He also will get good marks for picking up on the fact that two or more issues actually are related, and handling them accordingly. For example, he may discover in his basket a note from the commander telling him that Officer Mary Smith has used up all her accrued sick and other leave time. Further down in the stack is a memorandum from Mary Smith requesting approval to take on an off-duty job at a retail outlet. And at the very bottom of the basket is a letter from a citizen complaining that Mary was rude to him during a traffic stop. A good candidate will be expected to make some connections and perhaps move Mary up on his priority list of issues to be handled.

As in all of the other exercises he will face, the successful candidate will approach the in-basket by placing himself in the mindset of an individual holding the rank he is seeking. He will need to remind himself to see each solution he proposes in the light of how it might affect the whole organization, not just his corner of it. He will score extra points with the evaluators for his demonstrated ability to visualize the "big picture" and discern the distant repercussions of his actions.

Tactical Tests. This exercise gauges the candidate's handling of a mock crisis or other field operations problem designed by the coordinators of the assessment center. Typical problems of a tactical nature include make-believe hostage incidents, barricaded gunmen, terrorist attacks, multiple casualty accidents or crimes, hazardous materials incidents and natural disasters. The candidate must be prepared to demonstrate that he can make quick and logical decisions under stress. Preparations also call for a solid grounding in the agency's emergency operations procedures, mutual aid agreements and incident command system.

There are a number of things that the promotional candidate may do to make as good an impression as possible on the members of the board. In a way, the candidate is "on trial" in much the same manner as he was when he underwent his initial pre-hiring interview. Some of the same preparations he made then, bolstered by the lessons of his more recent law enforcement experience, should prove helpful for the oral promotional exam.

Dress Appropriately

A clean, pressed uniform may be the reasonable dress for the interview. If the uniform is inappropriate because of the nature of the position being sought or some other reason, then a neat, clean, conservative manner of dress is a must. A dark suit is preferable.

Whatever the specific mode of dress chosen, it is important that it be targeted at showing board members that the candidate considers the interview to be extremely important to him, and he is treating the occasion in a manner appropriate to that concern. Too informal a means of dress could create just the opposite impression.

Be Polite; Not Subservient

The interviewers will expect the candidate to answer their questions courteously and in a tone appropriate to their rank. At the same time, the candidate is not expected to lick any boots or stroke any swollen egos. A polite, straightforward reply could be the candidate's best ally.

Avoid Nervous Mannerisms

Nail biting, gum chewing, and smoking without permission are quite obviously out of the question for the oral board appearance. So are toying with garments or items on the table top and drumming the fingers on any surface. Slouching is out, but so is an unnatural, ramrod-stiff posture.

The candidate wants to avoid any sort of behavior (nervous or otherwise) that distracts from what he has to say. Anything that attracts attention away from his verbal presentation hurts his chances of favorably impressing the oral board. When the scores are added up and a promotional decision is reached later on, he wants to be remembered for what he said under adverse conditions, not for the fact that he tapped a dent into the table top.

Make Direct Replies

The promotional candidate should make eye contact with the person asking the question. A promotional board is not a staring contest, however, and the candidate must not confuse directness with a near-hostile stare that might be interpreted as a glare of arrogance or challenge.

An Attitude Is Showing

Confidence is fine; arrogance is unacceptable. Recent years have produced a sort of "guaranteed success formula" craze in which the practitioner is taught that everyone else will think he is great if he acts so convincingly that he believes it himself. Unfortunately, the student of this school of thought may never get the chance to prove his amazing abilities because an unimpressed board labeled him a know-it-all, correctly or otherwise.

There is room for the proverbial "middle ground" here. The successful applicant for promotion certainly does not hang his head, lower his eyes, and make self-depreciating remarks about himself to the board. Neither does he become a real bore by acting cocky, affecting an air of superiority, or rambling on and on about his own virtues. If his replies and presentation before the oral board are good, he will not have to concern himself with affecting appearances. His abilities and potential will be evident from his direct replies and demonstrated common sense.

One more note of caution: The entire promotional process should be treated as an important affair that will affect its participants' future significantly. (It will do just that.) The process is therefore deserving of the best efforts that the candidate can muster.

A promotional competition is certainly not a life or death matter or anything else even remotely approaching this degree of seriousness. It is, however, vitally important to the police officer's future and that of his department, and it deserves the participant's very best efforts.

A promotional exam should not be taken "just to see what it's like." The test taker should fully expect to win the desired promotion and have plans for his future after he does so. He should, in other words, approach the forthcoming examination in the same manner in which he would plan for any desired objective. He should seek promotion for the right reasons (using the proper techniques) to reach a desirable and proper goal.

A CHANGE IN OUTLOOK

The police officer anticipating a career as a leader of others should very early anticipate some necessary changes in the way that he will look at his job, his peers, and his agency once he dons the sergeant's stripes. He will no longer, for example, be free to participate in general gripe sessions with his buddies in which everything and everybody from the chief of police to the brand of ball-point pen purchased by the department is damned mercilessly. This kind of irresponsible behavior is not in keeping with the expectations of responsible leadership.

The newly promoted supervisor probably will find his circle of really close friends from the job shrinking in size. Remember the unwritten rule in supervision that the higher in the organization a person rises, the fewer his really close companions become. It does not have to be this way in every instance, of course, but the experiences of many police supervisors indicate that it probably will be so, at least to a degree.

On the more positive side, the new supervisor will see his agency in a wider perspective now. As he gains experience in looking at a somewhat bigger picture of the organization with its interrelated parts, he may see some reasons behind policies and procedures he had previously questioned. As a patrol supervisor works more closely with his counterparts in the detective bureau, he may see firsthand the difficulties posed by incomplete or imprecise crime reports forwarded from the street officer. Other things also will take on increased meaning as his scope of vision grows.

The big jump from line police officer to line supervisor is not an easy one. Its successful completion requires some trade-offs along with the considerable gains. There are sacrifices to accompany the rewards; hardships to go with the pleasures.

The jump is a big one that must be made, however, if American law enforcement is to obtain a steady supply of intelligent, capable, devoted leaders of police personnel. The jump begins with careful and thoughtful preparations for promotional consideration and competition. It really ends only with the honored retirement of a career leader in the police service.

SUMMARY

The upwardly-mobile police officer must alter a bit the way he thinks, feels and acts. As a supervisor, he will have to see the big picture, not a fragment of a snapshot of the total scene. His relations with his old peers will change, as will his associations with management.

The would-be police supervisor must prepare mentally for the change in outlook that he will face if promoted. In seeking that promotion he must master the knowledge of his profession, including pertinent statutes, case law, rules and regulations, policies and procedures and supervisory principles. He must hone his test-taking skills and practice his presentations for an oral board or assessment center. He must remain mindful that appearance, demeanor and sincerity will go a long way towards figuring his final score in the promotional process.

Most of all, he must remember to be himself and respond thoughtfully, courageously and honestly to the tests and trials of promotion.

POINTS TO REMEMBER

- Moving to the role of supervisor requires an alteration in the way a police employee thinks about his job and his agency.
- The smart individual goes for promotion for the right reasons.
- Not everyone is emotionally suited to be a supervisor.
- Correcting former peers can prove extremely uncomfortable for a new supervisor.
- There are specific information sources that the promotional candidate must master.
- The promotional candidate should digest a good text on supervisory principles.
- Mastering test-taking skills is vital to the promotional candidate.
- The candidate should practice the skills required by an assessment center or interview process.
- Some basic questions and answers should be expected and rehearsed.
- Dress and appearance are vital to the promotional candidate.
- Distracting habits and mannerisms must be avoided.
- The new supervisor will see his organization in a much wider perspective.
- The jump from first-line employee to first-line supervisor is the biggest leap in law enforcement.

Chapter Three

ETHICS OF POLICE SUPERVISION

There can be no doubt that the professional police officer works and lives by a code of ethics. If he finds that he cannot do so, he has no business in law enforcement. It is not unreasonable to expect that, in addition to following the canons of ethics for law enforcement officers, the police supervisor has his own extra set of ethics to adhere to as a leader.

Ethics may go by a number of other names and involve several things. Ethics have been termed "rules for proper conduct" and have been referred to as a set of moral principles. Ethics are said to deal with the nature of the "good and right." In their most formal sense, ethics are said to be the science of the human character in its ideal state of being. Ethics may encompass all of these things and more.

What about the source for what has been called ethics or codes of conduct? Such guidelines for proper professional behavior obviously are not handed down on stone tablets from some nebulous higher authority. Rather, in order to be most effective, any set of ethics or rules must be drawn up and supported by way of example by the very people most likely to use them.

Police officers have had their own Law Enforcement Code of Ethics since 1957 when the International Association of Chiefs of Police (IACP) adopted a code developed earlier by the California Peace Officers' Association and the Peace Officers' Research Association of California. Many other organizations and associations have since accepted and promulgated the code. Its concise, direct language appears to have contributed to its widespread acceptance in American law enforcement. It can be stated that very few contemporary police officers are unaware of the existence of the code and its meanings for practicing police people.

Perhaps the time is at hand for police line supervisors to draw up and publicize their own universally acceptable code of conduct to be relied upon not in place of, but in addition to, the Law Enforcement Code of Ethics. Consider, then, the following:

THE POLICE SUPERVISOR'S CODE OF ETHICS

I will be loyal.

I will be loyal to my employer. I will support his policies as my own. I will relay his instructions accurately and without expressed prejudice. I will tell him what I know to be true, not what I think he wants to hear. I will question him when I am uncertain as to what he expects of me and my subordinates.

I will be loyal to my subordinates. I will ask of them only what I am capable of and willing to do myself. I will evaluate them accurately and discipline them fairly. I will teach them what they need to know to succeed in the tasks I have set out for them. I will not lie to them. Neither will I cover up for them when corrective action is needed. I will truthfully represent their views and do everything I can about their real problems and valid complaints. I will lead by example. I will be just. I will serve as a positive role model.

I will be loyal to myself. I will accept the role of supervisor for the right reasons. I will be honest with myself. I will keep myself in a healthy physical and mental condition. I will set high standards of personal integrity for myself. I will strive constantly to reach those goals in my conduct both on and off the job. I will serve the community.

Above all else, I will be loyal.

A code of ethics of this nature makes no claim that the police supervisor is a superman or superwoman or should be one. It asks no one to become an angel. It allows for human frailties, but it also demands that the ethical supervisor work always to better himself and his job performance.

RESPONSIBILITIES TO MANAGEMENT

Just as the police sergeant has the right to expect certain things from his boss, that same boss and the organization itself have the right to count on certain behavior on the part of the ethical supervisor. It has already been noted in the proposed Police Supervisor's Code of Ethics that the organization and its managers are owed the honest loyalty of their supervisory officers. Loyalty here does not call for unthinking, bootlicking subservience. What it does require is that the supervisor place enough faith in his own superiors to grant that, in the absence of overwhelming evidence to the contrary, they are probably well-intentioned in the course of action they have selected. They may well be correct in their selection of options arrived at through the decision-making process.

At the same time, the intelligent supervisor will ask for clarifications of orders or policies that he does not understand. If he disagrees with a proposed course of action, loyalty commands that he question the directive *at the right time and in the right way.* This will mean that an order issued under emergency conditions will be obeyed now and questioned or discussed later, unless obedience calls for obviously illegal or immoral behavior.

If, for instance, the sergeant's superiors have decided that it is proper to execute a warrantless search in an emergency situation, it is not the sergeant's place to debate case law before carrying out the emergency search. At the same time, the sergeant receiving the unlikely directive to order his men to shoot on sight an obviously unarmed offender had damned well better challenge the order before implementing it! To do less would be to share in criminal conduct.

Loyalty also speaks to the issue of the proper way or place in which to question or debate orders and directives. The wise sergeant meets with his immediate supervisor in private to tell him why he feels that an ordered course of action must not be followed. He presents calm, logical arguments for his point of view. Best of all, he produces solid evidence and firm examples to bolster his viewpoint.

If, for instance, the street sergeant disagrees with the watch commander's decision to use a police traffic car on the all-night shift, the thoughtful sergeant might offer a logical list of reasons why the decision is not one he agrees with:

1. Manpower is needed for building checks due to an increase in commercial burglaries.
2. There have been few serious car accidents on the all-night shift.
3. Past experience with a traffic enforcement unit on that shift has

resulted in poor returns in good arrests and summonses for traffic offenses.

The sergeant must remain mindful of selecting a proper place to put forward his constructive criticism. He will not, for instance, challenge the validity of the plan of action when he and his superior are in front of a group of officers. This is an obvious taboo. Less obvious is the requirement that he must avoid belittling or ridiculing the plan or decision in front of others in the absence of his boss. The supervisor may feel that he is making points with the troops by attacking the validity of a plan or order in front of a roll call briefing of officers. He might mistakenly feel that he can make even more points by encouraging evasion of the unpopular directive by indicating, directly or by implication, that he will close his eyes to deliberate noncompliance. In doing so he is missing the point that many of his own subordinates will find his behavior disloyal and disturbing, although they may say nothing in his presence.

The supervisor encouraging noncompliance may soon find that his attentive subordinates are also finding it easier to avoid compliance with other procedures or regulations they disagree with in practice. In the final tally, the sergeant's own reputation will very likely suffer. It may become increasingly difficult for him to obtain compliance with those guidelines and policies he *does* support. His effectiveness as a supervisor has been reduced.

The loyal supervisor does not broadcast ill will about the organization of which he is a member. He has an obligation to address himself to its shortcomings, but in the proper places and at the proper times. Such places do not include social gatherings with other members of the community. If he shows little pride in his organization, it is doubtful that others will show much, either. They may make the logical assumption that since he knows the place from the inside out and thinks that it is awful, there must be some truth to the story!

The ethical police supervisor must develop a reputation for reliability with his superiors. This proven ability to "get it done" allows those superiors to concentrate upon other things, safe in the assurance that the called for work will be performed as requested. A reputation for reliability cannot help but strengthen the supervisor in his own chances for promotion through demonstrated merit.

Every police sergeant worth his chevrons owes his boss absolute honesty in all things. This truthfulness must survive even if the information being presented is unpopular, unfavorable, or downright unbelievable. One of the first-line supervisor's key responsibilities is the gathering and reporting of facts. Distorted or omitted facts can destroy the supervisor as an effective and reliable communicator. With this reputation compromised, the supervisor becomes of doubtful value to the police organization.

The honest supervisor is neither a blind "yes" man nor a perpetual "no" bird. He helps no one if he supports an idea or suggestion simply because it originates with the bosses. At the same time, he is not acting responsibly if he attacks every new procedure or change in policy just because it comes from above. The supervisor who sees nothing but negatives is just as off base as the individual who praises everything new just because it is new.

It takes supervisory courage to tell the boss that he is not correct about something. The supervisor has a better chance of seeing his "no" vote take effect if he presents his opinion in a constructive and carefully worded manner. It is not enough to tell the mid-level manager that his idea will not work. It is much more effective to tell him *why* it will not work, and illustrate the point with example situations or potential problems. A suggestion of an alternative or revised plan might then be appropriate.

For example, the experienced detective sergeant has a "gut" feeling that his lieutenant's new case flow plan is not as effective as it might be. Gut feelings are not enough, however. The sergeant must detail to his boss the significant problems he sees with the new plan:

1. Reports are delayed in getting to the assigned investigator.
2. There is a built-in delay before a follow-up contact can be made with the crime victim.
3. As additional time elapses from the time that the offense is committed until it is investigated, chances for solving the crime decline steadily.
4. Consequently, the quality of services rendered by the investigations unit is reduced.

At the other end of the scale, a few supervisors seem to feel that it is their destiny to oppose anything and everything that smells even remotely of management's influences. The doomsayer affecting the "angry young man" approach to supervision falls into this category. Perhaps attempting to impress either his peers or his subordinates by facing down the management "enemy," this self-appointed hero can slow needed progress and stifle change that is sorely needed for the betterment of the agency.

As implied earlier, it is not enough for the communications section supervisor to tell his boss that a particular piece of equipment is inadequate for the agency's needs. So far, he has completed only part of his duties with such a notification. The job is done only after the communications supervisor has offered sound evidence of the equipment's inadequacy and provided some suggestions regarding an alternative.

The police supervisor has a lot to gain by developing a reputation for being forthright and honest with management on *all* occasions. The leader whose behavior can always be predicted as being one extreme or the other will eventually lose both his believability and his audience. An earned reputation for a lack of credibility on the part of the supervisor will lessen his value to the agency and to the subordinates whose interests he supposedly represents.

The responsible supervisor keeps his own boss and, consequently, management as a whole, well-informed. Managers do not like surprises, particularly when those surprises tend to show them and their people in a bad light.

Keeping the boss informed requires a good deal of judgment ability on the part of the first-line supervisor. Minor difficulties and so-called "routine" situations generally need not be brought to the mid-level manager's attention. The first-line supervisor will handle them, instead. (Here, as elsewhere in this book, the mid-level manager will generally be a lieutenant or his equivalent in an organization not structured along quasi-military lines. The supervisor generally will be the sergeant or team leader equivalent.) The really difficult part is determining what the boss wants to know about and what can be handled at a lower level of command.

Such decisions will become easier as the supervisor's experience grows. He also will find that he will have to adjust to each new boss he works under. While one manager may want to be kept advised of personal problems experienced by team members, another boss may wish to leave such matters entirely within the realm of his sergeants. Many of the uncertainties of taking on a new boss can be eliminated if the supervisor and his superior have some frank and wide-ranging talks at the start of their association. In this way, each individual can get a feel for the expectations, abilities, and personality of the other.

No manager wants to create the impression that he does not know everything of importance that transpires on his watch. The supervisor who contributes to a shortage of knowledge on the part of his boss will not win that superior as his friend. Simple organizational survival instincts should tell the supervisor that bad feelings from the boss will not contribute to his job welfare.

The efficient and effective police supervisor needs more than the aid and good will of the boss to succeed in his leadership role. He also must have the help and combined wisdom of his fellow supervisors. The supervisor who cannot work and communicate well with his peers is not fulfilling his responsibility to his employer or to himself. There is no need for a supervisor to face each and every job crisis as a new and unknown problem. Such an approach is unnecessary when the solution may already exist at a convenient source: the bank of knowledge and experience contained within the minds of the agency's other supervisors. The supervisor who is loyal to his organization and himself also is loyal to his fellow supervisors. He gets along well with them, supports them, and strengthens them by backing their decisions and proper actions where called upon to do so. This is not to say that he must blindly back their every move, right or wrong, but he never attacks their decisions or personalities in front of his subordinates.

The supervisor who attempts to gain the friendship of a subordinate by joining him in criticizing another of the department's supervisors will gain little good in the end. His disloyalty probably will gain for him the eventual contempt of the employee he is attempting to befriend. When knowledge of his remark gets back to the target, as it inevitably will, he also will have lost the respect of a fellow supervisor.

Close and constant communication among leaders is necessary for very specific situations as well as for larger problems. An example: While it is certainly necessary for the supervisor to remain impartial and unprejudiced towards all of his subordinates, it is also necessary that he inform himself as quickly as possible regarding their strengths, weaknesses, and special problems. If a supervisor has learned by experience that a given officer is, for instance, a habitual liar, it would be foolish and wasteful for the man's new supervisor to have to learn the same thing for himself over a time period. The officer's old supervisor would not be showing loyalty to his organization or his fellow supervisor if he did not advise the new sergeant of the problem. By the same token, a sergeant who is aware of a special talent possessed by one of his troopers would be negligent if he did not inform his peers of that special ability when he knew it to be needed elsewhere in the organization.

Loyalty to management, then, means loyalty to the *entire* management team. Every supervisor–sworn and civilian alike–must be considered a member of that unit and treated accordingly.

The supervisor who is loyal to his superiors sees to it that he follows the existing chain of command and requires his subordinates to do the same. The leader who winks at shortcuts taken by his people or who sets a poor example by shortcutting the chain himself is of questionable use to the police organization.

No one should deny the supervisor the privilege of talking shop informally or socially with those above him and outside of his immediate chain of command. When such talk is intentionally aimed at sidestepping the supervisor's own boss, however, it begins to smack of disloyalty. Only the leader himself can say what the purpose of his contacts outside the chain of command is. It is up to him to see to it that the goals are proper and responsible ones.

A unique obstacle to following the established chain of command is found when personal, off-the-job friendships are involved between the persons doing the communicating. Again, the intelligent supervisor must use his own good common sense to tell him when, for example, a subordinate friend is using their relationship to help him second-guess another supervisor's actions or elicit an opinion of him. The smart supervisor will turn this sort of potentially dangerous conversation in another direction. He cannot afford to do less. The subordinate who fails to get the initial message may have to be told more directly to break off the line of discussion.

The responsible police supervisor combats the fostering and spread of rumors and unsubstantiated information in its many forms. While the supervisor may get as much vicarious delight out of the particularly "juicy" stories as anyone else, he is not being loyal to the organization that promoted him when he lets rumors run rampant through his personnel.

Some rumors start accidentally enough, and many have at their core a kernel of truth. An example comes to mind: the fact is that Sergeant X has been off duty for two weeks. He is clearly not on vacation. The rumor is that he is on a disciplinary suspension. (Here the rumor mill may insert a cause for the disciplinary action. No foundation in truth is required!) Eventually, the truth turns out to be that Sergeant X has taken emergency leave due to illness in his family. In the above-described situation, the supervisor would not be showing good faith towards Sergeant X or his agency unless he determined the true story and got the facts to his people.

Unfortunately, other rumors may be neither accidental nor benign. It is a sad trait of the human animal that he sometimes feels a need to hurt his fellow man, perhaps over a real or imagined wrong suffered at some time in the past. The instigation of a particularly nasty and vicious rumor is not infrequently the means for seeking revenge for such an old grievance.

The supervisor may find himself the target of such a barb tossed by someone he has corrected or otherwise obstructed in the past. Regardless of who is the target, cruel untruths must be tracked to their source whenever possible. If the author of the lie has concocted the scheme to cause misery to another individual, formal disciplinary action may be the only adequate response.

Tracing a major, malicious rumor to its source will require the knowledge and backing of the agency's managers. Fellow supervisors may have to become involved, as the various passers of the story will likely belong to various units of the organization. Where necessary, the disciplinary sanctions of the organization may have to be brought to bear to elicit from a "passer" his source. "I just heard it around someplace" cannot be an acceptable answer if rumor control is to succeed.

Rarely, however, should such drastic rumor-fighting measures be required. The supervisor should usually be able to fulfill his management obligations by expressing his concern about the truthfulness of stories brought to his attention. He can promise to find out what the real facts are and then follow up by doing so to the very best of his ability. In all of these ways does the police supervisor carry out his responsibilities to management by the use of his own good judgment and common sense.

RESPONSIBILITIES TO OFFICERS

The responsible supervisor owes his officers the same loyalty that he affords his boss and the larger organization itself. He is their routine link with higher authority. He must accurately and faithfully convey their grievances, thoughts, feelings, and ideas to the levels of the organization where they can be acted upon. In his role as a valuable transmitter of information of many kinds, the supervisor must be alert and responsive to his subordinates and their needs.

The careful sergeant must avoid paraphrasing his employees' words in the light of what he *thinks* they mean. He must repeat their words back to them and ask them to clarify points that he does not understand. When he is sure of their message, then and only then can he pass it along the chain of command. He is charged with the duty of relaying information accurately. He also is responsible for seeing that the message is not altered just to avoid provoking someone higher in the command chain. Accuracy, not consequence, is his worry at this point.

The good supervisor must always be truthful with his subordinates. He relays the bad news along with the good. He may soften a blow in the manner in which he presents his information. The message itself, however, must remain true in content and spirit.

The truthful and honorable police leader does not lie to a subordinate to save that subordinate's feelings. Neither does he give groundless and unwarranted praise. Deception never really solved anyone's problems. Lavish praise given when not earned soon causes all praise to lose its positive value to the employee receiving it. Honesty does, after all, remain the best policy, in matters of praise and commendation as in other areas.

The team leader must acknowledge responsibility for his actions, popular or not. It is disloyal to both superiors and subordinates to pass the buck on the source of an unpopular decision or order. As a part of management, the supervisor must not attack in public a decision or rule that he does not agree with, either. He instead must work quietly to get the improper decision or action reversed or neutralized by logically advancing arguments and evidence supporting his own viewpoint. It is permissible for him to tell his officers that he is going to speak out for a change on their behalf. He must not, however, argue and bicker for it in front of them.

It is not a valid defense for a police sergeant to claim that he lied to a subordinate only to spare that subordinate's pride or feelings. The unpleasant as well as the favorable in an individual's work performance must be made known to him, regardless of how uncomfortable it might make supervisor and supervised alike. It is unfair to the employee to omit telling him of a problem that needs some work, even if that problem may be of a somewhat sensitive nature. It is no fun telling a patrolman that his persistent aroma demands that he shower more often. Failure to tell him, however, is a disservice to the officer as well as to those who must be in close proximity to him.

The police supervisor owes his employees fair and impartial conduct in all of his dealings with them. The job of supervisor is not the place to even-up old grudges or pay back old and still open accounts. It is very likely that unfair, prejudicial actions on the part of the supervisor will be recognized for just what they are. At best, this sort of behavior will make the errant boss few friends and will bring him a deserved unsavory reputation. At worst, it may cost him his job altogether.

Fairness in all dealings means that even the appearance of prejudice or partiality must be avoided. It is enough that one's actions appear unfair in the eyes of others, whether they are actually intended that way or not. This would require that the sergeant avoid awarding an out-of-proportion number of choice assignments to his fishing buddy or the trooper who works on his personal car for him.

Being a good friend of a supervisor can be a trying experience for the friend, too. The supervisor should see to it that the friend does not suffer unnecessarily just because of the relationship. The relation is not always one that can be balanced with ease. This fact contributes to the maxim that having few close friends among subordinates is an unfortunate price the supervisor sometimes has to pay in exchange for his leadership position.

The responsible supervisor will show genuine concern for his workers' problems and worries. Even the unrealistic worries of his people deserve the careful and immediate attention of the supervisor. His experience may tell him, for instance, that the county's "reduction in work force" plans likely will not touch the sheriff's office. The fact that he is not worried personally should not blind him to the fact that some of his deputies with little tenure may be quite upset over the cost-cutting news. It is up to him to allay their fears as much as possible by explaining the basis for his own confident state of mind.

The leader should make it plain to his people that he is always available to them for talking about their difficulties and disasters, job-related and otherwise. Sometimes he will find all that is wanted is for someone to listen to a tale of woe and offer a little sympathy. On other occasions, the supervisor may find it necessary to investigate an alleged grievance or inquire into a very complex problem involving other personnel. Whatever his course of action, the reliable leader will make certain he fulfills his promise to get back to the involved employee with the requested information or response.

As in all other areas of his responsibilities to his employees, the leader must be sincere in his interest in their personal difficulties and concerns. Police officers are generally very perceptive individuals. Insincerity and sham are quickly sensed. A less than honest attitude on the part of their supervisor may bring about long-term bad feelings and an immediate loss of respect.

The responsible police supervisor attempts to further his peoples' abilities and aid them in developing their careers to full potential. Encouragement and advancement of those careers may take various forms. Continuing training and education for his officers are obvious means of preparing for the future. By helping find useful schools and training sessions for his people and encouraging them to sign up for further college work, the police sergeant is strengthening the agency at the same time that he is helping the individual to better himself.

The sergeant is also furthering a subordinate's career when he praises where appropriate and corrects where required. Outstanding work must not go unrewarded, even if that reward may be no more than some carefully chosen words on a given occasion.

Substandard work or improper conduct must just as surely be brought to the attention of those responsible. This must be done whether correction amounts to formal disciplinary action or an informal, "You shouldn't have been doing that." To ignore an out of the ordinary performance, good or bad, is to fail to carry out one of the supervisor's most vital functions: evaluation and review.

The supervisor interested in his employees' career outlook will seek new tasks for them when their talents and attitudes reveal their readiness for change of some kind. He will recognize that it is professionally and personally damaging for an aggressive, interested police officer to grow stale in a given assignment, and he will attempt to find new outlets for stifled or incompletely used energies. Such redirection may mean a shift to a new division, if the option is available. It may mean pursuing additional or different off-the-job distractions.

The supervisor may find, for instance, that the juvenile division has no current openings for a good patrol officer who may have become tired of his patrol duties. He may have to temporarily guide his officer into volunteer work with juveniles until a slot opens to suit his interests. In this case, many more persons in addition to the patrol officer himself could stand to benefit from the sergeant's concern for his officer's development. Meanwhile, the supervisor can stay in touch with the juvenile unit's supervisors in case the awaited opening should occur.

The sergeant interested in furthering his troops' careers should nonetheless keep in mind that some individuals are quite content to spend a very long time–perhaps a whole career–doing essentially the same thing. So be it. Rather than being pressured to try for a detective's badge, the experienced patrolman who truly enjoys working the street in a uniform should be allowed to do just that. If the officer's motives for wanting to remain in that role are legitimate ones (and most will be), then he should be encouraged to use his talents in the best interests of himself and his agency. There is not a police agency anywhere that has a surplus of talented, experienced patrol officers.

Instead of harassing the content, long-term veteran on patrol, the wise sergeant will attempt to involve such an experienced officer in patrol tasks for which his particular abilities are well suited. He might make a good acting supervisor. He could be an excellent choice for training rookie patrol officers. He might even be a good candidate for the departmental committee or work group reviewing some revised procedures for field officers. The practical experience he could bring to such a gathering could be highly valuable.

The responsible police leader is always a mouthpiece and translator for those under his command. He relays their feelings to higher authority in a concise manner. He gets answers for their questions and obtains clarifications for procedures that neither he nor they understand. All the while, he is careful not to rely strictly on his own interpretations of changes or additions to rules and procedures. He knows that to do so would be to run the risk of contributing to an atmosphere in which every line supervisor would be running the show according to his own opinions and interpretations. In the end, inconsistency leads to chaos. Instead of guessing, the smart supervisor confirms his own common sense beliefs and expectations with those in a position to know. He reports his findings back to his people in a timely fashion.

The concerned supervisor can serve as his employees' means of cutting through the strangling coils of red tape and the haze of bureaucratic double-talk which at times seem to reach into even the nation's smallest police agencies. It may be left to him to penetrate the often accidental, occasionally intentional, glittering generalities and obtuse language of the administrator who has had one too many "pop management" seminars. It may be up to him to get a definite answer out of a morass of confusing statements and contradictory information from an insecure manager.

To make his life just a little more complicated, the line supervisor must attempt to extract this needed information without hopelessly alienating the superior he is questioning. This kind of task is neither easy nor comfortable, but it is a necessary and responsible one that a good leader must perform.

Loyalty and responsibility to one's employees, then, requires hard work and sound character on the part of the police supervisor. Still, his responsibilities are not at an end.

RESPONSIBILITIES TO SELF

No police leader can serve his agency and his subordinates in a responsible fashion unless he is first responsible to himself. Just as he must be honest with others, so must he be truthful to himself. The successful police sergeant will not practice self-deception. He will not only acknowledge his weaknesses and shortcomings, he actively will search for symptoms of their existence by asking the opinions of his peers and superiors. More than a few good leaders of police officers have also sought the opinions of the officers they supervised.

The socially responsible police supervisor is self-confident about his strengths, but he is willing to examine the possibility of problems in his performance, too. Just as he is neither cocky nor arrogant about his good points, neither is he unduly embarrassed or defensive about his weaknesses. When he needs help with a given problem, he wisely finds a source of competent assistance.

The patrol sergeant who detects a lack of a sound background of search and seizure principles in his own job knowledge goes to the department's legal advisor, an attorney, the agency's legal library, or other reliable source of legal aid. The detective sergeant who sees himself developing an alcohol problem goes to the agency's psychological counselor, Alcoholics Anonymous, his physician, or another competent professional for much needed and career-saving assistance. The vice unit supervisor who finds that he just "can't stand" the eccentricities of one of his people sits down with the alleged culprit to talk about the problem and to see whether the difficulties are real or imagined.

Dishonesty in any form is something that the professional cannot afford. The ethical supervisor will avoid it at all cost.

The law enforcement officer intent on reaching a happy and useful retirement takes good care of himself both physically and mentally. The law enforcement supervisor presents no exception to this rule of survival. He cannot expect to do his best work if he is continuously tired, grossly overweight, and otherwise out of shape. A supervisor in such condition sets a poor example for his officers.

While the days may have passed in which a police sergeant had to be the biggest and meanest and able to whip any man under him, the leader must nonetheless set an example of physical well-being for his people to emulate.

It is not necessary to become a physical conditioning "nut" to stay reasonably fit and healthy. Virtually any individual of working age can attain a reasonable degree of fitness by instituting a moderate exercise program based upon five days per week. He can run a mile on each of these five days, or he can swim, walk, bicycle, or engage in any other reasonably exhausting pursuit in equivalent amounts.

He can improve and maintain muscle tone by a few weight lifting exercises. He can add some pushups, sit-ups, and squat thrusts to his routine. None of these, practiced in the moderation that his limited time probably allows, will develop showy muscles. These efforts will, however, make him feel better about himself while improving his overall body conditioning. He may add as much more work as he desires to reach higher goals of fitness.

The supervisor rightly concerned about his body will eliminate harmful habits such as smoking (at all) or drinking alcohol in excessive amounts. Both objectives are, of course, easier stated than done. When successfully accomplished, however, both also add greatly to a growing self-assurance and total health picture. The use of illegal drugs or the abuse of legal ones also will be on the intelligent supervisor's personal roster of banned behaviors.

The responsible leader does not overlook the importance of his mental and emotional health. He is careful to schedule himself enough free time to do those things that he does not *have* to do but *wants* to do. Having a healthful good time should not become a strange phenomenon to him. Release from job strains and worries is a must if he is to survive both on and off duty.

The supervisor who is properly concerned about his own welfare will take pains to develop friends and diversions totally unrelated to his work. Time away from the job may have little value as an emotional recharger if it is filled only with shop talk and on-the-job faces.

Supervisors who really know how to separate their work world from their playtime have been known to draw up lists of things they really take pleasure in doing. They then apply themselves to enjoying as many of these things as they can, both as fully and as often as possible. It is not coincidental that many of these same supervisors appear to be the most content as well as the most effective people when they are working.

A sergeant or other police leader who has learned the ways of responsibility to self consistently sets a good example for his troops to follow. He sets a good example in his personal morality. He does not, for instance, preach honesty to his officers while he collects a periodic bribe from the neighborhood bookmaker. He does not accept gratuities from the precinct's merchants while lambasting the practice to his underlings.

The exemplary supervisor leads by example in attitude, too. He does not lecture his men about the evils of starting and passing rumors while giving them the latest tidbit about the lieutenant's girlfriend. He does not damn the department brass to his subordinates and then expect his officers to lavish loyalty upon the organization or to him personally. Here, attitude and loyalty become one.

The really valuable supervisor sets an example of initiative and displayed job interest. His enjoyment of his work and his belief in it show. His enthusiasm for his job and his devotion to it can inspire imitation in his team. A laissez-faire attitude and bored demeanor also can be copied. What is to be imitated is left up to him.

The supervisor who displays responsibility towards himself and conviction for what he believes in does not wait to weigh popular opinion before making his own views known. He does not compromise his ideals. He asserts them and, where necessary, defends them intelligently and reasonably. He does not rage and shout but he does reason and persuade.

The supervisor who demonstrates consistent integrity in his actions does not seek out controversy just to espouse his own views and pet ideas. His sense for organizational survival tells him that he does not challenge his peers or his bosses just for the noise it may bring. When the situation at hand demands it, however, he does not shrink from the task of proper debate.

RESPONSIBILITIES TO THE COMMUNITY

There is yet another group to which the ethical law enforcement supervisor owes his very best efforts. Those who are paying the freight for the operations of the criminal justice system–the people of the community–also deserve his best performance. When he follows the chain of command back to its very beginning, it is to these people that he owes his first allegiance. What he does for them and how he does it will help determine whether or not he is truly living up to the demands of his ethical code.

The first-line law enforcement leader owes his constituents his best work, just as do his peers, subordinates and superiors who are also on the public's payroll. It is not likely that the hard-working police sergeant has any problem with that. But he owes the taxpayers more, as well. He is also responsible for assuring that they get their money's worth in the job performance of the team he leads. As likely as not, the law enforcement supervisor is at least as cynical as the next guy when it comes to voicing opinions on the quality and quantity of work turned out by the "average" government employee. Fair or not, he probably engages in at least a little of the verbal sniping at government employees that seems almost a hobby for the average American. At the same time, it is up to him to see to it that the verbal rocks tossed at government in general are inappropriate for *his* work because of the way he does it. In other words, it is his task to assure that he and his people produce results that may be atypical of what the public expects.

The veteran police supervisor also knows that the public loves a good scandal, particularly when it involves someone who has power and authority over others. The police leader knows that he and his people labor in an environment that presents the opportunity for unethical, improper and illegal behavior. Most cops deal with prostitutes, thugs, cheaters and other criminals a lot more often than they interact with nuns, professors and pillars of virtue. The opportunity to fall morally short and participate in the bad behavior he is sworn to suppress is ever present for the law enforcement practitioner. The ethical police supervisor knows this and remains alert for employee misconduct that will embarrass him, his agency and the public who are footing the bill for all of them. He knows that a well-placed word here and there may prevent an otherwise-honorable cop from starting down the wrong path. He also is ready and willing to blow the whistle on already-existing misconduct and seek justice for the police employee who has betrayed the code of ethics he swore to uphold. While this may be an unpleasant and unsettling task, the moral supervisor will do it because it is the right thing to do. He will do it because of the kind of person he is.

The ethical law enforcement leader also knows that he best serves his community as well as his subordinates when he acts as a positive role model for what a peace officer should be. By obeying the law, on duty and off, he sets a positive example for his troops to follow. By living his personal life in a moral way, he denies the rumor-mongers ammunition to destroy him and his agency. More important, he shows his people by example what a "real cop" is expected to be. At a time when too many young officers get their vision of what a cop's life is all about from really bad television shows and junk action movies, positive role modeling is more important than ever. A good supervisor will see to it that the picture they get from him is positive. An always-watching and quick-to-criticize public will see the same.

Most important of all, it is the right thing to do.

SUMMARY

Certainly more ethical responsibilities could be added to those already noted here. The supervisor who wants to do his job well is also responsible and accountable to the citizens he serves, whatever his jurisdiction happens to be. He owes them the best service he can render. The supervisor owes a certain debt of responsibility to the profession of policing itself. He owes that profession the most ethical, responsible, competent job he can possibly do.

Most of all, however, the police leader laboring persistently and ethically within the guidelines of his responsibilities must recognize his paramount obligations to himself. There is no one he should want to disappoint less. He must, in the end, satisfy himself and his own image of what he wants to be. If his actions please others, that's great. If his boss is happy about his performance, that is an added bonus.

Only when the supervisor knows that he is performing in a manner in which he can be rightfully and personally proud can he honestly lay claim to meeting the ethical requisites of his calling.

POINTS TO REMEMBER

- The law enforcement supervisor must adhere to his own Code of Ethics.
- The police supervisor demonstrates loyalty to his agency and its leaders.
- The suppression of rumors is a valid task of the police leader.
- The leader owes his loyalty to his subordinates and is responsible for their welfare.
- The leader also has obligations to himself and assures that he remains physically, emotionally and morally healthy.
- The law enforcement leader is aware of his obligation to serve his community in a moral and ethical fashion.
- Above all, the supervisor serves as an excellent role model of what a leader should be.

Chapter Four

QUALITIES OF A LEADER

Jesus Christ and Abraham Lincoln were effective leaders. So, for that matter, was Attila the Hun. It is thus not possible to single out extreme goodness or righteousness as being necessary requisites for leadership to exist.

Golda Meir was an international leader and was widely respected in her own nation of Israel. So, too, was the young girl, Joan of Arc, an unknown who became a notable leader of her times. Thus, age and stature cannot necessarily be isolated as required elements for leadership.

Sergeant Jones, a much decorated military veteran, civic leader, and holder of a master's degree in public administration, is a well-respected leader at the Los Angeles Police Department. Sergeant Smith, a high school dropout unwanted during the last war, is held in extremely high esteem by his subordinates and superiors at the Truck Stop, Texas Police Department. He is every bit as effective a leader in his agency's environment as is Sergeant Jones in his. Thus, it would appear that advanced education and advanced formal training are not absolutely reliable indicators of leadership potential either, although their presence would certainly increase the likelihood of its presence.

What, then *is* a real police leader made of today?

One school of thought advances the notion that leaders are born, not made. This group of thinkers offers the idea of the *natural* leader: massive of muscle, marvelous of mind, this hero exudes charisma aplenty and wit as sharp as his intellect.

The natural leader is frequently seen by these theorists as embodied in the persons of some of the ancient military and religious leaders. These old-time heroes (the theorists might point out) had no opportunity to attend seminars on managerial and leadership skills, but nonetheless did some very efficient leading. How can this be explained other than by natural abilities and inherent talents?

Another group of thinkers speaks in favor of leadership as a science. They emphasize the value of *learned* skills over any natural, built-in traits. They remind that some very effective and remarkable leaders have been short, fat, physically unimpressive, and perhaps even downright ugly. Nevertheless, some of them have overcome all sorts of physical handicaps to lead successfully.

These people, it is claimed, have not been natural or born leaders. They have been persons capable of learning from life's experiences and the printed word. Perhaps, too, they learned early the value of leading by example. It is with this second group that a more in-depth examination might reveal some interesting facts applicable to the contemporary supervisor's role. Some of the characteristics exhibited by the experienced supervisor as opposed to a "natural" supervisor are worthy of further inspection.

CHARACTERISTICS OF A LEADER

The importance of setting a good example for one's subordinates has been stressed. It is obvious that proper legal, moral, and ethical behavior is a must for the police supervisor who intends to succeed as a leader. Just which specific characteristics the successful supervisor needs to show his people is a fair topic for argument. While a poll of successful police leaders and administrators might turn up a few variances in the qualities listed, a certain core of vital traits is practically guaranteed. The components include:

Integrity

The police supervisor has heard it many times throughout his or her career, and it is true: the law enforcement officer who does not have integrity has nothing. He cannot succeed in a career that requires the trust of his peers and the public at large. The same holds true in spades for the individual who would call himself a law enforcement leader.

The law enforcement supervisor must in all things set a positive example for his subordinates to copy. Not in any area of endeavor is this principle more important than in the requirement that the leader must set an example of honest, moral and upright behavior for his subordinates to follow. This mandate holds true for both on and off duty conduct. The sergeant who comes to work with liquor on his breath is in no position to challenge the patrolman who does the same. He thereby loses his moral authority to do anything about the bad behavior by his subordinate. Likewise, the supervisor who drives drunk while off the job or cheats on his spouse is setting precisely the wrong kind of example for his subordinates, who likely will learn of his misconduct sooner or later. Because of his lack of integrity and personal moral courage, this individual is not qualified to hold supervisory rank.

Integrity means doing the right thing for the right reasons even (or especially) when no one is watching. It means refraining from doing wrong when likely no one will ever know. It means passing the "video test" on every occasion: would you be doing this if your boss or your loved ones were watching your actions on the big-screen television? If they are to succeed in choosing right over wrong, the police leader's subordinates must have a positive example set for them by their boss. He must at all times role model for them the character and behavior expected of a twenty-first century law enforcement professional. Nothing less will do.

Personal Courage

The law enforcement officer must be willing and able to enter a darkened building in search of an armed offender. He must on occasion put his own life on the line in order to save another. He must, in a word, be brave. The individual who would lead other law enforcement officers must, of course, be willing to share their physical risks and dangers. He, too, must be brave. Most police supervisors recognize that reality of their job and accept it without complaint. The few who do not are quickly found out and held in low esteem by those they supervise. Cops are hard on peers whom they feel lack the courage to do a sometimes dangerous job. They are even harder on those who profess to lead them but lack in the guts department.

But there is another meaning of personal courage for today's law enforcement leader. It is the segment that demands the supervisor have the ability to make the unpopular or difficult decision. In some circles this trait is called administrative courage. In others it is simply referred to as having the backbone to make the really tough calls and then accept the responsibility for having made them, regardless of the outcome. The calls that result in favorable outcomes, of course, are the easy ones. It is much tougher to acknowledge being the parent of a decision that went bad. The courageous supervisor accepts accountability regardless of the results.

Another element of personal courage for the supervisor requires that he must be ready, willing and able to acknowledge as his own a decision or action that will be unpopular with his subordinates or others. This sort of courage requires that he must be capable of telling a subordinate who is perhaps also a good friend that "I am suspending you," not that the captain or the chief is doing so. It requires that he is able to announce the new but unpopular decision about wearing hats or ties to his people without slipping in an editorial comment or making a face that says "I can't believe it, either." Having the courage to do the job of an ethical supervisor requires acceptance of the reality that the boss cannot play to his peoples' desires, particularly when those wishes conflict with getting the job done in the expected way. A courageous supervisor seeks the respect of his people. He does not prostitute himself to win their affection.

Loyalty

The necessity for absolute and sincere loyalty to one's department, superiors, and subordinates has already been noted. It is unreasonable to expect subordinates to show devotion for their boss if he demonstrates by his attitudes and actions that he cares little for their welfare. The loyal supervisor corrects them when they are in error, but he also defends them against all comers when they are wrongfully accused or otherwise subjected to unfair treatment by the police organization. The supervisor who abandons an unpopular or politically uncomfortable defense of a deserving subordinate will earn the distrust of his troops. Equally damaging in the long run will be the loss of respect he suffers with many of his peers and superiors.

Vision

Some have defined leadership as the ability to envision and inspire others to see and seek the accomplishment of that vision. For the police supervisor, vision may mean simply knowing what it is he wants to accomplish, on a short- or (especially) a long-term basis. The vision is the grand goal or objective he is seeking. The patrol sergeant may envision a city or sector in which the residents have a decreased fear of crime and disorder. If he can move his subordinates to share and act upon that vision, they as a team may be able to take measures to reduce the likelihood of someone becoming a victim in that area. The 911 dispatch center supervisor may envision a more customer friendly workplace in which her call takers display excellent telephone courtesy and top-notch customer service. If she can enlist her work group in seeing that vision as well as feeling ownership in it, the citizens calling 911 for help should be the beneficiaries of improved service and remember their contact with the agency in a favorable light.

The best leaders know where they want to go and have at least a rough idea of how they plan to get there. They will fill in the details as they learn more and engage the target. If fulfilling the vision is truly a team effort, some of those details for success will be provided by subordinates who are even closer to the work than is their leader.

Common Sense

It is subject to debate as to whether or not common sense really can be taught. Certainly there is general agreement that life experience and being a skilled observer of the antics of the human animal can help build it. For the police supervisor, common sense contains an element of political sense. That simply means that the seasoned police leader has a good feel (once again based partially on experience) for what will get him, his people, his boss, and his organization in trouble. Common sense tells the patrol sergeant that he should not have his people routinely writing speeding tickets for two miles an hour over the speed limit. Common sense tells the detective sergeant that she needs to let her boss know that her investigators just busted the city councilman's son for rape. And common sense alerts the evidence section supervisor that allowing one of his employees to borrow a shotgun from the evidence locker for some weekend bird hunting could well cook his goose and his boss's, too. None of these supervisors may find a written proscription on any of these activities in the department's rule manual. But all have the common sense to know that permitting any of these missteps to occur will come back to haunt them and the organization.

Common sense permits a leader to look at a problem for which, at times, no formal set of handling guidelines exists. It allows him or her to draw on native intelligence, previous experience, training and a "feel" for the situation to arrive at a solution. The solution may be neither traditional nor perfect, but it addresses the issue and at the very least makes things better. For the full benefits of common sense to be realized, of course, the supervisor must have self-confidence enough to put what his brain has devised into action.

Truthfulness

What a sergeant has to tell one of his officers about job performance will not always make the officer happy. Yet, the supervisor owes his subordinates and his organization total honesty in all things. To give less is to cheat everyone concerned. The employee who has not been told of his apparent shortcomings cannot be expected to improve. The agency itself, uninformed by the supervisor's incomplete rating on an employee's performance, has no opportunity to assist in correcting substandard work. As a result, the public receives police service of diminished quality. Everyone involved suffers as a direct consequence of the supervisor's lack of truthfulness.

It may be much easier at the moment for the police supervisor to avoid the unpleasant confrontation or the uncomfortable counseling session. These tasks, however, go with the turf of those who would be their organization's leaders. The individual who cannot handle the sometimes harsh consequences of reporting, relaying, and speaking the truth has no business remaining in the supervisory ranks.

Reliability

When a manager delegates a task to his sergeant or other first-line supervisor, he should be able to assume that the task will be completed as requested. The manager should not have to think of the matter again until and unless it becomes necessary for him to add or clarify points. Otherwise, his next contact with the situation should be when he evaluates his subordinate's finished work.

Subordinates have an equal right to expect reliability from the line supervisor. When a police employee entrusts a job-related problem to his supervisor for help with a solution, that employee should be able to count on the supervisor to report back to him on the resolution (or non-resolution) of the difficulty. The reporting back should be done in a timely manner. This means that he should not have to be continually jogging his supervisor's memory to check on the status of the issue. A lack of reliability or follow-through on the part of his subordinate often tops the list of the CEO's complaints.

Reliability is a quality that the supervisor cannot afford to be without. Its absence can all too quickly offset whatever other beneficial traits he might possess and employ.

Job Knowledge

The effective leader should know the technical in's and out's of his field. The patrol supervisor is a sort of "master patrolman" and much more when it comes to the specifics and mechanics of getting the job done. The detective sergeant is likewise a "senior investigator" in addition to being a leader.

If the supervisor is a patrol sergeant, he should know how to properly search prisoners, buildings, and vehicles. He should know how to handle violent subjects. He should know his agency's rules, regulations, and procedures for getting the job done. He should, in brief, know the patrol task.

If the supervisor is assigned to a detective unit, he should be well versed in the law regarding his particular area of concern. For example, while the supervisor of the burglary team should have a good working knowledge of criminal law in general, he should have an excellent understanding of the statutes relating to burglary. He should be current in his knowledge of case law regarding laws of arrest, search, and seizure. He should be knowledgeable in the techniques of scientific evidence collection and processing. He should, in other words, know the detective's tasks.

It will take the supervisor himself to determine which specific skills and knowledge he must bring to his work assignment. No one resource can tell him precisely what he needs to know for his particular jurisdiction and position. Having determined just what it is that he needs to know, it is up to him to acquire that job knowledge and apply it accordingly to his supervisory tasks.

Interest

The really top-notch police leader is alive with interest. Interest in his job, interest in his people, interest in the twists and turns of life itself help to motivate him. The person who desires only to be left alone while surviving in a small, limiting world of his own making has little prospect for a successful leadership career.

The interested leader is constantly striving to further his knowledge of his work and the much larger world at large. He reads a lot, he stays up on current events, he is able to carry his end of a discussion on something more substantial than the sports pages. He uses the television set for something more than a sleep inducer and lives life fully. His interest in life itself is contagious to those around him.

Patience and Empathy

The effective leader of police personnel is probably not a saint, but he is an individual capable of empathetically placing himself inside the problems and shortcomings of others. As a result, he is understanding and patient with them. The wise supervisor is acutely aware of his own weaknesses. This awareness may cause him to realize that what may look relatively simple to him may be a complex problem indeed to a less experienced or personally involved subordinate. The patient supervisor then governs accordingly his handling of that subordinate and his problems.

Tact

The truly capable supervisor knows more than what to say in a given communication with another human being. He also knows when, where, and how to say it. The sharp supervisor knows that the manner in which he passes along criticism as well as praise can be extremely important to the feelings of his subordinates. It is also vital to his own reputation as a fair and compassionate leader.

The tactful supervisor praises his people in public and criticizes or corrects those individuals in private meetings with them. He extends to them the same courtesies he would expect from his own boss.

The smart supervisor never uses an individual as a model or example of either good or bad to others. Such a performance by the leader is practically guaranteed to bring the displayed employee the ill will of many of his peers if he is being praised and their sympathy if he is being labeled as the "goat." Such a performance also likely will bring the initiating supervisor the undying malice of at least a part of the group hearing his message.

The tactful leader chooses his words carefully. He knows that useful counseling sessions avoid inflaming the emotions by omitting such people-baiting words as lazy, fat, dumb, stupid, careless, and their kin. All of these insulting words have synonyms that are a little less unpleasant and emotional to the ear. Those substitutes should be used carefully in place of their more aggravating cousins.

Trust

A wise supervisor does not require that the honesty, integrity, and ability of his subordinates be conclusively proven to him at the outset of their relationship. Instead, he assumes that all of these qualities are present in his people until and unless solid evidence proves the contrary to be true.

This is not to say that the police sergeant must be blind to his subordinates' faults. Just the opposite is true: he must be aware of their weaknesses and help them to overcome these difficulties. Even while doing so, however, he believes what they tell him and show him unless his trust is proven to be unfounded. In a field where justice is all-important, the supervisor believes in their innocence until guilt is proven beyond a reasonable doubt.

Trust is not expected to be deaf, either. The citizen who complains to the sergeant that one of his officers has performed improperly cannot be rebuffed with a "My man can do no wrong" attitude. The complaint must be investigated. Nonetheless, even while probing his subordinate's actions, the common sense supervisor communicates an attitude of trust and empathy for the involved officer. Impartiality in the misconduct inquiry does not rule out trust until such point as trust is shown to be unwarranted. Impartiality does, however, call for open-mindedness and a feeling for the citizen's point of view.

In all things, the supervisor counts on the faith and trust of his officers. He cannot count on either unless he first grants them the same considerations.

Fairness

The effective supervisor's strong sense of justice is not limited to the victims, witnesses, and offenders who are the stuff of the police job. He directs that same sense of justice to his dealings with the police personnel entrusted to his leadership.

A keen sense of fair play is a necessity for the contemporary law enforcement supervisor. It must guide him in the assignment, evaluation, reward, and correction of his subordinates. There is no room for preferential treatment of an off-duty pal. There is no place for a grudge satisfied in excessive amounts of disciplinary actions handed to an employee. There can be no tolerance for an undeserved reward given or a much deserved one passed over. The term "unfair" must never be accurately used to describe the supervisor's actions where his subordinates are involved. Even more difficult, perhaps, the very appearance of unfair or otherwise tainted treatment of subordinates must be avoided.

There is nothing wrong with bouncing a supervisory opinion off of a fellow police supervisor or two before implementing it. An uninvolved, largely disinterested observer might be able to see points missed by someone more closely involved in the situation at hand. Recommendations for disciplinary actions are excellent examples of situations calling for more than one opinion as an assurance of fair play.

Any given supervisory act is not worthy if it is not also fair. Any supervisor who is, for whatever reason, incapable of an impartial and just response in a given situation is equally unworthy for his role as a trusted leader. He will be obliged to either work to overcome any unfairness in his actions and attitudes or remove himself from the leadership role entrusted to him.

BARS TO LEADERSHIP

There are significant pitfalls if not gaping tiger traps awaiting the unwary or careless police supervisor. Just as there are important strengths he must cultivate in himself, there are dangerous traits and tendencies that he must avoid. To succumb to any of them could destroy his ability to lead effectively. At the very least, failing to overcome the bad effects of one or more of these enemies will compromise his position as a leader. Some of the more dangerous offenders are not hard to identify:

Frequent Displays of Temper to Subordinates

To get really, visibly angry occasionally shows that an individual is human. To direct the anger at a subordinate or coworker in a tirade of verbal abuse is an indicator of a lack of maturity and self-control that a supervisor cannot afford to display.

No one likes to be yelled at or belittled, especially in front of others. The police sergeant above all people should know all too well the dangerous effects of leaving the recipient of verbal abuse with no opportunity for a face-saving retreat. The culprit confronted on the street is liable to strike the officer who treats him in such a demeaning manner. So, too, is the police officer who is assaulted by his boss likely to respond in kind. He probably will not retaliate physically against the supervisor attacking him, but his response may be verbally hostile, at best.

Long-standing ill feelings can easily result from a harsh show of emotional frustration directed at a subordinate. Those ill feelings can come from the subordinate himself, others present, and perhaps from those who hear about the incident, as they surely will.

It is not much better to verbally abuse a recalcitrant employee in private. The intense resentment will still be there. Future working relations with the employee will be strained at best and hostile at worst. Other employees who were not present will hear all about it just as soon as the "victim" can get to the department grapevine.

Any supervisor who finds himself greatly angered or otherwise upset by a subordinate's performance needs some cooling-off time before confronting the offending individual. Reason needs time to push more emotional feelings into the background.

The supervisor who has perhaps gone over this incident or a very similar one with the same employee on a previous occasion may initially want to throttle him for his newest misdeed. Common sense will hopefully take over, however, if it is just given time to assert itself.

The very pressing nature of much police business may require that a supervisor take corrective action immediately in a delicate field situation. An example might be found in the case of the patrol sergeant who has happened upon unsearched and unsecured prisoners being placed in a patrol car. Field survival and common sense safety practices demand that these prisoners be removed from the vehicle, searched, and secured right away. This is an issue that cannot wait until later for debate and discussion. What the sergeant on-scene *can* do, however, is instruct the officers present to carry out the necessary corrective action. Any counseling or disciplinary actions should be handled later. The twin goals of (1) remedying a dangerous situation, and (2) obtaining a desired change in employee behavior have been achieved without a disruptive scene or confrontation.

The field sergeant will encounter situations requiring immediate corrective action, as found in the foregoing instance. However, he should seldom encounter a situation requiring public, immediate and summary tail-chewing of his personnel. Good supervision simply is not done that way anymore.

Discipline should not be administered when the one administering it is still angry about the transgression involved. An emotionally inflamed mind is sometimes not a very logical one. The previously mentioned cooling down time, whether it amounts to minutes or more, allows all parties involved to view the incident in the calmer light of "later." All sides can be heard, including that of the accused employee. What sounded like an unreasonable course of action when only some of the facts were known may appear considerably more reasonable when all participants have been heard, and all the facts are at hand.

The employee obviously has a right to present all evidence favorable to his cause before any punitive action is visited upon him. There may be some neutral observers to be heard from, too.

Playing Favorites with Subordinates

The extreme importance of impartiality in the makeup of the competent supervisor has already been stressed. That very same powerful sense of fair play found in most police officers will surely cause them to rebel at the first sign of partiality displayed towards a team member. The supervisor unwise enough to "pick on" or discipline unreasonably an officer under his command may find that he has made that employee a virtual martyr overnight.

By the same token, the leader who favors a subordinate over his peers has probably sealed that employee's fate as far as his coworkers are concerned. They probably will ridicule and isolate him and his supervisor both—at least to the extent of their ability to do so. If the supervisory favoritism is obvious enough, news of the leader's indiscretion will spread throughout the organization. As the word reaches the higher echelons of command, management may find it necessary to deal with the overly partial supervisor.

No one can say that the police supervisor's subordinates cannot also be his friends. Off-duty friendships and relationships cannot be allowed, however, to influence the way in which the leader treats his subordinates at work. Perhaps without even realizing it, the supervisor may be placing more credibility in his pals' statements than those of their peers whom he may not know as well. He also may be awarding them preferential treatment in assignments and the like without being aware of what he is doing. Meanwhile, he is building up resentment directed at himself and his employee friends because of this unintentional but real special treatment.

Police work is difficult enough without adding to it the bad feelings and internal squabbling brought about by preferential handling of subordinates. The supervisor who practices favoritism is probably hurting the recipient of such favors far more than he is helping him. Isolation and abuse of the officer from his fellow employees are rather stiff penalties to pay for special favors from above.

It goes almost without saying that the police supervisor must exercise even more discretion where off-duty friendships with police employees of the opposite sex are involved. Male police officers–in spite of the convincingly macho image they enjoy portraying–are among the working world's worst gossips and scolds. Many like nothing better than a good tale to carry and perhaps embroider a bit for added interest. If sex can be injected into the story, it's even better.

An actual or strongly suspected sexual relationship between the supervisor and a member of the work unit can be devastatingly harmful to the job atmosphere. The sergeant who is courting intimate terms with a subordinate is headed for problems. It is well and good to say that his off-duty pursuits should be of no concern to his peers, subordinates, or bosses. An awareness of the real world, however, should convince the intelligent supervisor that such is not the case in reality.

Whether true or not, claims of on duty special treatment for one's intimate friend are almost certain to surface. If the relationship is one that the supervisor and his or her friend want to maintain, a change in assignment for one of them is probably a necessity. The change must be significant enough that the supervisor/supervised work connection is broken entirely.

In the end, it may seem grossly unfair to require the responsible supervisor to carefully monitor his friendships, particularly his off the job associations with his buddies who are coincidentally his subordinates. The burden might be lightened a little if it is remembered that the "too close" friendship with a subordinate may bring that subordinate real grief, and unnecessarily so.

The subordinate who is suspected of receiving preferential treatment from a friendly boss really is getting heat from two sides. Beyond the unpleasantness that his co-workers may accord him, the employee may also catch unintended but real abuse from the boss himself. This state of affairs can come about if the police supervisor, suspecting group feelings against his perceived special treatment of a friend, counters by setting a tougher set of standards on that friend than the other employees are required to meet. In attempting to show others that his friend at work is just another employee, the boss may instead select the unfortunate employee for another sort of special treatment: a kind of reverse discrimination. The employee's unnecessary discomfort is the end result.

Holding a Grudge or Getting Even with Subordinates

The human animal tends to remember when it has been wronged. The same creature also frequently displays a very real if unpleasant tendency to seek revenge for the real or perceived wrong. Inasmuch as it is a safe assumption that police supervisors are quite human it may be reasonably expected that revenge is no stranger to their repertoire of feelings and drives.

Human or not, grudge-holding and ploys to "even the score" are not things that the ethical supervisor can afford to indulge. They can destroy his effectiveness as a respected leader and, when carried to extremes, can cost him his job.

The police supervisor must above all else be true to himself. Nothing is going to make him feel affectionate towards someone who has clearly wronged him through words, deeds, or other means. It is rather obvious that the sergeant intent upon survival in the police bureaucracy cannot afford to display hostility towards a superior officer. That is just good common sense. It is no less true, however, that the supervisor cannot direct such displays of ill will towards his peers or subordinates, either.

A hostile or conniving approach by the supervisor towards others within his agency is not acceptable. Frankness and openness when problems arise should be the acceptable substitutes. There is nothing wrong with the supervisor confronting his antagonist at the proper time and place. He then calmly describes his beef to the individual and makes a serious effort to end the problem there and then. Whether success or failure is the result of this attempt at clearing the air, he does not retain a grudge or plot retaliation.

Perhaps some honest talk will show both parties to the dispute that they are not as far apart as initially believed. Perhaps there has been a genuine mistake or misunderstanding. Maybe the whole thing can be resolved with little pain.

Barring such a happy ending, the participants to the disagreement can at least agree to disagree in an acceptable manner. The subordinate should be told that any bad feelings, such as they may be, will not result in any unfair treatment of the subordinate. The future working relationship will be on a professional basis. Then, with the air cleared and the issue directly addressed, it is up to the supervisor to carry out his promises: fair treatment, no revenge games, no behind the scenes maneuverings intended to hurt the employee.

Distorting the Truth with Lies or Intentional Omissions

Police supervisors routinely expect their charges to be truthful with them. It is certainly not too much for those subordinates to expect the same honesty in turn.

To many police leaders, there is no greater sin than that committed by a subordinate officer who lies to his boss. The same supervisor who may tolerate occasional derelictions in other areas will explode self-righteously if he catches one of his officers lying to him. On the other hand, the police officer may realize that he cannot afford the luxury of blowing up in his supervisor's face when and if he catches the boss in an untruth. He will feel just as badly, however, and his peers will quickly hear of the leader's "forked tongue" tendencies.

The unethical leader can find a number of reasons to lie to his subordinates: he can divert his peoples' criticisms by claiming that one of his own unpopular or unwise rulings actually came down from above; he can swear to take up the matter of his officer's overdue merit pay raise with the lieutenant, and then promptly and intentionally forget the promise; he can keep the peace by telling his detectives that nothing became of the citizen's complaint on them, while quietly inserting letters of reprimand in their personnel files.

The police supervisor can pull all kinds of stunts and tell various lies to make his job seem easier at the moment. Such peace is, however, an illusion, and even that is liable to be short-lived. Any respite an intentionally deceitful leader might feel will be temporary in nature. It may sound trite to say that most lies require even more lies to support them, and that eventually most of the untruths come home to haunt their author. Life experience would show, however, that both of these statements are very frequently true.

The police supervisor cannot work effectively when he has a reputation for questionable credibility among his superiors, peers, and subordinates. A reputation of that sort can be just as fatal to his career as a reputation for perjury on the witness stand. Both faults are incompatible with a profession based upon ethics, trust, and personal responsibility.

Setting a Poor Example

It is necessary to stress once more the extreme importance of a supervisor who sets a good example for his employees to emulate. The emphasis is well deserved. It is absolutely inexcusable for a police leader to expect his people to perform in a given fashion while he sets an example in just the opposite direction. It is a cardinal sin for any person who would call himself a leader to perform in such a manner.

If the patrol sergeant wants his officers to remain alert, awake, and active during that all-night tour of duty, then he had better not be napping himself. If the detective sergeant expects his investigators to arrive at work sober and stay that way while they are on the job, then he had better get rid of the bottle in his own desk. If the evidence section superintendent is going to demand that his clerks maintain the integrity of the evidence entrusted to their care, then he had best not go "shopping" through the parcels himself.

The examples cited above are relatively simple, homely ones. They make a point that carries over quite well to more complex, sophisticated issues of supervision by example. The unwavering point remains that the old adage "monkey see, monkey do" is in full effect here. A leader expecting proper and ethical behavior from his followers sets a good example for them to emulate.

Any manager worth his rank should immediately scrutinize his first-line supervisor when that supervisor's people all show similar weaknesses or faults. If they are routinely late getting to work, when is the sergeant getting to *his* post? If they show little interest or initiative for their jobs, what is their supervisor's expressed and demonstrated attitude in that regard? There may be some interesting correlations. The alert manager will look for them. The smart supervisor will know this and see to it that what the boss sees in his officers speaks well of them *and* their leader.

Good work, a good attitude, and a pleasant disposition really *can* be contagious. It is up to the conscientious supervisor to guarantee that his approach to leadership is one of "do as I do." A poor example set by a leader is unbecoming, unethical, and unacceptable.

Showing No Loyalty to Anything or Anyone

The rookie patrolman was issuing a summons to a traffic violator when he was approached by an irate individual. The angry man told the officer to move his patrol car from the driveway, which the officer was temporarily blocking, or he would "run over it." The officer replied that he would do so as soon as he was finished writing the summons. With no further words, the man got into his vehicle and nudged the side of the patrol car, denting it slightly.

Summoned to the scene by a more than slightly agitated young officer, the patrol sergeant arrived and assessed the situation. Despite the rookie's protestations that he had been deliberately rammed, the sergeant listened briefly to the still angry citizen and directed that an accident report be taken. He proceeded to apologize to the man for the whole encounter and chastised the patrolman for failing to move when asked to do so.

The sergeant continued to berate the patrol officer back at the station. The chief of police happened to walk by and inquired as to what was taking place. The sergeant related his version of the story, after which the chief exploded and demanded to know why the offending motorist was not in jail for damaging city property. A soundly shaken sergeant was at a loss for words and could not explain his actions. He had assumed that the chief would presume the citizen correct and the officer at fault in any such dispute. Obviously, the luckless sergeant had assumed incorrectly. The supervisor could now not move fast enough to make plans for the "fiend's" capture, while congratulating the suddenly exonerated rookie for his cool handling of the crisis.

This true story illustrates a point. The sergeant in the case demonstrated no loyalty whatsoever to his shaken subordinate involved in the "accident or crime?" caper. He quickly abandoned the patrolman in an attempt to satisfy what he thought would be the whims of the Big Boss. In placing his own welfare considerably above that of his subordinate, he displayed a lack of ownership in standards of ethical conduct. He abandoned his officer when he felt it was politically expedient to do so. He attempted to "fade the heat" for himself while leaving his underling to bake. In the end, this supervisor was loyal to nothing beyond his desire for job survival with what he assumed to be a tyrannical boss.

The police supervisor who is capable of little loyalty to anything is in the wrong line of work. The acceptance of the rank of unit or team leader implies immediate and concurrent acceptance of the problems, faults, and difficulties of that unit's members, as well as ownership in the unit's successes and strong points.

The would-be leader who would abandon his ethics, his employees, or the welfare of the agency itself when faced with controversy or other discomfort has no place in the leadership ranks of law enforcement. He is not up to handling difficult tasks.

It is all too easy to desert the employee who is in trouble, or disclaim responsibility for the unpopular rule or management decision. It is much more comfortable initially to join in the condemnation of the troubled individual or blame the controversial rule or decision on the "ignorance" of the command officer who imposed it.

It may be much more uncomfortable, though more professionally responsible, to advance the good points of the accused employee or list the merits of command's new project or plan. Such demonstrated responsibility is required of the competent supervisor. Comfort cannot be his all overpowering concern in all things. Morally courageous actions do not emanate from wishy-washy supervisors.

The police supervisor who is both loyal *and* responsible does not tirelessly defend that which is clearly wrong. Nor does he make excuses for misbehavior or poor judgment on the part of his bosses. He does, however, utilize the proper chain of command channels for his protests.

Loyalty also means that the supervisor will not use his subordinates as stepping stones or expendable tools to reach a higher position in his agency. The individual who utilizes his employees' talents only to further his own career will leave a trail of hostility and distrust behind him. A good leader cannot afford such reckless irresponsibility.

The leader who makes use of his subordinates' talents and then claims their accomplishments as totally his own is heading for a certain fall. The deceptive supervisor who selfishly capitalizes upon the work of others to ascend to his new position may find himself in trouble when asked to repeat his performance, but this time without the aid of his former, "ghost" helpers.

The loyal supervisor always renders honors where they are earned. He does not actively seek honors or acclaim for himself. If he is doing his job well, credit enough should come to him through his established connection with his subordinates' accomplishments.

COMMAND PRESENCE

Command presence is not an easy thing to define. It is widely considered to be an invaluable asset for a police officer to possess. This goes double for police leaders. Its precise nature remains somewhat hazy, all the same.

It is perhaps a little easier to say what command presence is *not.* Command presence as applied to law enforcement and law enforcement supervision does not call for the ramrod-stiff backbone of the storm trooper—who has an equally rigid personality to match. It does not require arrogance in a leader, nor does it mandate an arrogant attitude.

At the same time, command presence is not to be found in the scruffy, sloppily uniformed, foot-dragging patrol sergeant whose appearance and demeanor suggest that he has slept in the clothes he is wearing. A mentally lazy attitude and a disinterested approach to whatever task is at hand identify the perpetrator as very poor leadership material.

Command presence is missing in the would-be police supervisor who shuns self-assertiveness and follows the crowd rather than leading it. This rather dull character waits until a consensus of opinion has formed and then pledges allegiance to it. He determines a subordinate's political ties in the organization before challenging him. He avoids making decisions whenever possible, allowing his troops to make them alone and suffer the consequences when they choose poorly. In other words, he exerts about as much command presence as a marshmallow.

Command presence has been referred to as the ability to appear in total control of oneself, regardless of how confused or confounded the surrounding situation may be. Command presence is not, however, reflected in a saintly expression of absolute peace on the face of its owner. (Such a demeanor in a situation of real disaster would probably reveal a true lunatic, not a true leader!) Rather, the leader with considerable skill in displaying an air of command presence exudes an attitude of self-confidence as well as self-control under stressful surroundings. From his first days in the recruit academy, the police officer learns to control his emotions to at least some extent as he goes about performing some of the less-than-enjoyable duties among his job responsibilities. He practices a degree of self-control as he handles obnoxious drunks, long-dead corpses, and gruesome wounds from varied versions of mayhem. The police supervisor will be asked to display some of those same skills as he goes about his duties of providing an example of calm and competent leadership at various scenes of disorder and disaster, whether natural, manmade, or bureaucratic in character.

Command presence demands a lot from the leader who would practice it. First of all it calls for command ability. Command, in turn, speaks of authority, control, mastery, and confidence, to list just a few of the average dictionary's terms used to describe it.

Presence, meanwhile, may refer to personal bearing, carriage, demeanor, or appearance. It may denote the emotional or attitudinal atmosphere around a particular individual.

Put together, then, the terms *"command"* and *"presence"* speak of an overall attitude, appearance, or demeanor exhibited by a person. In the case of the police supervisor, that demeanor on display may range from a quiet, take-charge manner at a major crime scene to a still quiet but very firm facial expression which announces, "The boss is here–shut up and pay attention," in a crowded patrol briefing.

The effective supervisor cannot afford to allow indecisiveness or timidity to become part of a facial mask for him. He cannot permit disabling fear or unreasoning anger to control his actions or dictate his

words. Rather, he must remain obviously in control and visibly confident in his outward expression and attitude. Depending upon the situation at hand, such a display might require the talents of a polished
actor to supplement those of a talented leader.

Calmness, self-confidence, and self-control must remain the most
valuable assets of the police supervisor intent upon developing a
deserved reputation for ample command presence. The supervisor
himself may be unable to say when he has acquired the traits and abilities referred to collectively as command presence. It is more likely
that the first to notice the presence of this quality will be the subordinates who work under his leadership. When this kind of a reputation
has been built, the supervisor who owns it will find himself in posses-
sion of an irreplaceable tool for police leadership.

MORALE AS A TOOL

Although police officers may not always excel at attaching formal
dictionary definitions to words, most could quickly tell what "morale"
means to them personally. The uniformed officer might say that to
him, "good morale" means that he actually looks forward to going to
work, hitting the street, and making a decent pinch or two. To the
plainclothes investigator, good morale may mean that he feels good
because his caseload is no heavier than anybody else's, his boss recognizes his clearance rate as something more than a numbers game,
and his hours of overtime worked are kept within reasonable limits. To
the vice cop, "good morale" might mean that he has a good feeling
about what he is doing because the boss does not pile unnecessary
paperwork on his desk, backs him when he makes a good faith (but
sour) judgment call, and has his best interests at heart when reassign-
ment time rolls around.

The officer might have to think awhile before telling someone exactly why it is that he feels good about coming to work. He might then
say that he feels good about his work because, for one thing, he feels
he is accomplishing an important task that most people are incapable
of doing well. He might say that he feels pretty good about being left
alone to do his job as he sees fit, so long as he does it properly. He
might even tell his listeners that it is a good feeling knowing that his
sergeant trusts him, supports him, gets him what he needs to do his job

well, and straightens him out when he is off course.

The police supervisor who would be a successful and useful leader could do far worse than to heed the words of this officer and also adhere to some of the other recommendations for effective leadership noted earlier in this chapter. He will be avoiding some of the pitfalls pointed out, too. He will know that a sense of well-being—call it morale or whatever—can come from working for a boss who sets reasonable objectives, lets his subordinates know what those objectives are, and leads them in reaching for success. He also will know that poor examples, unfairness, disloyalty, pettiness, and selfishness on his part can all too quickly destroy that sense of well-being among his employees.

The police supervisor can contribute a lot to good morale by encouraging a good work environment and good working relationships. A good work environment does not call for Lincolns for patrol vehicles and steak and lobster at coffee-break. From the subordinate officer's viewpoint, it means the chance to do his job with minimal unwarranted interference from the boss, having the proper tools to do a proper job, having adequate training and sound procedural guidelines to apply to work problems, and having a supervisor who is available when needed and who is not an omnipresent hindrance when he is not required.

Good working relationships do not require that every officer love every other member of the work team. Good relationships do, however, require that team members respect the varying abilities, opinions, and feelings of their workmates. Neither prejudices nor more overt hostilities have any place in a unit of working police employees. The employee must know that his supervisor will not tolerate either.

The wise police sergeant knows that he often cannot lead a team of personal friends, even if such an arrangement was desirable. He also knows that it is his responsibility to help his people get along by confronting personality clashes and personal grievances as they come up. He brings antagonists together to attempt a resolution of their differences, realizing all the while that the troubles are possibly not as grave as believed by those directly involved.

The supervisor serves as a sympathetic listener and an intelligent confidant when personal difficulties begin to affect an officer's job performance. He helps personally where he can and makes careful referrals for help in areas where his own knowledge is limited.

It is important for him to get along with his subordinates while encouraging an atmosphere where they can get along with one another. He emphasizes team effort over individual glory, but is available when help is needed. When the occasion demands, he will accept his troops' support, in turn.

SUMMARY

This chapter presented a virtual laundry list of what being a supervisor requires of the would-be leader. As a leader, the police supervisor will have many and diverse tasks, none of which is more vital than his obligation to prepare his subordinates for their work. He will strive to accomplish this preparation through adequate and continuing education and training. It is this obligation that the next chapter will deal with.

POINTS TO REMEMBER

- Integrity and personal courage are among the most important traits that a law enforcement leader can demonstrate.
- Vision, common sense, loyalty, truthfulness, reliability, job knowledge, interest, patience, empathy, tact, trust and fairness are also vital characteristics of an effective leader.
- Frequent displays of temper and playing favorites among subordinates are highly destructive to a leader's effectiveness.
- Gossiping and rumor-mongering are not games in which the ethical supervisor can participate.
- Holding grudges and seeking revenge against others will sabotage the leader's effectiveness.
- Lying or setting a poor example also will destroy a supervisor's ability to lead effectively.
- The best leaders display ample command presence without appearing arrogant.
- The subordinates of a strong and effective leader are more likely to display high morale than the subordinates of poor leaders.

Chapter Five

THE POLICE LEADER AS AN EDUCATOR

Just a few decades ago, the newly hired police officer could expect little in the way of formal preparation for his new job. If he was lucky, he might be given a weary, ragged set of departmental rules and regulations. These attempted to warn him of any behavior that might get him (and possibly his superiors) into serious trouble.

If the new officer had a particularly interested sergeant, he might even get a "canned" talk on the unwritten "do's and don'ts" of his job. The talk probably focused upon how he could best stay out of trouble with his real boss: his sergeant.

Then, without much further fanfare, the new man was thrust out into the world of good guys and bad guys, virtue and evil. If he was fortunate, he might be paired with a more experienced officer in order to learn the ropes of street policing. It was expected that the rookie officer would learn the veteran's good habits and imitate them. Unfortunately, he probably picked up the less desirable ones, too. Mistakes and improper practices were thus perpetuated.

Virtually all law enforcement agencies retain some form of the old "do as I do" training for new police officers. This training is conducted by Field training Officers, or FTOs. Much of value can be passed on in this way. The practice is invaluable to common sense police work, though there are additional, equally valuable sources of job knowledge available to today's recruit officer. His primary supervisor is one such source and plays a large role in preparing the novice police officer for a useful career in an increasingly complex profession.

RESPONSIBILITY TO INSTRUCT

It is by now no surprise to the reader that the police supervisor plays a vital part in the welfare of both his subordinates and the organization of which they are components. He helps his people to learn their jobs and sees to it that they perform their tasks properly and well. He helps his agency by eliciting the best work possible from his subordinates as he guides them in their work towards accomplishing the police agency's goals and objectives.

One way in which the supervisor aids his employees and his employer is through his efforts in education and in-service training of the work force. The police supervisor may become involved in the training function at any of several levels. The sergeant may, for instance, be assigned to the police recruit academy where the information and skills taught will be of the most basic sort. At this level, he will be operating on the assumption that his pupils know virtually nothing about law, law enforcement or policing.

At another level, the sergeant may become involved in training for experienced officers, which may consist of a yearly block of refresher instruction. As a part of such a program, he may assist in briefing "old hands" at new techniques, procedures, and departmental guidelines that have come about as a result of changing technology needs and resources. He may take part in an update session on changes in statutes and case law affecting police operations, or he may even be responsible for demonstrating the proper operation of new equipment, such as the latest generation of in-car computer terminals or mobile breath-testing devices for alcohol violations enforcement.

At yet another level, the police supervisor may be giving advanced instruction in a specialized field of endeavor. He may (depending upon his own background and expertise) teach a course in evidence collection and processing to a class of patrol officers being schooled as crime scene technicians, instruct a session in supervisory techniques for new sergeants, or lead a group of officers in exploring crisis intervention techniques.

Whatever the subject matter for instruction, the police supervisor may safely assume that he will be (or should be) an integral part of the instruction effort. Such teaching may be found in a variety of formats. It may find the supervisor-instructor in a classroom setting at the police academy, in the field on a mock crime scene, or at the front of the patrol briefing room conducting roll call training for a team of uniformed officers. Some of the areas that might be covered are explored next.

TOPICS FOR POLICE INSTRUCTION

There are as many potential topics of study for a police educational program as there are areas of human knowledge. Generally speaking, however, a certain core curriculum can be found at the heart of most police recruit academies. Running anywhere from 600 hours of classroom instruction to double that figure and more, the recruit academy devotes time to such diverse yet vital subjects as the following:

Department and academy orientation
First aid
Cardiopulmonary resuscitation
Criminal investigative techniques
Mechanics of arrest
Laws of arrest
Laws of search and seizure
Code of criminal procedure
Penal or criminal code
Juvenile law
Evidence collection and rules of evidence
Narcotics and dangerous drugs
Firearms policy and use
Personal defensive tactics
Departmental policy
Departmental rules and regulations
Operational procedures and orders
Handling of intoxicated persons
Handling of the mentally ill
Community-oriented policing
Courtroom demeanor
Professional ethics
Interviewing skills
Identification and collection of evidence
Crime scene processing
Radio procedures
Traffic accident investigation

Vehicle code
Civil law and proceedings
Patrol techniques
Domestic violence
Child neglect and abuse
Crowd control
Traffic management
Report writing
Computer skills
Police driving
Observation and recall skills
Investigative skills and techniques
Field survival
Car stops and vehicle searches
Municipal (or county) statutes and ordinances

Depending upon the particular agency or jurisdiction involved, this very basic list of instructional topics may be added to or deleted from as circumstances or problems unique to a given locale may dictate. A department located near a national border might, for instance, wish to add a substantial section on United States Customs and Immigration Law.

In addition to the topics certain to be covered in any basic academy, just about any of the same subjects of study are fair game for inclusion in any refresher training program in law enforcement. Evidence collection and preservation techniques do change over time, for example, as do state and local laws on all sorts of topics. Revisions in the code of criminal procedure may even bring major changes in the police officer's authority and responsibility under law.

The agency and its supervisors interested in preparing the working police officer to the greatest extent possible for the complex tasks ahead will pay close attention to the demands of continuing education in current legal guidelines and issues. They will not permit him to become outdated in questions of constitutionality of various laws or procedures. Only in such a fashion can the working officer receive a full measure of the support, direction, and protection which his sensitive position deserves.

Besides his important role in preparing and presenting the recruit academy curriculum, the police supervisor's abilities will be drawn into the preparation of the in-service instructional effort. He may find himself called upon to instruct any of a number of possible refresher or specialized topics for veteran officers. Such a listing of in-service subjects could be practically endless, but might include the following:

Latent fingerprint processing and evaluation
General crime scene processing
Extrication and rescue
Major crime scene investigation
Fraud investigation
Intelligence operations
Forged instrument evaluation
Counter-terrorism
Firearms
Legal update
Use of force
Crisis intervention
Undercover operations
Surveillance techniques
Building searches
Crime prevention
Special weapons and tactics
Advanced accident investigation
Disaster scene operations

Once again, depending upon his background, experience and over-all job knowledge, the police supervisor could be expected to handle several of these topics for specialized instruction.

The sergeant who has the best interests of his people at heart will not wait until his own boss demands that some attention be paid to the in-service education endeavor. Instead, he will assess his peoples' needs for training and get it scheduled for them. An assessment may be conducted by evaluating their work and its readily apparent strengths and weaknesses. He also will ask them what they want and need in the area of further schooling and job preparation.

The supervisor should temper his subordinates' requests for training within the known limits of resources available. It is one thing to arrange for the veteran officer who feels he is weak in accident inves-tigation skills to sit in on the next academy's accident investigation ses-sions, but it is quite another matter to send him to a month-long seminar out of state. No supervisor has all the training resources at his disposal that he would like to make available to his troops. The wise supervisor makes judicious and careful use of the education and training to which he does have reasonable access.

Whatever the additional resources and capabilities of his agency, the police supervisor probably will find that a whole series of constraints—time limitations, available personnel, limited funds for "outside" schools—will require that he handle many training duties himself. Much of this instruction will be accomplished at the team or small unit level.

In order to best perform his tasks as a competent teacher of police officers, the supervisor will find a need to develop and refine a specific set of skills. He will need to know: (1) how to organize what he is going to teach, (2) which instruction method he is going to use, and (3) how he will evaluate the results on his officer "students." The next section will help the supervisor prepare for his or her role as instructor of law enforcement topics.

PROPER USE OF LESSON PLANS

The average patrol sergeant would show no surprise if told that he needed a plan of attack before leading an assault on a barricaded gunman. The average detective supervisor would likewise readily accept the fact that he required some sort of planning and organizing of a major case investigation before presenting it to the Grand Jury. Neither of these police leaders should express shock, then, when told that a plan is also a must for instruction in police subject matter.

Good instructors put together a lesson plan before they commence their teaching efforts in front of a class. An effective lesson plan can range from some hand-printed notes and plans on a lined card or a single sheet of notebook paper to a comprehensive, typed outline with supporting notes and material in a fancy binder. Regardless of the format, the aim is the same: to provide instructor and instructed alike with an idea of what is to be accomplished, how it is to be done, and in what ways the student will show his mastery of the material covered. The plans also include the instructor's notes to be used in his presentation.

In the attempt to accomplish these objectives, the lesson plan may be divided into five categories: (1) **Overview,** (2) **objective(s),** (3) **outline and/or notes,** (4) **evaluation,** and (5) **sources.**

Each part of the lesson plan plays a role in the actual presentation of the material to a class. If the supervisor is presenting his material at a large police academy class, the academy's staff may want a typed and bound outline of the proposed presentation well in advance of the actual class date. If the supervisor is planning on presenting the training to his team at a roll call briefing, then his planning will probably be for his own benefit only and may be more informal. It may consist of little more than roughly jotted notes and an outline.

Formal or otherwise, each of the five steps of the typical lesson plan deserves further explanation and description. Each can serve to guide the instructor in improving his presentation.

1. Overview

Here the instructor should present a short summation of what he hopes to accomplish with the lesson. This can be a general statement and should be no more than a couple of sentences in length. A sample overview might read: "The lesson will teach the officer how to protect and recover physical evidence of a crime."

The overview is something that can (at the instructor's discretion) be given to the students at the beginning of the training session. They will thus have some idea as to what is expected of them and where the instructor is planning to lead them.

2. Objective(s)

The overview offers a broad statement of what the lesson will attempt to achieve. The objective(s) should list the *specific* skills or knowledge that will be imparted in order to attain the aims of the goal. The objective(s) will get down to specifics.

Using for illustrative purposes the overview of "Teaching the officer how to properly protect and collect physical evidence of a crime," this particular lesson's objectives would get into exactly how the goal is to be met:

OBJECTIVE ONE: The student will learn four methods of doing crime scene searches.

OBJECTIVE TWO: The student will learn how to recognize potential physical evidence.

OBJECTIVE THREE: The student will learn how to avoid contaminating evidence.

OBJECTIVE FOUR: The student will learn how to properly package and preserve physical evidence.

The prospective evidence collector now has an idea of the skills he will be expected to develop. He is given the instructor's assumption that, once he masters these skills, he will have accomplished the broad aim of the lesson and will be able to properly recover and handle physical evidence of a criminal act.

3. Outline/Notes

This is the real meat of the lesson plan, i.e., the outline or notes on the material to be given to the class. This is the factual information that will enable the student to meet the requirements and expectations noted in both the overview and objectives of the lesson plan.

In the case of the sample "evidence recovery" lesson previously used here, the outline or notes section might list and then describe the types of crime scene searches available to the police evidence collector.

TYPES OF SEARCHES:

1. Concentric search (description follows)
2. Grid search (description follows)
3. Strip search (description follows)
4. Line search (description follows).

Skipping further along in this part of the lesson plan, one might discover the instructor's explanation for the proper recovery of, say, spent projectiles:

a. The bullet must not be marked by the officer. This could obscure its ballistic striations or dislodge trace evidence clinging to the surface of the projectile.

b. The bullet should be covered with cotton and placed in a cardboard pillbox or similar container.

   c. The pillbox should be sealed with evidence tape or evidence seals.

   d. The recovering officer shall print on the pillbox the following information:
   - his initials and employee number
   - time and date recovered
   - case number.

   e. The recovering officer shall note in his accompanying written report the circumstances under which the projectile was recovered, including:
   - exact location of recovery
     witnesses present
     how the projectile was removed and handled
   - relationship of the evidence, if known, to the case
     any photos taken of the recovery
     tests or procedures desired for this piece of evidence.

4. Evaluation

When the lesson presentation is complete, the instructor will want to know how successful he has been in obtaining the desired changes in knowledge and/or job skills performance of his students. There are various means of evaluation available to the instructor. Probably the best known types are written and oral tests given to the class at the completion of the presentation. The test is an efficient means of monitoring short-term results, such as whether or not the students recall the names of some particular evidence-gathering devices.

Any field that places as much emphasis on practical application as police work does also must call for a long-term evaluation process. In the case of an officer's desired improvement in evidence-gathering skills, further evaluation will call for future monitoring of the officer-student's field work by his primary supervisor.

For the sample lesson plan featured here, the evaluation section might read as follows:

1. The student's knowledge of evidence collection procedures will be evaluated by a short, objective test given after the last class session.

2. The student's application of lesson contents will be monitored by

his primary field supervisor who will observe his evidence collection work on the job.

Every training effort is made to achieve some kind of a change in the student: he will be more attentive to detail; he will shoot better; he will write better reports. In the long run, however, it will be the job of the student's supervisor to determine if the desired changes are really taking place. This remains so, even if the supervisor doing the monitoring is not the one who initially communicated the skills.

If the employee is a newcomer under his command, the evaluating supervisor may find it desirable to know precisely what the employee was supposed to have learned from his training. This information is available from the instructor, the lesson plan, or the employee himself. So armed, the supervisor can successfully address the question of whether or not the material was really learned and is being employed on the job. A continuing, follow-up evaluation is thus carried out.

5. Sources

The instructor should conclude his lesson plan with a listing of sources from which the material was derived. Once again (depending upon the subject) the list may be lengthy or brief. One veteran patrol sergeant listed his sources for a talk on "Patrol Observation Techniques" very simply: "personal experiences in 25 years of police work." Other topics might call for a bit more effort in the listing process. A discussion of a complex legal issue might cite a number of law publications as sources.

The sources portion of the lesson plan can do more than provide backing for the facts related by the instructor. A teacher who lists his sources carefully can aid the next instructor who handles the same or a similar topic. The sources section can also provide a direction for further study by the interested student. The ideal classroom presentation should end with the instructor supplying information on where the pupils can go for more details.

In the sample lesson plan addressing the finer points of evidence collection, an attached sources page might list several pertinent documents:

1. Department Procedural Manual.

2. "Evidence Handling for Police," a lecture by Sergeant Sam Snerd, Basic Recruit Academy, Anytown Police Department, March 12, 2008.
3. O'Hara, Charles E.: *Fundamentals of Criminal Investigation,* 7th Ed. Thomas, Springfield, 2003, pp. 87–103.

The sources portion of the lesson plan serves the student in much the same way a bibliography in a textbook serves its readers. With the completion of the sources documentation, the supervisor should have in mind his method of presentation of the selected topic of instruction.

THE PRESENTATION

With the prepared lesson plan in hand, the police leader is ready to embark on his instructional enterprise. There are a number of ways in which the chosen training can be presented. Certain types of presentations are more appropriate for certain types of subjects. A brief look at the approaches available to the supervisor might be in order at this point.

Lecture

One of the oldest methods of teaching something to someone is to explain it orally. This way of communicating knowledge is known as the lecture approach, particularly when used in a formal setting, such as a classroom.

In the lecture, the supervisor serving as instructor presents information to the class, which will, with luck, be accepted and assimilated. The students play a rather passive role in the pure lecture approach. This sit-down, classroom approach is traditionally used for handling topics such as law, procedures, rules and regulations, and background information for mechanical skills.

The lecture has one advantage. It conveys a volume of factual knowledge in a no-nonsense fashion in minimal time. Its limitations lie in the students' abilities to remain engaged, take notes and grasp the points being made.

The lecture is mostly one-way communication. The teacher talks and the students listen. The lecture also suffers from its uncanny ability to induce boredom (if not outright unconsciousness) in some of its listeners. Unfortunately, lectures seem to exceed an hour in between breaks while the chairs in most police classrooms are only good for about forty minutes of continuous occupancy!

There is no rule that says the lecture must be painfully dull. Some techniques for keeping any kind of classroom presentation from becoming unnecessarily uncomfortable will be discussed later in this chapter. The lecture, with its limitations upon student endurance, is probably most useful when used with another instructional approach.

Discussion

This approach works well when used with the lecture. The instructor who allows a general discussion of the topic under study is making use of the collective knowledge of the class members in addition to his own insights. Virtually everyone knows more about *something* than anyone else. The open class discussion allows the opinions, insights, and feelings of various people to be heard.

It is not necessary that every discussion contribution be factually correct. Without belittling the contribution's donor, the instructor can seize on incorrect assumptions or answers to illustrate common errors or misconceptions. The wise and thoughtful instructor is generally able to accomplish this feat without antagonizing anyone.

An open discussion can alert the police supervisor to any misconceptions or incorrect information that his students may harbor. This problem may never surface in a straight lecture setting. The lecture and discussion methods of instruction can be used together to the betterment and strengthening of each.

At the outset of the talk, the supervisor-instructor makes it clear that he should be interrupted with pertinent questions as they arise. Pauses may be necessary after covering a particularly complex or difficult part of the lesson. As the instructor leads the group in a discussion of the material covered, he may rely upon examples, "war stories," or similar anecdotes. Many a discussion on police pursuit driving procedures has been made more pertinent as well as more interesting by the inclusion of a few colorful tales of disastrous car wrecks and the consequences.

The discussion method also can be used to allow several different instructors to take part in a group presentation. A discussion of damage suits against police personnel might, for instance, be headed up by an attorney, a member of the agency's command staff, the department's insurance claims handler, and a line supervisor, each person bringing a viewpoint on the subject pertinent to his particular area of expertise. The end product will be more interesting and more informative as a consequence of the wide-ranging discussion approach.

Demonstration/Participation

Many of the skills that must be taught to law enforcement officers require some physical participation. One cannot teach a student officer how to fire a handgun properly and accurately while seated in the classroom, though safety rules, weapons nomenclature, and principles of proper shooting can be taught there. Demonstration and practice on the firing range always should be the most important area of such training.

The demonstration/participation phase may follow the lecture and discussion phases as one of the final steps in the instructional process. Having been given background information and the agency's procedures for handcuffing and searching a prisoner, and having been given a chance to discuss the problems and finer points of the operation itself, the recruit officer will now have the mechanics of the act demonstrated to him by a training officer. After he has had ample opportunity to observe the techniques involved, he will be expected to imitate the performance. Following the demonstration, he is expected to participate.

This sort of "watch me first and then you do it" training is very old and is by no means unique to police educational efforts. As a matter of fact, prison officers have reported seeing the older "cons" schooling their juniors inside the walls on how to spring out of the old "hands on the wall" search posture. It goes almost without saying that the police officer cannot allow himself to fall behind his adversaries with respect to participation-style training. Also, the supervisory police officer cannot let his own attention to demonstration and participation lag in the vital instructional process.

The well-prepared instructor checks ahead of time to make sure that everything he needs is ready for his presentation. If markers and a whiteboard are needed, he sees to it that they are made available. If he is going to distribute some printed material to the group, he makes sure enough copies are on hand. If he needs a computer projector and screen for his lesson, he determines in advance that both are available and properly functioning.

Many successful teachers rehearse their lesson before employing it before a group of people. While rehearsing a presentation at home is probably unnecessary for the experienced instructor, the beginner may find it helps him pace himself, determine how much time the session will take, and discover any rough spots in the presentation.

The conscientious instructor will not end his involvement with the material nor his students as soon as the presentation has been completed. It has already been noted that the instructor must evaluate the student's grasp of the information covered. He generally accomplishes this via written examination, oral questioning, or informal discussion with individuals or small groups. He also looks for long-term change in the students' behavior through continuing on-the-job monitoring of their work.

Evaluation should not be limited to the students' performance. The skilled instructor will be equally interested in grading his own performance. Did he really get the message across? Was he boring? Was there adequate discussion and questioning? Was the lesson too easy or too complex? To answer these queries, he will need to question his students.

Some police academies routinely use a printed form with which the students grade each of their instructors. The questions asked generally include at least the following:

1. Did the instructor seem interested in his subject?
2. Did the instructor speak clearly and audibly?
3. Was the material too easy or too hard?
4. Did the instructor appear to have a good understanding of the subject?
5. Did you learn anything worthwhile from the material covered?
6. Did the instructor hold your attention?
7. How could this presentation be improved?

Such evaluations can be helpful in a number of ways. They allow the student to have some involvement in selecting the highest caliber of instructors available. They allow the agency to either improve or remove the poor teachers from the instructional staff. Finally, they enable the interested instructor to identify his own weak points. For this to occur, of course, the written, anonymous evaluations are passed on to the teacher after the academy director or departmental training officer has had a chance to review them.

Evaluations do not have to be highly formal affairs in order to be effective. Equally useful to the instructor is the opportunity to talk with individuals who were students in his class, whatever its content or nature. Candid responses should be encouraged, and when given, they should not be met with arguments or excuses. The student is doing the instructor a favor here, and he should be treated accordingly.

The instructor need not accept every criticism as valid. His own common sense should help him determine those opinions that are not soundly based on factual observations. One instructor looked at his student evaluations and learned that while one pupil thought that he used too many video materials, another complained that he had used too few. All criticism, however, should be accepted and acknowledged at the outset. If a critique is unclear or vague, additional questions may be asked to clarify the student's complaint or comment.

The instructor may discover that he has committed one of a variety of minor sins in his instructional efforts. Fortunately, all are to a large extent curable. The list of most frequently encountered shortcomings of police instructors includes few surprises:

1. The instructor talked too fast.
   Solution: Slow down.
2. The instructor's voice was monotonous.
   Solution: Add a few anecdotes, change positions at the podium, use facial expressions and hand gestures occasionally.
3. The session was too long.
   Solution: Have one ten-minute break per hour; condense the material.
4. Difficult or new words were unclear.
   Solution: Use a whiteboard or flip chart. Slow up the presentation for new words, and make sure that they are understood. Definitions may be needed.
5. The instructor did not know his subject.
   Solution: Know the material before beginning the presentation. Do not bluff. Admit shortcomings, but get the needed information later and put it out.
6. The instructor spoke too loudly or too softly.

Solution: Engage in some self-monitoring. If in doubt, stop and ask the class if voice level is about right for everyone.

7. The instructor appeared to be bored or uninterested.
   Solution: Learn the material thoroughly along with some practical examples or anecdotes to illustrate vital points. Attempt to relate the material to be learned to the officers' practical needs.

Self-evaluation can be of great worth to the instructor. By using it he can improve both his performance and the student officers' success rate in absorbing the material presented.

AIDS TO INSTRUCTION

The supervisor should be aware that there are a number of devices and techniques available to help in keeping his teaching efforts interesting and productive. The value of audiovisual equipment should not be overlooked. Any presentation can be made more interesting and more clear if its highlights are demonstrated visually.

The instructor can also make excellent use of a chalkboard or whiteboard to illustrate important words, figures, or diagrams in his lecture presentation. The mere act of putting particularly difficult terms or vital phrases on the board often will forestall many requests to repeat or clarify such points. The judicious use of the board, along with visual aids of other kinds (color slides, PowerPoint presentations) demonstrates to the students the instructor's concern that they get the material down pat and in as painless a manner as possible.

The supervisor/teacher also should have copies of the material being discussed available for each student to examine during the session itself. It is much easier to explain the proper completion of a new report form, for instance, if each employee has a copy at hand and there is an enlarged, easy-to-see copy of the document on the screen for the instructor to utilize. An overhead transparency or computer projector can be used for this. Computer-generated "slides" provide excellent learning tools.

Audio cassette tape recordings can be very effective teaching aids. For example, a presentation on the proper and improper use of the police radio comes home to its listeners much more effectively when some concrete evidence of the issues under discussion is provided.

However, the instructor must take care to balance his examples of poor work with some instances of good work, too.

Videotape and video disc presentations should not be overlooked for their valuable contributions to realistic police training. There are plenty of quality, up-to-date productions available today, as well as some not-so-good imitations. Officers can learn a great deal about what to do and avoid doing by watching scenarios played out on a screen. But a word of caution: video presentations can teach a lot in the realm of how-to information. Nonetheless, they are no substitute for hands-on practice in such areas as safe driving, handcuffing, baton use and firearms training. Used along with hands-on training, video is an excellent tool for the supervisor-trainer.

An extension of video training may be found in the firearms simulation training that permits an officer to interact with threat scenarios played out on a screen. The best versions feature bifurcated responses in which reactions from the actors vary. Responses depend on whether or not the officer-student shoots accurately, or shoots at all with his nonlethal, laser-equipped weapon. The stressful realism provided by this training is generally highly-praised by police students and their instructors. These systems and similar setups are not inexpensive. But neither is a successful lawsuit for "failure to train" following a bad shooting by officers.

Role-playing exercises also can bolster the training effort. The most realistic ones use outside actors unknown to the law enforcement students. There is probably no better way to teach the proper handling of a nasty domestic dispute than by exposing the trainee to actors who are working from an informal script crafted by a creative supervisor. Indeed, role-play training is limited only by the imagination of the designing supervisor and the talents of the actors.

The smart instructor will not overlook the usefulness of tangible objects in his teaching efforts. A discussion of problems to avoid in completing fingerprint cards will be much more useful to the officers in attendance if some examples of good and poor cards are on hand for close inspection. Normally, a couple of hours talk about the appearance of counterfeit money might be cut down to half an hour if sample pieces of the bad money are available for close scrutiny, including handling by the class members.

Instructional endeavors are affected by much more than the teaching method or approach employed. Extremely crucial to effective learning is the instructor's application of good common sense to his preparation and presentation. He will, of course, dress appropriately for the occasion. For a classroom session, it would be inappropriate in many jurisdictions for the instructor to show up in a sweatshirt and jeans. Likewise, manner or attitude in presentation can have considerable impact upon the students' reception of the material delivered. The instructor who has skimped on his preparation and has to read his material word for word is not showing much regard for his audience.

The considerate instructor answers his officers' questions to the best of his ability and gets answers to those queries he cannot immediately address. This same instructor also knows that such responses as "because that's just the way it is" or "because I say so" are generally shallow and unacceptable responses in the classroom setting. Fair questions deserve fair answers. There is no room in the instructional ranks for bullies or smart alecks.

The instructor who gets results attempts to stay in close touch with his listeners. He makes eye contact with each member of the group, he watches his class members for signs of extreme restlessness or discomfort, and he stays flexible enough to go into a break period early or start a lively discussion session if he senses that he is losing his audience's interest and attention.

Sitting for long periods in any sort of classroom is no fun. Rather than get angry about losing the attention of one or more class members, the talented supervisor-instructor tries to regain the misplaced attention through modification of his own approach.

The capable police instructor is concerned enough about the welfare of his class to see to it that their surroundings allow them to be at their best. He ensures that the temperature of the classroom is comfortable and the lighting is adequate for the activity underway. He does his best to eliminate distracting noises or actions in or near the room and works to prevent interruptions to the session by cell phone calls, messages, or uninvited visitors. In sum, he tries to encourage what the professional educators refer to as a "climate conducive to learning."

The supervisor does all of these things in his role as educator of police personnel. Whether as a classroom instructor dealing in principles and theories or as a field trainer demonstrating the finer points of the police rifle, the supervisor serves in the highest traditions of his profession as he labors to guide and prepare the employees entrusted to his care.

SUMMARY

In his role as a facilitator of learning, the police leader assesses his employees' training needs and then works to help meet them. If he is fortunate, he may find skilled instructors on needed topics inside or outside the agency to handle the teaching chores. If not, he may need to handle the task himself.

The effective instructor utilizes a carefully prepared lesson plan, complete with identifiable learning objectives that can be measured to help guide him in his work. Likewise, he uses demonstrations, class participation, field exercises and learning aids such as video presentations to get the message across. Finally, he questions, talks with and observes his student officers after the training is given to see if the desired results have been attained. In so doing he recognizes that the learning process for a law enforcement professional never ends.

POINTS TO REMEMBER

- The supervisor's job includes that of training his subordinates.
- His role includes discovering where his people need additional training and helping them attain it.
- A good training lesson plan includes an overview, objectives, outline, evaluation and sources section.
- Teaching methods include lecture, discussion, demonstration/participation and a combination of more than one type of method.
- There are effective troubleshooting techniques for some common instructional problems.
- Technological aids can make the law enforcement instructor's efforts more effective and his task easier.

Chapter Six

THE POLICE LEADER AS AN EVALUATOR

The police sergeant may be the single most important individual employed by the law enforcement agency. Without him, the directives, orders, and designs of the upper ranks would go unimplemented, and the concerns and problems of the working police officer would be much more difficult to identify and address.

It is the police sergeant who must translate the broader concerns of top management into concrete, effective action at the line level. He or she also must accurately and promptly relay employee grievances and problems that cannot be solved at a lower level to those higher up.

This may also be one of the most difficult jobs in the police agency. Not only must the leader be aware of proper procedures and departmental guidelines, he also must be capable of quickly improvising and adapting to fit the unique situation, which perhaps no pre-existing directive or order fits exactly. He must possess a great deal of common sense and bring it to bear in a whole cross section of practical problems and related supervisory crises.

If the police sergeant in general is indispensable to the effective and efficient operation of the police agency, then the uniformed sergeant on patrol is the most important subsection of that larger supervisory group. Frequently, without the luxury of time for consultation or advice enjoyed by his superiors or even his cohorts in specialty assignments, the street supervisor must bring his knowledge and common sense instantly to bear on an incident or situation which his bosses, the courts, and perhaps the news media may have months to analyze. No stranger to the barbs of the "Monday morning quarterbacks," he nonetheless moves quickly to solve routine disasters and mini-crises alike.

In no area of his job description is the competent field supervisor more relied upon by both management and subordinates than in his role of work performance evaluator. Here he will strive to improve the organization as a whole by helping its component employees under his direction to do their jobs better for the benefit of the agency and the community as well as themselves. It is in his role as evaluator that the supervisor must identify employee strengths and weaknesses, recommend rewards for excellence, recommend help for difficulties, and report his objective findings to employee and employer.

PURPOSES OF EVALUATION

In all too many instances the employee evaluation is hesitantly written by a supervisor who really had rather be doing something else. All too often, the evaluation is then promptly forgotten until the next one is due. Instead of being used as a tool to help the employee do better work and receive increased personal satisfaction, it is all too often viewed as something used to expose and punish failure. Little wonder, then, that most supervisors do not particularly care to prepare evaluations on their people. There should be even less surprise that many employees dread receiving them.

While the formal, written performance evaluation can help the police employee when properly used, it also can help the police organization in utilizing the officer's abilities in the service of the community and can identify weaknesses in the organization itself to allow for their correction.

After identifying the strengths and weaknesses of his personnel, the supervisor will in extreme cases identify those employees who must, for the good of the agency, be removed from police service. For instance, when in three successive six-month evaluation reports a continuing and unacceptable level of citizen complaints is tallied regarding an officer's attitude and demeanor, responsible service to the public and protection of the agency's reputation demand that decisive corrective action be taken, and at once. If negative evaluations are in hand and previous corrective measures have failed to change the employee's behavior, termination of employment may be the ultimate result. Although no supervisor takes great pleasure in administering an evaluation destined to have a terminal effect on a subordinate's employment, he can take consolation in knowing he may have saved the public, the agency, and, ultimately, the employee himself from continuing grief.

A good performance evaluation program can identify more than individual strengths and weaknesses. Properly administered and closely monitored by command staff as well as line supervisors, the performance evaluation system can identify problems in the department's selection, training, or operational procedures.

If, for example, a large number of employee evaluations of police patrol officers shows a consistent lack of ability in accident investigation skills, it might be safely assumed that the agency's basic police training academy needs to look at its presentation and content of accident investigation instruction. A refresher course in accident investigation skills might be required in order to solve the present difficulty.

Another lot of evaluations–this one of telephone complaint clerks–might reveal a uniformly high number of citizen "beefs" about police discourtesy or poor customer service received when calling the police department. Assuming that the number of employees rated "weak" in courtesy and service categories of the evaluation is significant, the law enforcement agency's bosses may safely assume that the problem may lie with the organization itself rather than with the individual quirks of specific employees. Perhaps a mandatory course in telephone courtesy would be beneficial or more clerks are needed to reduce the wait for service. Perhaps more telephone trunk lines and modified equipment would help. However the problem is eventually diagnosed, the fact remains that it first came to be recognized as important through a careful and continuing evaluation process.

Procedures, not just people, can be evaluated and strengthened through a good evaluation system. The question persists, though, as to what form this evaluation should take. With policies, procedures, and other guidelines, perhaps the best method of evaluation is a continuous monitoring of the *end results.* Are the calls for service being handled promptly and efficiently? Are citizen complaints against police employees rising disproportionately with the number of police/citizen contacts? Are the crime clearance rates at or near the national average? Almost inevitably statistics will measure to at least some extent the agency's overall effectiveness.

But what about the individual police employee? How might he be evaluated? What means will be employed to rate the employee's work product and ability? These questions will be examined next.

MEANS OF EVALUATION

All police employees–sworn and civilian–should be evaluated periodically. Obviously, exactly the same criteria cannot be used for all. There may be only a few common criteria in the civilian complaint clerk's evaluation and that of the patrol officer. Courtesy and punctuality might be a couple of these common factors. The uniformed officer and the detective might have many more similar categories to be rated, but differences in factors being measured still will exist. It would be rather useless to rate most patrol officers on case filing skills, while it would be an equal waste of time and energy to attempt to measure the average detective's abilities at accident investigation.

At the same time, every individual police employee must be rated on the same criteria as his peers who are in the same category or job description. It would be unfair to have one patrol supervisor rating on one set of criteria while a different patrol sergeant used a different set of performance standards.

Perhaps a little unfairness is built into the very best of evaluation systems through the unavoidable differences in personalities, abilities, and other qualities of the individual supervisors involved. Partiality and distortion can be kept to a minimum, however, by the consistent use of a uniform set of rating criteria designed to measure the skills necessary for a given task.

First of all, the agency's leaders must decide what is to be measured. Different departments may place varying degrees of importance on particular skills and traits. Technical skills may be highly valued at one agency, while skills at dealing effectively with human factors may be stressed at another.

Second, it is vital that performance appraisals look only at behavior or results that are tangible, observable and capable of being measured in some way. Results can be measured; attitudes cannot. It is not sufficient to write that an employee "has a bad temper" or a "poor attitude." It IS possible to describe the results of temper tantrums by referring to documented and described complaints received on the individual from peers and citizens. Example: "Complaint clerk Jones complained that Dispatcher Smith stated 'Stick it!' when she asked her to answer the 911 line." By the same token, it won't do to say that some-one has "a poor personality." (What does *that* mean, anyway?) It *is* acceptable as well as informative to describe exactly what is objec-tionable about the person's actions: she throws objects, curses her co-workers and belches into the telephone!

It is desirous to have the line supervisor continuously evaluate the evaluation system itself. He may well be more knowledgeable than his bosses on what is needed to do the job in the most effective and effi-cient manner. He and his peers should be given the opportunity to suggest modifications where necessary to existing evaluation forms and procedures to fit the real world that police employees deal with daily.

While keeping in mind that there will continue to exist differences in what is considered important enough to be rated at differing police agencies, a core of important traits or abilities stands largely unop-posed as necessary characteristics of a good police officer. They might be grouped for convenience:

General Knowledge and Skills

Applicable Laws and Ordinances

Does the employee demonstrate a good working knowledge of the laws utilized in his job? Does he understand the elements of the crimes he is dealing with? Does he show an ability to translate the meaning of laws to the actual applications he faces in the field?

Departmental Procedures

Does the employee obey the established guidelines and procedures for his job position? Does he routinely apply these formal procedures to his work in an intelligent fashion?

Tools and Equipment

Is the employee able to operate properly all tools and devices required of his position? Does he apply adequate safety procedures when working with them? Does he take good care of the equipment placed in his charge?

Interviewing Skills

Can the employee obtain information from those with whom he comes into contact on the job? Can he obtain cooperation without unduly antagonizing people? How good is he at placing his interviewee at ease?

Current Events

Is the employee reasonably familiar with what is going on in the world around him? Is he up-to-date on criminal intelligence and crime information as it pertains to his particular assignment? Does the employee make this information available to his fellow officers and show an interest in their contributions?

Oral Communication

Can the employee communicate orally in an effective manner? Does he get the message through with a minimum of distortion? Is he able to stay on the subject at hand? Is he accurate in relaying information passed along to him? Is the employee courteous, clear, and concise when speaking over the radio or telephone?

Report Writing

How clear and complete are the employee's written efforts at communicating facts and ideas? Does he routinely follow the effective "who, what, when, where, why, and how" formula for reporting? Is the employee's writing, printing, or keyboarding easy to read? Are his grammar and spelling efforts acceptable? Does his written report accurately reflect what actually happened, or are there gaps and distortions? Does he avoid both shortcutting and padding in his writing?

Knowledge of the Area

Does the employee show a good comprehension of the geographic layout of the jurisdiction? Can he quickly get to or direct others to a given location? Does he demonstrate a good understanding of the *human* makeup of his area?

Personal Characteristics

Job Interest

Does the employee show a desire to learn more about his job and his growth in it? Is he enthusiastic about his work?

Relations with Others

Does the employee get along well with the public, fellow employees, and supervisors? Does he draw an unusually large number of citizen complaints of discourtesy and misconduct?

Punctuality

Does the employee arrive at work on time? Does he complete assignments when due and meet all other job deadlines?

Handling of Stress

Can the employee perform satisfactorily under job stress? Does a stressful situation expose bad traits, such as quick anger? Do peers see him as a stabilizing influence under stressful circumstances?

Patience

Does the employee demonstrate patience and tact under trying conditions? Does he lose his temper easily or display impatience quickly?

Judgment

Does the employee utilize mature reasoning in his thought processes? Are decisions based upon logic and common sense as opposed to emotion? Do decisions reflect thinking more than guesswork or luck? In short, can he really "think on his feet?"

Self-confidence

Does the employee show faith in his own talents and abilities without appearing arrogant? Is he a good leader? Does he set a good example? Does the employee exhibit belief in and responsibility for his work and his decisions?

Acceptance of Supervision

Is the employee resistant to constructive criticism and direction, or does he accept it as useful to him? Can he work under both close and loose supervision? Can he adjust to a change in supervisors? Does the employee become either sullen or overly defensive when corrected by a supervisor?

Appearance

Does the employee dress appropriately for his work assignment? If he is a uniformed officer, does he keep his uniform clean and well-maintained? Is his leather gear shined? If he is a plain clothes officer, does he wear neat, clean garments suited to his job? Is he neat and well-groomed at all times while on the job?

Doubtlessly, numerous other job-related traits could be added to the list for measurement. As noted previously, whatever is being measured, it is vital that the criteria be examined consistently throughout the job classification. An evaluation program cannot be successful if it attempts to compare water with gasoline.

It is equally important that guidelines be provided to a group of supervisors in determining what is being critiqued under a particular evaluation category or heading. The preceding listing of some sample evaluation criteria with attendant questions to be answered provides one form of guideline. There are others.

The important thing is for each supervisor to answer the same set of questions when he pauses to rate an officer in, say, appearance. All patrol officers should be rated by one standard. Otherwise, a bewildered and disillusioned police officer might find that while his old boss graded him on the way in which he maintained his entire uniform, his new leader was most interested in the shine on his leather gear. The need for consistency in evaluation standards cannot be overemphasized.

What form is the evaluation itself to take? It is worth saying one more time that the format chosen should be relatively *uniform* throughout the agency. Most law enforcement organizations have elected to use some sort of a printed form for the evaluation work. If such a prepared form is used, it should have built-in flexibility to allow for the evaluation of various job descriptions throughout the police agency.

One way to do this might be to leave some blank space in each category so that the supervisor in that particular assignment can add pertinent detail to the basic, core criteria measured throughout the department.

Variations of at least two major rating or scoring formats are often used in law enforcement employee evaluations. The first uses a kind of numerical scoring system. Although the number of points to be awarded for good, fair, or poor performance may vary from department to department, there are some distinct similarities.

The form in its simplest state provides a listing of job-related skills, abilities, and performance indicators. These are presented on the left side of the page. Many of the things listed here would be found among the criteria for job performance measurement listed earlier in this chapter.

On the page beside each trait or characteristic, the supervisor or rater enters the designated number that best describes the police employee's job performance in that area. A sample scoring system might award 3 points for excellent performance, 2 for good work, 1 for fair performance, and 0 for inadequate or unacceptable work.

The simplicity of the form makes it relatively easy to complete and explain to the rated employee. This can be a distinct advantage to supervisor and supervised alike.

The form can be made even more effective if provision is made for the supervisor to comment in narrative form on any unusual strengths or weaknesses noted. The evaluation can then assume increased value and clarity for both the employee and employer. Numbers simply cannot compare with words in descriptive value to all concerned.

Another type of printed evaluation form utilizes a similar listing of personal traits and performance characteristics, but dispenses with the use of numbers in the rating process. Instead, the supervisor uses word descriptors to describe job performance. The descriptors may vary from one locale to another, but the terms often used include the unsurprising "excellent," "good," "fair," and "poor." Other printed forms using this format may substitute the words "strong" and "weak" as general performance descriptors. Still others may rely upon simply "exceptional," "satisfactory" or "unsatisfactory" as labels placed on job performance.

Agencies using such a written evaluation format sometimes add the label "non-applicable" or "does not apply" to the supervisory rater's list of available choices. With this added ability, a single printed form might be used for the entire agency. The supervisor doing the rating needs only to mark appropriately he unneeded categories (N/A) and move on to the ones that do apply.

There might not be a predetermined "pass-fail" point in this sort of evaluation format. At the same time, an evaluation with an overall negative tone would require some kind of help or correction for the concerned employee. Just *what* would be done and *how* would depend upon the established procedures of the agency. Whatever the response, the leader who rated the employee in the first place and who works with him on a regular basis should be fully involved.

There is yet another form of written evaluation of law enforcement work performance. It requires no preprinted form; only a plain sheet of paper or two. The supervisor sits down and, using a predetermined set of criteria and/or guidelines, writes a narrative describing the employee and his work. There are no numbers to total up, blocks to check, or labels to attach. A written discussion of perhaps a couple of pages is all that is involved.

This type of evaluation's greatest strength is its direct approach to the rating task. There is no necessity to translate numbers or labels into descriptions or words. Citing specific examples of performance is vital, however.

With this sort of evaluation, the supervisor approaches the issues directly and describes performance in his own words. The employee (and whomever else may eventually read the evaluation) is told openly where the pluses and minuses of perceived job performance lie. If the evaluation report is well written, this approach can simplify the process of evaluation for all concerned.

The "open narrative" evaluation does have a disadvantage. The drawback is, in reality, an open admission of weakness in some supervisors' communicative abilities more than it is a true fault in the evaluation format itself. This weakness is centered around the unfortunate inability to express oneself clearly in writing that afflicts many persons today, police supervisors among them. All too often, the leader who can counsel effectively and lead decisively has a problem in reducing his observations and opinions to written form.

It is possible to trace the blame for the general population's inability to engage in effective written communication all the way back to the public schools of contemporary America. Within the last two decades or so, schools (including many colleges) appear to have radically de-emphasized the importance of correct written communication. It has even been claimed that classes of largely illiterate graduates have been turned loose on society after spending some sixteen years or more in the education machinery of this country.

Whether such accusations are justified or not, it remains a harsh fact of life that some supervisors cannot write well, and what they may damn in their rookies all too often they share themselves. A police agency can and should set down a list of criteria to be commented upon in the "blank page" evaluation. The same categories will be used here as in the other kinds of evaluations. Beyond providing such necessary guidelines, however, the agency should not have to teach its supervisors how to write.

There are, of course, a practically limitless number of ways to do a performance appraisal narrative. One format identifies the job element to be evaluated and then requires the supervisor to record several examples justifying the rating he has given the employee in that category. A supervisor completing the performance review might elect to list the examples as bullet points. For instance: Teamwork and Cooperation–I have rated Detective Jones as EXCEPTIONAL in this area. Examples of his performance this year include:

- Bob provided assistance to the D.A.'s office by teaching a course about police interview techniques to several new deputy prosecutors.
- Bob assisted the Muleshoe Police Department by conducting several local interviews concerning a sexual assault case that actually occurred in their jurisdiction.
- Detective Jones helped the Property and Evidence Section manager by doing an audit of drugs and money stored in that unit.
- Bob volunteered to be the police department coordinator for the Red Cross blood drive in December.

In the final analysis, the department will have to base its decision on which kind of written evaluation format to use upon the writing capabilities of its supervisors. Only the agency with supervisors of strong writing ability will want to attempt the 100 percent narrative form of evaluation.

Fortunately, there are some things that the sergeant faced with preparing a narrative-style evaluation can do to make his task a little easier and his final product a clearer, more useful one:

1. An outline to organize thoughts along the lines of the set criteria or guidelines to be followed may be helpful in getting started.
2. Keep sentences and paragraphs short. Break up a long and complex line into two or more simpler, shorter sentences.
3. Do not try to use technical words, the meanings of which may be unclear. The supervisor possessed of an ample supply of common sense will refrain from using "pet" phrases and catch words and instead use clear and concise terms, which get to the point.
4. End with a summary that stresses good points while listing again the areas of needed improvement.
5. Watch for spelling errors and keep a dictionary handy while writing the evaluation. A computer word processing spelling and grammar check program will not catch every error.
6. A finished evaluation should be proofread carefully at least twice by its writer; once for content and clarity and once for errors in spelling or grammar. The writer should check to be sure that nothing has been omitted by accident.

There also exist guidelines for the preparation of performance evaluation reports of all kinds and formats. Likewise, there are lists of known pitfalls awaiting the unwary evaluator. Some of these guidelines as well as the potential stumbling blocks will be explored next.

GUIDELINES AND PITFALLS

It has been said that performance evaluations are inherently unfair to the employee being evaluated because they place him on the defensive at the outset. He is allegedly left no recourse but to defend himself or his actions from a critical supervisor. The same critics of performance evaluations also will state that many of the supervisor's "complaints" contained in the evaluation have been accumulating over a long time period. All too often, suggest the critics, the employee has been given no hint of his shortcomings or a warning to improve himself before evaluation time comes around.

The same individuals who attack the fairness of the employee's evaluation may say that the system is unfair to the supervisor as well. The critics believe that the evaluation system traps both employee and supervisor into a role that each must defend. According to them, the supervisor may find himself defending his evaluation to a vehemently objecting subordinate. Just as bad, the disagreeing employee may say nothing but will form resentments and bad feelings about the supervisor he sees as callously wronging him.

In the worst possible scenario, say the critics, the supervisor ends up justifying and protecting his evaluative work while the employee defends and explains his performance, all of which escalates into an argument. In this scene, nothing is gained but bad feelings.

Performance evaluation sessions do not have to even faintly resemble this picture. The wise supervisor will have assured that the employee has shared in the establishment of his goals and objectives, and thus has interest in carrying them to a successful completion. The smart leader also will have assured that he can support his statements in the evaluation with factual observations, records, and other evidence.

The supervisor-rater can do a number of things in preparing an effective and meaningful evaluation of a police employee, whether civilian or sworn, support or line. Some of the more vital steps, all of them reflecting the rater's prudent use of good common sense, are worth noting:

1. Furnish Evidence or Backing for All Evaluation Statements or Opinions. If the rater states that an employee is consistently late for work (or "weak" in the evaluation's "attendance" category), he must be able to substantiate his claim with specific, cited incidents. If he writes that a subordinate loses his temper easily, once again specific episodes should be cited as a sound defense against a challenge from the rated employee.

One effective means for keeping a running account of an employee's strengths and weaknesses is the supervisor's log or notebook. Some agencies maintain such a book for every employee. Other agencies issue the supervisor a single binder in which to keep notes on all his subordinates. Yet others rely upon computer files. Whichever device is used, it is utilized to keep written, dated notes on the employee's performance.

If the patrol officer makes a quality arrest, it should be documented here. If the detective successfully puts together a complex inquiry, it should be so noted in his log. Likewise, those repeated episodes of being late to roll call or that incident of appearing out of proper uniform should be documented therein.

More routine record keeping to be used in the eventual evaluation also should be included in the supervisor's log pages. Pistol range scores, results of inspections, and case clearance statistics might all be noted.

The rated employee should have the opportunity to review his log's contents periodically. Ideally, he should initial and date each entry to indicate that it has been read. In addition, the officer should be provided with the opportunity to discuss any entry with the supervisor making it. Also, the officer should be allowed to make his own entries in the book by way of explanation or disagreement with the supervisor's written comments.

2. The Evaluation Session Must Be Treated as Very Important. The supervisor should consider the presentation of the evaluation to be an important event for the employee. Before discussing the evaluation with the subordinate, a private place free of interruptions and distractions should be selected. The evaluation should not be presented when either party is pressed for time. For this reason, it is sometimes best to avoid the start or end of the work day as a time for the presentation. Frequently, too many other things are going on at these times for attention to remain focused on the matter at hand.

The supervisor should stress the employee's strong points and assets, and praise him for them. Praise must be used only when deserved. Otherwise, it will soon lose its meaning for the employee.

Weaknesses and areas needing improvement must be covered, too. The rater must be careful to communicate that it is the employee's action or inaction in a given area that is being criticized and not the employee himself. Words such as "sloppy," "lazy," "reckless," and the like are unacceptable in the evaluation discussion. Other, less emotional words exist that carry essentially the same message without the virtual guarantee of hostility evoked by these bombshells.

3. Stay on the Subject. The evaluator should not stray afar from the topics covered in the written evaluation. He should guide the employee back to the subject under discussion if unrelated incidents or opinions are brought up. Past behavior should have no place in the current evaluation unless it is a continuing problem. The same limitations should be placed on the employee's comments or arguments with the present evaluation.

Relevancy is the password in the evaluation process. The fact that the officer feels his past sergeant mistreated him should have no place in the current evaluation discussion with his new supervisor. Nor should the fact that the rater and the rated are golfing buddies have any bearing on the evaluation report's content.

4. The Evaluation Must Be Fair and Accurate. Nothing will destroy a supervisor faster than substantiated claims of prejudice or gross inaccuracy in the evaluations he writes. Obviously, personal grievances have no business surfacing in the performance evaluation. The rater must be truly objective. He must criticize or praise only with proof in hand.

Employees taking their grievances into civil courts have become a common sight in recent years, and the police field has not been exempt from the effects of a lawyer's bonanza. A proven claim of bias in the case of an unfairly rated police employee could cost both the supervisor and his employer dearly.

Accuracy is vital in the evaluation. If the sergeant writes that Patrol Officer Smith was late for work on a certain number of occasions, then he had best be able to document the dates and circumstances in each instance. Precise statements and examples are preferable to generalized remarks. Exactness becomes even more critical when the evaluation's remarks are of a negative nature.

5. The Evaluation Should Not Spring Surprises. The employee reading his written evaluation should not encounter any critical remarks for the first time. Before a supervisor can be fair in "dinging" a subordinate in his yearly or six-month evaluation report, he should have first notified the employee at least verbally and preferably in a written supervisor's log entry of his observations at some earlier time. This, too, must be documented.

Any early warning of unsatisfactory performance should, of course, be accompanied by advice on what sort of improvement or behavior change is expected. It is of some use to tell a detective that his mode of dress is improper for the job. It is considerably more useful to tell him that consistently shined shoes, a clean shirt, and a tie that does not have an illuminated pig's head for a tie holder are appropriate for a working investigator's attire on the job.

6. Statistics Should Not Be Overemphasized. Some police agencies have attempted to measure their officers' performance almost entirely in numbers. While it is certainly vital that each police officer carry his or her fair share of the work load, measuring employee effectiveness in numbers alone can be quite misleading. The rookie who turns in a dozen field interview cards of dubious value should not be rated more competent than the officer who completes only five cards in the same time period–all of them on known burglars and thieves. An evaluation system paying too much attention to quantity alone could unfairly rate rookie and veteran alike.

Generally speaking, the individual officer should be rated more on his demonstrated capabilities and performance than solely against any set standard. It can be truthfully hypothesized that quality cannot be claimed without at least some quantity to choose from, but quotas and rigid targets set in numbers are poor yardsticks when used alone for evaluative purposes.

7. The Evaluator Must Not Play Santa Claus. Most everyone finds it much easier to write nice things than bad ones about associates. All too many times, the supervisor's log becomes a praise book, and the evaluation report begins to resemble a proclamation of congratulations. The supervisor's tendency to praise his employee may become even more pronounced if he knows that his subordinate's much-needed merit pay increase or bonus check is tied to the requirement of an outstanding performance report.

The police supervisor is helping no one, including the employee, if he grants more praise than the performance deserves. A weakness overlooked or a bad performance concealed in order to win his employee a reward or spare him some kind of punishment often will come back later to haunt rater and employee both. The sergeant who lacks the supervisory courage to tell the truth about a poor performance may be greatly complicating the job of his fellow supervisor who will be required to take a firm stand somewhere down the line. In the end, no one has benefited from misplaced praise or deferred criticism.

Ideally, evaluations should in no way be tied to longevity pay. Merit pay raises and length of service salary increases should be kept entirely separate. Bonuses or other performance incentives arising out of good evaluation reports should reflect truly extraordinary work, not a meeting of routine job demands.

8. Evaluations Should Be Completed on Time. The supervisor must remain mindful of the due dates for his subordinates' evaluations and get them in on time. It may appear to the employee that his supervisor does not consider the evaluation effort very important if it is not done in a timely manner.

Common sense dictates that the sharp supervisor will give himself plenty of time (weeks, not hours or minutes) to think about what he is going to say before he actually puts it to paper. A last ditch flurry of effort, hours before the evaluation is due, does not speak well of the supervisor's planning abilities.

If the employee is to be given the chance to participate in the setting of goals and objectives for the evaluation, he, too, must have adequate time for thinking about his choices and putting them into words. Again, this cannot be a last minute undertaking if it is to work well and retain its credibility. As a result, the employee must be made aware of the approaching evaluation well in advance of its due date. If the completion of the performance review is linked to a merit pay raise or other benefit, its timely completion becomes still more vital to its recipient.

At this point, a sample evaluation may be of use to the supervisor as an illustration of points made. The one shown here is the combination labeling/narrative variety. This one was prepared by a patrol supervisor and covers the job performance of a uniformed patrol officer of a municipal police agency.

SIX-MONTH PERFORMANCE
REVIEW OF PATROL OFFICER
BILL JONES

Evaluation Key:

+ = Strong   - = Weak   X = Standard

Courtroom Testimony (+)

The volume of work produced by this officer makes him a frequent occupant of the witness chair. A log entry by this rater on 2–17 reflects upon Officer Jones's abilities in court: "Officer Jones received a letter of commendation from a city attorney regarding his testimony in a recent liquor authority hearing. The attorney notes that Jones was well prepared, an excellent witness, and convincing in his knowledge of the case."

Patience (-)

Officer Jones is, at times, rather quick to display his displeasure at the inferior work or attitudes of other patrol personnel. This has been reflected in a stinging remark to a less-than-brilliant colleague in a voice inflection on a radio transmission from Jones.

Officer Jones is extremely competent as a police officer, but he must attempt to show more tact and understanding when dealing with those of lesser abilities or poorer attitudes. He is too valuable an asset to the department to have his effectiveness reduced in such a manner.

City Geography (+)

Patrol Officer Jones can be utilized anywhere in the city with confidence, as he is familiar with the problem spots and points of particular police interest.

Current Events (+)

Patrol Officer Jones displays a good knowledge of the local "Who's Who" of shady characters and has demonstrated his recall for current crime problems and specific criminal MOs by his frequent contributions at roll call briefings.

Teamwork (+)

He has been an effective contributor to the team effort, both in his demeanor and in work completed. A log entry by Sergeant Garner on 12/24 refers to this effort: "He has shown excellent initiative, has done clear and complete reports, and has been a real benefit to the team. An assault report he completed on November 5 was described by Det. Smith as the best written work he had seen from Patrol. Jones also displayed teamwork and initiative in obtaining a supply of blood alcohol test kits for Detox when he learned they had run out."

Leadership (+)

On several occasions, Officer Jones acted as field training officer for recruits. In each instance, he provided a good example through his own behavior and guided the recruits in proper procedures and tactics.

Self Confidence (X)

Officer Jones displays a considerable amount of command presence as he deals with each task at hand. From this rater's observations, Jones appears to be making some progress in assuring that his self-confidence is not mistaken for arrogance or "cockiness." The matter has been discussed with him at length, and Officer Jones states that he understands the situation. I have observed that he is being much more courteous with his peers these days than in the past.

Report Writing (+)

This officer's written reports are above average in both content and form. Excerpts from several log entries over a span of several months support this conclusion. A couple of examples:
"Officer Jones turned in an excellent burglary report that was easy to work from and helped in the eventual solution of the crime." (Sgt. Smith, 7/12)
"The daily evaluation reports that Jones has written on his recruits have been complete and thorough." (Sgt. Evans, 11/12)

Relationship with Co-workers (X)

Some casual observations of personal on-the-job relationships have convinced this evaluator that Officer Jones is highly regarded by most of his peers. He does need to pay special attention to avoiding giving offense to others when their mistakes irritate him, as has already been noted.

Work Environment (X)

No particular strengths or weaknesses are noted in this area.

Field Survival (+)

Officer Jones exercises good control of the thin line between self-preservation and provocative overreaction on the street. He appears to be passing this ability on to his trainees.

Field Initiative (+)

Patrol Officer Jones is clearly increasing his officer-initiated activity. A log entry of 11/18 by Sergeant Gray on this trend: "Officer Jones, without a complainant, initiated enforcement action at a troublesome local lounge that resulted in four illegally parked cars being ticketed and towed and a fleet of others being hastily removed by their owners. This in itself is no 'big deal' outside of the fact that the parking problem was one that is often ignored by other officers who are no busier than Jones. I feel this is a good example of the initiative of this officer."

Evaluation Summary

Patrol Officer Jones continues to perform at a successful level for someone at his level of experience. He has been rated "strong" in such areas as city geography, current events, teamwork, leadership, self-confidence, and field survival. His only "weak" area is patience, where needed improvement is indicated. When he is able to improve his performance here as well, Officer Jones will be even more valuable to the department.

Based on his consistently successful performance, Officer Jones is recommended for a merit pay increase.

Here is another example of an officer job performance review. This agency utilizes some of its organizational values as performance guideposts to be reviewed in the periodic employee evaluation completed by a first-line supervisor.

Performance Review of Officer Fred Fox

Leadership. Fred is recognized by his peers as an informal leader on the shift. I also count on him for his leadership abilities. When Corporal Twinkle and I were both on sick leave on September 5, Fred volunteered to handle the roll call briefing and make the beat assignments for the Patrol team. Lt. Smurf later told me that Fred did an excellent job of handling the shift. I have encouraged Fred to compete for the next sergeant's position, but he says he is not interested at this time.

Integrity. Over the past five years that I have worked with Fred I have never had cause to doubt his honesty. I have not known him to lie about anything. In October I received a note from Judge Dork who said that Fred had requested that one of his summonses be dismissed in court because he could not identify the defendant. The Judge was impressed by Fred's integrity, and so am I.

Attendance/Punctuality. Fred has used approximately the department average in sick leave this past year. However, he has been late to briefing by at least 15 minutes on several occasions. I noted that he was late without an acceptable excuse on the following dates: April 4, April 12, May 19, August 5, August 6 and November 11. I have told Fred this is unacceptable and that he will have to fix this problem in the coming evaluation period. He assured me that he will and he made no excuses for his tardiness.

Job Knowledge. Fred displays solid knowledge of the laws, policies and procedures we use on the job. Junior officers have told me that they turn to Fred for advice on how to handle a complicated call, especially those dealing with motor vehicle accidents. Fred is a Level Two accident investigator and is looked at as a subject matter expert by his peers and supervisors.

Patience/Tact. Officer Fox demonstrates excellent patience with the people he contacts on the street, even when they are less than cooperative with him. In September, I watched Fred working with an obnoxious drunk who called Fred numerous obscene names and was generally verbally abusive and uncooperative. Fred remained professional and courteous with this character and processed him into jail in record time. The subject acted to me like he was actually disappointed that he could not get Fred's goat.

Cooperation. Fred is willing to assume his share of the work on Watch Two, and then some. On October 19, I heard him take over a radio call for an officer who was already backed up on reports. On November 20, I observed Fred volunteer to stay over and help a rookie officer book a huge volume of property from a burglary case. These instances are not unusual for Fred.

Safety/Risk Management. This department emphasizes the importance of officer safety, and I have never seen Fred fail to demonstrate good safety and risk management practices. He drives carefully and has not had a preventable vehicle accident in seven years. On the calls I have made with Fred, I have observed that he utilizes excellent approach and positioning as well as prisoner control. On November 13, I saw him carefully re-search a prisoner I gave him after I stopped a wanted party. He found a small knife that I had missed. He did that without worrying about embarrassing his sergeant, which is just what I expect him to do.

Communication. Fred gives clear oral instructions. He is easy to understand on the radio and uses the proper radio codes. Fred's written work is generally good. His reports contain the necessary details and elements of the crime. Fred does need to watch his spelling and realize that the computer won't always catch his errors. Virtually every week that we work together I have to return at least one report to Fred for spelling corrections. Proofreading his work more carefully and carrying a pocket dictionary in his bag will help him do better.

Appearance. Fred looks like the professional he is. His shoes are spit-shined and his uniform is clean and neatly pressed. His brass is well-polished. His grooming is excellent. Frankly, I have used Fred as an example of what a cop should look like when I talk to new officers. In an inspection conducted on August 21, I recorded that Fred received an "Excellent" rating for appearance.

It should be noted that this performance review properly uses specific examples to document specific employee performance. Concrete examples are required if an employee is to understand what behavior is to be sought or avoided. They also are required if the supervisor is to successfully sustain a challenged performance review.

INSPECTION AND FOLLOW-UP

The preceding sample evaluation did not mention a couple of areas worthy of further note. First of all, it did not establish a specific set of goals and objectives for the employee in his next evaluation period. In other words, he was not given objectives to achieve in order to better his job performance and overall skills. Second, the evaluation did not report on the employee's success (or lack of same) in meeting the targets set for him during the preceding rating period. Part of any police agency's plan to reward or correct its employees on the basis of performance appraisal reports must of necessity consider that employee's success or failure in achieving preset objectives of performance or skill.

To be truly useful, any performance evaluation tool must be part of a continuing process. There is little value in establishing goals and objectives if no one ever checks to see if they are being met. Likewise, there is little value in noting that an employee is rated "weak" in patience if his supervisor never checks to see if improvement is being made.

To be complete, an effective employee evaluation report needs a section for the rater to comment on the employee's progress towards meeting established goals and objectives. Perhaps no more than a paragraph in length, this narrative cites continuing difficulties, if present, in addition to progress made. The "Performance Review" section of Officer Fox's evaluation report might look something like this:

OBJECTIVE: Complete training and obtain certification as a speed radar operator.

RESULTS: Patrol deployment and the employee's shift assignments did not permit him to undergo training to meet this objective. The objective will be carried over into the next rating period.

OBJECTIVE: Increase officer-initiated enforcement activity.

RESULTS: A review of enforcement statistics reveals that Patrol Officer Fox has accomplished this objective. His officer-initiated enforcement work now exceeds that of the majority of his fellow officers on the patrol team.

OBJECTIVE: Improve knowledge of techniques of accident investigation.

RESULTS: Officer Fox has been turning in accident reports that are consistently thorough and accurate. However, he did not complete his suggested reading of Northwestern University's Accident Investigation Manual, as called for by his previous supervisor. It is vital that he complete this objective and it will be carried over into the next rating period with the expectation that it will be accomplished without fail.

This part of the evaluation reveals that Officer Fox did a good job during this time period, but his performance in meeting all of his preset objectives has not been flawless. The supervisor-rater must make this known to Fox and then attempt to assure that the objectives become accomplished as soon as possible.

The supervisor must be cautious not to let any favorable feelings towards Officer Fox cause him to report a rosier picture of goal accomplishment than actually exists. To distort the evaluation picture could hurt employee and organization alike.

At the same time, he must not allow any personal, unfavorable impression of the employee to taint the objectivity of the evaluation report. Few employees fail to do *something* well, and any good review of goal and objective achievements will keep that fact in mind.

Patrol Officer Fox must, therefore, have some areas of expected improvement outlined for him for the upcoming evaluation period. The length of this period will have some effect on the goals and their nature. It would, for example, be unreasonable to expect a rookie patrol officer to develop the skills of an experienced specialist over the short span of a six-month evaluation period.

The officer himself should, whenever possible, assist in setting reasonable goals that are important to him as well as to his supervisor and the department. The employee generally will labor much harder to achieve an objective if he shares in the recognition of its importance and its relevance to his job. A detective likely would share his sergeant's concern that he write better reports, for instance, but would likely balk at the idea that he should develop additional accident investigation skills in his current assignment.

It is particularly urgent for the supervisor to connect past inadequate or lacking areas of job performance with future goals and objectives tailored to produce significant improvements. In the case of the highly talented but impatient Officer Jones, one such future target might read:

Objective: To exhibit more tact and patience in working with fellow employees.

There is no requirement for a specific number of goals and objectives to be listed on each employee evaluation. The complexity of the skills or abilities to be mastered by the employee must be considered, as must the time length of the rating period itself.

Goals and objectives from the previous period that have not been met for some reason generally should be regarded as an opportunity for another attempt during the oncoming period. The importance of having the employee agree that these are, in fact, worthwhile targets is evident if eventual success is to be the end result.

If the police employee is in sharp disagreement with his supervisor about the relative value of a given objective set for him, further discussion is in order. Compromise may, on occasion, be necessary. A set of goals and objectives that looks pretty and sounds good may be nearly worthless if the employee himself feels it has been forced upon him with little or no real participation. Such an arbitrarily established group of targets may be doomed to failure from the start.

Generally, employee evaluations connect excellent job performance with some sort of a reward system. A given score or rating brings a resultant increase in pay, rank, or position in the agency. There are probably as many variations of reward systems as there are law enforcement agencies around the country.

Every police agency should have some kind of a reward system operating to recognize extraordinary job performance of employees at all levels and assignments in the organization. Whatever the system in operation at a particular agency, the supervisor serves as the gatekeeper for the employee seeking deserved awards—monetary or otherwise. Once the actual evaluation is complete, the supervisor must see to it that the necessary procedures and paperwork are completed to get the deserved recognition to the employee recipient.

The sergeant also is fulfilling his role as a competent and thorough evaluator when he follows up the evaluation session with inspection and review actions to assure that whatever changes in performance or behavior were called for are actually put into practice. For an officer who has had a problem keeping his sidearm properly maintained, follow-up may mean periodical inspections of the weapon. For the supervisor who has the radio room clerk who just cannot get along with her co-workers, it may mean frequent consultations with her regarding her progress.

SUMMARY

The police supervisor's job as an evaluator is obviously a multifaceted one. He must be a keen observer, a fair and accurate reporter, and a patient and tactful leader. He must, in the final analysis, be one who effectively rates, records, and, where necessary, requires improvements in the efforts of his police subordinates.

As an impartial and accurate evaluator the supervisor will furnish hard evidence and examples to back his opinions. He will stay focused on the subject at hand, assure completeness of the assessment and emphasize its importance by getting it done on time. Then, he will follow up the performance appraisal session with inspections and observations as required. If indicated, he will apply appropriate rewards and sanctions.

POINTS TO REMEMBER

- Performance appraisals help both the employee and the organization.
- Preparing clear, impartial and informative performance appraisals is a key task for the supervisor.
- To evaluate performance effectively, the supervisor must be a good writer.
- Employee performance appraisals must contain clear examples of employee behavior, both good and bad, to back up the ratings given.
- The evaluation session must be seen as very important and adequate, uninterrupted time provided for it.
- The evaluation must be fair and accurate.
- The evaluation should stay on the subject at hand and contain no surprises.
- Performance reviews must be completed on time.
- Evaluations should not overemphasize the value of productivity statistics.
- The supervisor must not give undeserved praise to win his employee's favor.

Chapter Seven

THE POLICE LEADER AS A DISCIPLINARIAN

Most people (police supervisors included) tend to view the term discipline in the same category with such words as flogging. It would be something of an understatement to note that, over the years, the term has taken on a decidedly negative connotation. The word "discipline" is often used interchangeably (and not always properly) with the word "punish." Given these considerations, it is not surprising that many supervisors and supervised alike view discipline as a harsh, unpleasant, and painful part of the work scene.

To hold discipline in such a light is incorrect and self-defeating. Discipline entails much more than punishment. It involves correction and allows for a beneficial change in behavior. To a great degree, it involves an attitude and a feeling for the job, the law enforcement agency, and one's fellow police employees. It is this sort of favorable attitude that military leaders refer to when they speak in glowing terms of brave and elite units or individual soldiers who have displayed the favorable results of perhaps life-saving discipline under harsh conditions. In such praise, discipline begins to take on a very positive meaning.

Discipline as it pertains to police work might then be defined as training and preparation that help develop self-control, sound character, and job efficiency in the police employee. Discipline as described here is an attitude that assures prompt and complete obedience to direct orders, and, at the same time, results in an attitude or demeanor that causes an employee to initiate proper and effective actions in the absence of close supervision. The disciplined police officer does a job properly because he knows that it's the right thing to do, not because he's actively fearful of being punished for failure to perform properly.

When a disciplined attitude is lacking, whether in an isolated incident or on a more widespread basis, discipline in another of its forms will be necessary. In an instance of intentional or negligent misbehavior, correction and/or punishment will be invoked for the good of the employee and the organization.

PURPOSES OF CORRECTION

• The patrol sergeant, making his rounds in the quiet early morning hours, spots an occupied patrol car "blacked out" and parked in an alley. As the supervisor pulls alongside the parked vehicle, the lone officer inside jerks upright; his embarrassed greeting to his boss confirms that he has been dozing.

• The investigations sergeant, locked in a close quarters conference with one of his detectives, notes an apparent odor of alcohol on his subordinate's breath. This is not the first time he has noticed this while the detective was on duty.

• The state patrol supervisor has just arrived at the scene of a car crash that concluded a high-speed pursuit of several miles distance. In telling his excited recap of the chase to his supervisor, the trooper explains his captured traffic violator's bloody scalp: "He wouldn't get into the felony search position so I clipped him with my gun."

In each of the foregoing incidents, some kind of supervisory action is indicated. In one instance, such action may amount to no more than an inquiry. Another may call for counseling and follow-up. Yet another may require a careful investigation into possible unethical or unlawful conduct by the officer involved. The incidents share a common denominator, however, in that each demands supervisory attention with a potential for corrective action.

When he was promoted to the supervisory ranks, the police leader lost the ability to hear a story of employee misconduct and then shrug off the problem to the "bosses" of the department. Now that he is a part of the agency's leadership structure, the police supervisor must be concerned for the agency's interests, the public's legitimate concerns, and the employees' welfare, all in addition to *his* personal realm of interest and concern. In short, he can no longer afford to be as selfish with his worries and interests on the job.

A fellow officer confronted with any of the problems illustrated in the three incidents noted earlier may retain the option of discounting them, starting rumors about them, doing absolutely nothing, or bringing it to a supervisor's attention. The line supervisor's options are not so numerous. As a designated leader sharing in the responsibility for the organization's welfare and effectiveness, he must act in a decisive and responsible manner. This action may involve correction of improper, unethical, or illegal conduct. The supervisor may act alone or with help from others.

In the first incident cited, the patrol supervisor has unexpectedly come across an officer who was apparently not prepared to continue performing his street duties, at least not at the moment. While he cannot ignore the safety hazards and temporary duty derelictions of an officer who was asleep on the job, neither can he as a supervisor afford to "blow up" and reprimand the officer without giving him a chance at explaining.

What the supervisor must instead do is calmly, quietly, and carefully inquire into the obvious problem: sleeping on duty. Is the officer ill? Is there a valid reason why he got too little sleep before reporting for work? Is he being "gassed" by a patrol car with a defective exhaust system? Is he a chronic sleeper on the job? There are many questions that have to be answered before any sort of effective corrective action can be taken.

The corrective action selected must fit the known totality of circumstances. Rare is the police officer who has not "dozed off" while on duty at some time during his police career. If this is the patrol officer's first time, the sergeant's attention is in itself probably enough to shake the culprit out of his doldrums.

If the officer is sick or there is an illness at home, assignment to sick leave for the rest of the duty tour may be mandatory. If he is quite ill, he should be taken home rather than allowed to drive himself. If the illness appears serious, the trip home should come only after a trip to a hospital emergency room.

If the sleeping on the job problem turns out to be a chronic one, further action is indicated. The supervisor may be able to suggest some changes in the sleepy employee's schedule to allow for more rest. In the case of the repeat offender who has clearly disregarded previous warnings and offers of help, formal corrective action may be required. A letter of reprimand, suspension without pay, or other disciplinary action may be indicated in order to get the resistive employee's attention.

Whatever form of corrective action is chosen for a specific incidence of misconduct, the first-line supervisor must be closely associated with it. If the line supervisor is to retain his authority, as well as his image as one who can help, he must be able to recommend formal corrective actions to higher authority.

Corrective measures arbitrarily dictated from above can destroy the effectiveness of the first-line supervisor. Any corrective action in which the supervisor's honest recommendations are not considered will be less than wholly effective. Any department policy that allows a first-line supervisor to shrug and point upstairs to the source of any corrective measure detracts from that supervisor's faith in his own ability and sense of personal responsibility. It likewise belittles him in the eyes of his subordinates as a rather impotent figurehead whenever really important matters are to be decided.

At the same time, the supervisor must merit the faith and responsibility placed in him by his employer. Personal friendships, grudges, or prejudices can take no part in decisions regarding correction of personnel. Whatever corrective action is recommended, it must be appropriate for both the employee and the organization as a whole.

Too harsh a corrective response may embitter the employee and destroy the morale of his co-workers. Too lenient or laissez-faire a response may create the impression among officers and supervisors alike that improper conduct will be overlooked and tolerated. If corrective action is extreme in either direction, the overall discipline and effectiveness of the employee's peers will suffer as a result.

The second incident portrayed tells about a police supervisor who has just learned that a detective of his may have a drinking problem. Once again, the sergeant's official response must be a carefully measured one. A false accusation of this nature could ruin a working relationship forever with the officer concerned. Yet if a real drinking problem does exist as suspected, the employee is not the only one who is compromised and in danger.

Alcoholism, as hinted at by a need for liquor early in the day, will not get better on its own accord. Its gradually worsening effects on the officer will sap his vitality and slowly erode his ability to control his own life. The supervisor must first identify the alcohol problem before any corrective assistance can be obtained. When the supervisor has sufficient information from his own observations that such a problem exists, then is the time to act. Although unpleasant, a direct and private confrontation with the officer is the fairest and, in the end, most humane approach the supervisor can take.

Anger, denial, and perhaps even personal insults and abuse aimed at the supervisor may be the result of the initial confrontation with a victim of alcoholism. The supervisor must persevere even under barrages of excuses, justifications or even harshly-worded attacks from the employee.

Professional help is available, whether it is from a private physician, mental health counselor, department psychologist, Alcoholics Anonymous, or a combination of sources. The point is that the responsible supervisor must persist until the need for help is recognized.

Demonstrated personal concern and involvement of the line supervisor may be all that is needed to convince the troubled police employee to seek and stay with a program of professional assistance for the treatment of alcoholism. All too often, however, the sergeant may find it necessary to employ the law enforcement agency's quasi-military control over its employees to urge the employee into treatment. At the same time, the employee's condition requires that he be treated with understanding and compassion. It also must be kept in mind that like any other dangerous illness, alcoholism has symptoms and side effects on its sufferer which can be harmful to those around him. An employee who is intoxicated at work should be promptly removed from the workplace for the safety of his peers, the public and himself. Obviously, he cannot be allowed to drive himself home.

In such a situation, the police supervisor's ability to correct and change through well-informed intervention is brought to bear. As a result of this kind of correction, a personal problem can be treated and a hardship and danger to others can be eased.

A note of caution for the supervisor confronting the effects of what he suspects to be alcoholism displayed by one of his employees: drug and alcohol addiction are covered under the provisions of the Americans with Disabilities Act (ADA). These conditions are viewed as medical matters and their diagnosis, treatment and record keeping are granted confidential status under ADA. The wise supervisor will consult with his organization's Human Resources or Personnel Department specialists for assistance with a situation that appears to involve alcoholism or drug addiction in a police employee.

The ADA does NOT prohibit a supervisor from acting immediately when he has cause to believe he is dealing with an under-the-influence police employee. Whether he is dealing with an addiction or simply the results of over-imbibing, the leader is obligated to intercede in conduct that is affecting an employee's ability to function safely and effectively in the workplace. The ADA was never intended to curtail an employer's ability to supervise its people and correct inadequate performance, and it does not do so. The ADA does not give an employee license to violate his employer's rules with impunity. The supervisor who detects alcohol on a subordinate's breath or develops other evidence (slurred speech, bloodshot eyes, unsteady gait, etc.) that he may be under the influence is required to intervene promptly for more than one reason. First, the immediate safety of the employee mandates it. If he is under the influence or impaired by alcohol consumption, the prospect of on-the-job injury is present. Second, as noted, the safety of the employee's peers and the public is potentially at risk. Finally, the employee may be in violation of agency rules that prohibit, for example, showing up for work with alcohol on one's breath.

It is worth repeating that it is quite possible that the employee with the alcohol smell about him may not have a problem with alcoholism. His problem may be much more localized in nature, perhaps no more serious other than too much partying the night before. Nonetheless, identification of the problem remains the job of the supervisor who must detect potential trouble and inquire into its nature.

In his information-gathering role, the supervisor who has reasonable grounds to think his on-duty employee is intoxicated or under the influence of alcohol or drugs may want to confirm his fears with a breath or blood test to determine the level of intoxication or impairment. Naturally, he will need to have solid cause for ordering the exam. He also will be well-advised to notify his own chain of command of the situation before ordering such a test. Assuming the exam is authorized, the organization's procedures for ordering and conducting it must be followed to the letter. Whether or not a test is conducted, the supervisor will have additional obligations to assure that the incident is thoroughly documented and provisions made to get the impaired or intoxicated employee safely home.

The third sample situation places the state patrol supervisor at the scene of what, at face value, appears to be an episode of use of excessive force on a traffic offender. Was it really that or was it something else? The supervisor, being familiar with the possible results of adrenaline flow after a dangerous pursuit, looks at all facts of the case. He does not leap to hasty conclusions.

With an unresisting but verbally abusive and quite uncooperative traffic violator at hand, the state trooper has come face-to-face with the sobering reality faced by many an officer before him: a gun in hand with no justification to use it. Confronted with an offender who perhaps knows that the officer has no basis for the use of deadly force, the trooper must now "put up or shut up." He likely must now put away the weapon and control the offender with lesser force.

The state patrol sergeant mentally reviews all of these things as he elicits further details on the encounter from the participants. He also will need to question any other witnesses present.

What the supervisor hears in this little scenario confirms the tentative picture of the events as they unfolded: The patrol officer tried to force a passively resisting motorist into a kneeling position for a search. A struggle ensued, and the firearm still clutched in the officer's hand was brought down on the offender's shoulder blade. Or so it was intended. The blow missed the intended target on the writhing individual, and a lacerated scalp and a suddenly compliant prisoner were the results.

Improper tactics were perhaps more the cause of the prisoner's injury than was excessive force. In deciding what sort of corrective action to take here, the trooper's supervisor must look at several things. Does the trooper have a past history involving an unusually large number of excessive force complaints? How much training in hand-to-hand defensive tactics and prisoner control techniques has the officer received? Had the trooper been fully informed of statutes and policies regarding the use of force—deadly and otherwise? What other circumstances—aggravating or mitigating—existed in this instance? All of these questions, and probably some others, must be answered satisfactorily before the supervisor can take any action.

In this case, additional training in personal defensive tactics might be advisable for the involved trooper. An employee who possessed a record of abuse of force from previous occasions would mandate a more punitive approach from the supervisor and the organization. Suspension without pay, mandatory counseling, discharge from employment, or even criminal charges could result from a continuing pattern of abuse of prisoners by a police officer.

The purpose of correction here, as it is in most cases of improper, lacking, or excessive police action, is definitely multifaceted. Problems in employee behavior must be corrected to help and protect the employee and his fellow workers. This, in turn, benefits the entire agency and its reputation even as it protects the public at large from law enforcement misconduct.

REQUISITES OF FAIR AND EFFECTIVE DISCIPLINE

Behavioral psychologists have known for a long time that in order to be effective, reward/punishment must be sure and immediate enough for the person being rewarded or punished to connect his actions with the results. A bureaucratic disciplinary mechanism that requires months to employ corrective action for improper conduct cannot possibly adhere to the very basic teachings of common sense, as well as to the tenets of behavioral psychology.

Corrective action should be swift, because otherwise the supervisor finds it an unpleasant task and may postpone it for as long as possible. Nor should it be delayed in hopes that the misbehavior will go away or cure itself–it generally will do neither. Likewise, the responsibility for corrective action should not be sent up the chain of command when it can be handled by the primary supervisor, which is by far most of the time.

As has been suggested, the immediate supervisor should know more about the employee than anyone in the chain's higher reaches. Removing him from a very central role in the correction process is almost certain to lessen the likelihood that the corrective action chosen will be appropriate and fair. At the same time, the supervisor's absence from direct and visible participation in the disciplinary process may well diminish his stature and importance in the eyes of his subordinates. His ability to direct and control the employee in the future may diminish proportionately.

Corrective action should be delayed until all pertinent facts are available to the supervisor. The wise leader will never act rashly on the basis of rumor, gossip, or hearsay. Then, with all of the confirmed facts in hand, he will give his employee an opportunity to tell his side of the story.

The good supervisor will, over a period of time, develop and expand upon his ability to separate extenuating circumstances and justifiable deviations as things apart from self-serving excuses and outright fabrications. The fact remains, however, that the employee must be given an adequate opportunity to explain his actions or lack of them. The supervisor must avoid giving the impression that the issue has been decided and the judgment rendered even before the employee has had a chance to relate his side of the story.

Corrective action should be delayed until the supervisor can be alone with the employee in a setting offering adequate quiet and privacy for discussion. Such an environment is not found in the locker room or roll call briefing hall in front of the officer's peers. Nor is it on a crime scene or elsewhere in front of suspects, witnesses, and other citizens. (The author can recall a particularly irritating prisoner driving his arresting officer near the point of homicide because the arrestee had heard his captor being reprimanded by a lieutenant over an unrelated matter. The belligerent prisoner badgered the officer over the next two hours by continuously rehashing and embroidering upon the overheard chewing out.)

The location chosen for a supervisory inquiry and/or verbal reprimand need not be excessively formal. Inquiry and correction can be just as effective in the car, at coffee, or elsewhere when the two are alone without interruption. The formality of the closed-door office session can sometimes do more harm than good.

Occasionally, an ongoing situation will require immediate correction at the time and place that the problem is detected. A street search of a prisoner–improperly and incompletely carried out–cannot be corrected later and still get the job done. Officer safety requires that the supervisor observing such a problem intervene at once. Likewise, the patrol sergeant directing a building search for a burglar cannot debate the propriety of his orders with an officer who feels it should be done another way. At that time and place, the sergeant's orders must be carried out without delay. Discussions or disagreements must wait until the volatile situation at hand is secured.

Later, the sergeant will want to further explain precisely why he corrected a subordinate "on the spot." Questions and discussions are now proper. The supervisor who wants to retain his employees' respect will be sure that the involved employees are told why correction could not safely wait for privacy and an absolutely polite approach.

Corrective action, to be accepted as fair and just by the party on the receiving end, must be consistent with what has gone before. In other words, the supervisor and the agency must avoid meting out one punishment for misbehavior by one employee and then turning around and doing something very different with another employee who has committed the same misdeed under similar conditions. A sense of fair play demands that disciplinary action be consistent in both kind and severity. This is often referred to as *comparative discipline.* It means simply that identical or similar infractions earn identical or similar penalties. Police unions and other employee groups are often very sensitive to the issue of comparative discipline and will vehemently object to corrective measures seen as overly severe.

The phrase *progressive discipline* also comes into play here. It requires that more severe penalties are imposed for repeated improper actions on the part of the employee. The old maxim of "start light, get progressively heavier as required" applies.

At the same time, the police supervisor must recognize that there can be no all-encompassing "shopping list" for discipline, though certain general statements *can* be made: the first time an officer misses court, he gets a warning; the second time, he gets a letter of reprimand, and so on.

Leeway must remain available to the supervisor for the out of the ordinary situation. It would, for instance, be blatantly unfair to award the same degree of discipline to an officer who missed court because he worked overtime the night before as might be given the absent employee who was hung-over from his off-duty pursuits.

The supervisor concerned with promoting consistency in disciplinary practices can rely upon the experiences and recollections of his fellow supervisors who have handled similar situations in the past. Where accessible to the supervisor, personnel records and the transcripts of trial boards or formal disciplinary hearings can sometimes provide the same kind of information and insight.

In order to be recognized as fair and just by its recipient, corrective action must be handled in an atmosphere devoid of anger or other strong emotion. This generally will require that a brief cooling-off period must elapse between the behavior being corrected and the counseling or correcting session itself. No set standard in minutes, hours, or days can be provided. This must be added to the factors demanding that (1) correction be closely tied to the improper act itself to be psychologically effective, and (2) some field situations require immediate intervention for safety or legal considerations.

If there can be anything resembling a general "rule of thumb" regarding the supervisor's attitude in administering corrective action, it might be this: Before confronting an employee who is to be corrected through counseling, verbal reprimand, or formal administrative penalty, the police supervisor must analyze his own emotions and motives to be certain that neither anger nor revenge nor a desire to "put down" an employee are among his motives for acting. If he feels any of them the session should be postponed until such a time when hostile feelings have dissipated.

The supervisor also should monitor the employee's reactions to discipline. While the employee must be given his opportunity to be heard fully, a corrective session that deteriorates into an argument is of use to no one. The supervisor who detects a counseling session headed in the direction of an emotional, head-on collision would do well to adjourn the proceedings until later. This may mean finishing the discussion later in the work shift or not until the next day.

Corrective action that has been carefully formulated, thoughtfully administered, but then immediately forgotten is worse than useless. To be effective, corrective action must be followed up to determine if a change in behavior or performance actually results. Such a follow-up requires the cooperation of all of the agency's supervisors. If, for example, Sergeant Jones had to counsel Detective Whodunnit about turning in his assignments late and poorly done, it may be that the follow-up evaluation will be done by Sergeant Smith if the detective has changed supervisors in the intervening time period. Only through communication with his fellow sergeant will Smith be aware of the need to pay particular attention to Detective Whodunnit's punctuality and thoroughness.

Supervisory follow-up to detect a change in performance (or the absence thereof) can be as informal as an occasional look at the work being done or a conversation with the employee to see what his own feelings are about his progress. At the other extreme, follow-up can be as formal as a special written evaluation by the supervisor coming at the end of the period allowing for the employee to, in effect, "clean up his act." Whatever form it takes, continuing and thorough monitoring of the effects of past corrective action is an important part of the police supervisor's job.

Corrective action, in order to be most efficient, must be something else in addition to being timely, fair, sound, privately administered, devoid of anger or spite, consistent, and followed up. It also must be *documented.* This helps insure fairness, because it makes the action subject to future review by the employee and other supervisors on a "need to know" basis.

What type of record to keep will depend on several things. The agency itself probably will dictate what sort of records or disciplinary files are to be maintained. The seriousness of the infraction being corrected may affect the kind of record made. A relatively minor employee problem may be reflected in a brief entry in the employee's log. A more serious problem may invoke a suspension without pay, mandating a written accounting of the whole incident in the employee's permanent personnel file.

There is sometimes disagreement among police supervisors as to what should be in written form and what may be handled verbally. Probably the best guidance available for the supervisor faced with the dilemma goes something like this: If the incident or infraction is a serious or repeated one, it should be recorded. If a continuing or worsening problem is indicated, even though the problem may have begun as a relatively minor one, it should be recorded.

The written record becomes invaluable if later difficulties blossom and the question arises as to whether or not the employee has been previously warned or counseled. The written (including computerized) record is equally priceless in its ability to inform future supervisors and evaluators of past trends in employee performance, good or bad. Such a solid record can inform the future boss when he wonders if stronger corrective measures are needed because past, milder reminders have not brought about the desired results.

A final prerequisite of effective disciplinary action is that it be recognized as fair and proper by the person receiving it. This is often the hardest part of all. No amount of convincing in the world is going to change the mind of the officer or civilian employee who truly feels that he or she has been maltreated by the disciplinary system and its agents. As a result, the supervisor must avoid placing himself in the role of a huckster attempting to "sell" the corrective action to the employee. He can explain the reason behind the action. He can attempt to show that it is fair and in line with what has gone before. He can explain that the action was aimed at changing a particular employee's conduct, and not the employee himself.

All of these things the good supervisor can and must do as a part of the disciplinary/correction process. The leader also knows, however, that sometimes all of his best efforts will not sway the employee in his belief that he was treated unfairly. Faced with such a situation, the effective leader must settle for a complete explanation of the discipline for the employee, along with an honest rendering of the reason behind it.

The supervisor may wish to reiterate again in different terms or from a different viewpoint if he senses that he is not being understood. When confronted, in the end, with an employee who understands what is being said but just does not agree with it, the wise supervisor knows when to cease in his efforts at gaining concurrence from that employee. Perhaps another time the matter can be brought up with better results. For now, however, the supervisor has honestly met his obligation to be fair with the interests of agency and employee alike.

While there is no magic formula for discipline that is both fair and effective, a few time-tested guidelines for good disciplinary procedures can be helpful. When executing corrective action of any sort, the supervisor should adhere to some basic commandments:

Have the Necessary Information and Know the Full Story. In other words, be sure of the facts of the incident before assigning blame or responsibility. It can be awfully embarrassing for the disciplinarian if it happens that a disciplinary action was based on rumor or incomplete information. A supervisor's reputation for fairness and competency can be seriously damaged by a false start or an erroneous assumption.

Have the Required Official Support Before Taking Corrective Action. It is more than embarrassing to have one's corrective actions overruled by a superior. It is destructive to future effectiveness as a supervisor.

To prevent this problem from happening, the supervisor should check an unusual disciplinary situation with his superior(s) before attempting to place sanctions into effect. It also can be helpful to have a proposed corrective action reviewed by fellow supervisors. If the recommended corrective measures are, in fact, unreasonable or otherwise improper, the problem is detected before any real damage is done. Alterations can be rendered with no loss of face to anyone.

Know the Recipient Well. The supervisor should attempt to anticipate how his subordinate will react to correction. Knowing this will help him in tailoring the corrective action to best suit its recipient. In this way the supervisor will know when formal action is needed and when an informal "word to the wise" will suffice.

Knowing the employee to the fullest extent possible also will prepare the supervisor for the reaction to expect from him over the corrective matter. While one employee may be angered or insulted, another may be embarrassed or emotionally hurt. Knowing what to expect in advance will help the supervisor to plan his words and approach to the chore of correction.

Remember to Praise the Good Points, Too. A smart and sensitive leader will not overlook the troubled employee's good points and strengths while pointing out his shortcomings or errors. If possible, corrective counseling sessions should end on a positive note. (It certainly does not hurt anything if they start that way, too.)

Even the most problem-ridden employee probably has some good points. He may have a number of them. If, for example, it is necessary to counsel and correct an officer about his poor spelling and grammar in the written work he submits, the supervisor may want to compliment the same officer for his thoroughness in including all of the pertinent details and elements of the offense. Presented in a relaxed and informal manner, this kind of correction mixed with deserved praise will not sound false or contrived.

Massive Doses of Authority Should Be Avoided Whenever Possible. It is neither necessary nor desirable to shout, get red in the face, pound tables, and otherwise carry on an emotional tirade to get a point across. "Because I said so" is almost never an acceptable answer to a subordinate's challenge, just as "because I'm the boss" is equally useless.

The employee does not have to be reminded of his supervisor's ability to reward or punish; he already knows this. The supervisor who has mastered the skill of displaying self-composure, self-assuredness, and overall command presence does not have to tell his people that he is the boss–it shows in his mannerisms, actions, and moderate speech.

To be respected by others, the supervisor must first respect (and maintain control of) himself. A leader who is secure and comfortable with himself will be secure and comfortable when working with and leading others.

Try for Agreement From the Employee. As noted, to be most effective, discipline must be accepted as fair and proper by the person receiving it. The effective police supervisor will not discourage the employee from discussing the corrective action thoroughly, even if the subordinate indicates initially that he strongly disagrees with it. A thorough and open discussion hurts nothing. As long as people are talking, a chance remains that they will reach agreement.

IMPORTANCE OF THE SUPERVISOR IN DISCIPLINE

The conclusion of this discussion on discipline is a good time to reemphasize a very important fact of supervisory life: The primary supervisor must be intimately and realistically involved in the whole disciplinary process. Whatever action is to be taken to resolve a problem in employee behavior, the police supervisor must have a big role in deciding what the action will be. To eliminate the supervisor from this vital process is to reduce the likelihood that the corrective action taken will be fair, appropriate, and effective in achieving the desired results.

If he has been doing his job properly, the first-line supervisor will be more knowledgeable than anyone else in the agency regarding his employee's problems, strengths, weaknesses, and general personality and character makeup. To ignore this personal knowledge in favor of correction/punishment handed down from above is to hurt the employee, supervisor, and agency.

The immediate or primary supervisor has much to offer the correctional process. Having him thoroughly involved in it can accomplish a number of things:

Correction Is Personalized for the Employee. Discipline in the form of correction does not flow from some nebulous and perhaps out of touch higher authority. Correction is devised and dispensed most often by the individual whom the employee knows well and works with regularly: the primary supervisor.

Correction Is Appropriate. No one should be as familiar as the first-line supervisor as to what will work to bring about a desired change in his employee's performance. "Overkill" therefore is eliminated from disciplinary actions. Which worker needs only a verbal counseling session and which one merits more drastic measures can best be decided by the person closest to the employee and his work;

that is, the primary supervisor.

Correction Is Timely. Several months must not pass while various layers of the police bureaucracy attempt to reconcile their differences over the appropriateness of a particular corrective action. Heavy emphasis upon the first-line supervisor's fact-based recommendations can cut drastically the time needed to decide upon a course of action.

Participation in Correction Strengthens the Supervisor. The primary supervisor is more effective on a day-to-day basis when his subordinates know that the police organization regards him as a vital member of the leadership team whose opinions and recommendations are worth heeding. The subordinates are shown the supervisor's importance (and thereby his value to them) when his recommendations on corrective actions are valued and enacted. The same subordinates will be more likely to heed the supervisor's requests, warnings, and guidance in the future.

Finally, the supervisor must make sure that any disciplinary action he takes is done "by the book" and according to existing departmental procedures. He must be careful that all of the employee's rights to a hearing or grievance process are protected and explained in detail to him. In a world where union contracts and civil service regulations have at least some impact on what the supervisor can and cannot do, the first-line leader will be wise to seek the advice of his boss and Human Resources staff before he launches a corrective measure that will deprive its recipient of pay or other benefits. The supervisor must keep careful documentation of the entire disciplinary process and what led up to it so that he can testify accurately in a grievance or civil court proceeding, if need be. If he does give testimony, it is his responsibility to approach that task with the same fairness, honesty and courage that he draws upon when he appears in any other legal arena.

SUMMARY

The police supervisor's role as disciplinarian is a key one. Allowing him to meet his full potential boosts the organization as a whole and its employees and leaders as individuals. It is the first-line supervisor's responsibility to guarantee that he meets his obligations through a judicious application of fairness, intelligence, job skills, and plain common sense.

POINTS TO REMEMBER

- There are both positive and negative forms of discipline.
- Self-discipline is the highest level of discipline.
- Disciplinary action must be appropriate for the infraction involved.
- The ADA does not restrain a supervisor from disciplining an under the influence employee.
- Comparative discipline assures that different employees involved in similar misbehavior are corrected in a similar fashion.
- Progressive discipline assures that discipline increases in severity for repeated incidents of misconduct.
- Efficient discipline is timely, fair, devoid of anger, privately administered, consistent, followed up and documented.
- Appropriate discipline requires the participation of the first-line supervisor.

Chapter Eight

THE POLICE LEADER AS A PLANNER

Planning plays a large and critical role in modern police work. Its effects are found at all levels of the police organization.

When the chief and his associates sit down to determine next year's budget, they are engaging in a vital planning effort. When the patrol sector commander drafts a work schedule for the upcoming shift, he is engaging in planning. When the investigation division sergeant delegates individual assignments on a tough case to teams of detectives, he is wearing his planner's hat. Finally, as the patrol officer thinks about his strategy of approach and positioning while responding to a burglary-in-progress call, he, too, is being a law enforcement planner.

Managers define a planner as "one who plans." To carry the exercise in definitions a little further, one generally finds the act of planning itself referred to as *the preparation of some sort of scheme, design, or manner of operating, to achieve some end goal or objective.* In this sense, just about everyone has planned something at one time or another.

The burglar plans exactly how he is going to break into a building. The police officer is a planner when he prepares a trap for that burglar. The patrol sergeant is a planner when he devises a personnel deployment schedule designed to put the most officers on the street during the burglar's prime operating time.

Planning is clearly a part of life's every endeavor, to one degree or another. How it appears in the lives of police supervisors is discussed here.

ELEMENTS OF A PLAN

Every plan is a design for action aimed at reaching an end result or objective. Regardless of what the proposed result or objective might be, the plan for getting there will contain certain elements that are common to each and every other plan, whether it involves how one responds to an emergency police call or how one teaches an academy class in defensive tactics. Most of these common parts or elements are rather easily identifiable. The would-be planner must consider each phase as he constructs his own plan of action.

First of all, the supervisor-planner must identify the end objectives he seeks. If his plan is aimed at the resolution of a particular problem, that problem must be identified before he can successfully go about solving it.

For example, the detective supervisor might determine that his investigators are not getting enough useful work done. Cases are piling up, "call backs" are not getting made, and the unit's crime clearance rate is dropping unacceptably.

Upon questioning his subordinates, he learns that they are having to cope with an unrealistic amount of paperwork in doing their jobs. As one detective puts it, "We're pushing a lot of paper, but we're not putting any crooks in jail."

The detective sergeant now feels he has identified the perceived problem (based upon his subordinates' comments and bolstered by his own observations): excessive paperwork is bleeding away his officers' valuable crime-solving time. He is now ready for the next step in the planning process.

Having identified the potential problem, which here appears to be an excess of paperwork, and having formulated a reasonable, logical objective (reduce the paperwork), the supervisor must further refine the problem. It's a good start to know that excessive paperwork is hampering his unit's work, but he must now be more specific in his problem definition. Is paperwork of all kinds to blame, or is a particular type of report or written assignment the main culprit? Which reports are vital, and which ones can be dispensed with or reduced in size?

Is the problem one of mechanics (too few computer terminals and/or desks to get the job done quickly) or is it one of agency procedures (detectives are given an unreasonable caseload to handle)? Does the problem and its potential solution involve people, things, or both?

At this point, the supervisor-planner may wish to call on some advice and assistance if someone within reach has already tackled a similar problem. The wise planner will consult his fellow supervisors and superiors for their counsel. Solutions and plans previously developed by others may prove equally effective in the new situation, and perhaps they can be made to fit with only minor alterations.

Failing to find useful advice from a peer, the planner may find aid in the professional literature available through his departmental library or on the Internet. It has been said there are few really unique problems in law enforcement. If it is a problem for someone today, almost certainly it has been a problem for someone in the past. It may be that someone else discovered a solution or made some observations applicable to the current problem. The literature may well contain an accounting of previous efforts and their outcomes.

Once a plan of action is put together, the police leader should once again take advantage of the knowledge and experience of his colleagues. Discussion of the proposed plan is vital. It is much better to learn of any possible weaknesses and potential difficulties in the plan now than after it has been placed into operation. For example, the troubled detective sergeant may have decided by now that the best solution for getting his investigators' paperwork done more quickly is to hire more clerks and secretaries for support purposes. It may take one of his peers to point out that there is no money budgeted for the hiring of more people. Another friend may note that there is no office space for them to work in even if there was money to bring them aboard. Still another colleague may suggest the use of volunteers, police cadets or Explorer Scouts to help with the more mundane paper tasks of the investigator's livelihood.

The advice of fellow supervisors is critical to the eventual success of any plan. Such assistance must not be omitted from the planning process.

If the planning task is to be a long one, perhaps covering weeks or months of work time, a timetable or schedule will be helpful to the supervisor. Such a schedule does not have to be exhaustive. Rather, it might be just a set of guideposts or markers to let the planner know how he is doing and how much time is left in which to do it.

A schedule or timetable should be as flexible as possible. It is supposed to help its user, not unduly confine him. It should allow for unforeseen complications and new problems which may be unveiled as the planning continues.

As an example, a patrol sergeant devising a plan for a new beat structure might find the creation of a rough timetable to be very helpful. Initially, he could give himself a week to identify the need for a new beat configuration. Then he should allow a couple more weeks to gather the crime statistics and call-load information, which will be used in setting the new beat boundaries. Another week may be set aside for the production of a rough draft of the new beat plan. The following week may be reserved for review and discussion with other supervisors. A final week could then be utilized to produce a refined version of the plan for presentation to his boss and the agency's command staff.

Much shorter schedules can work to the supervisor's advantage, too. For example, a tentative schedule may be used to plot out how much time to allow for each anticipated duty of a busy work day.

There is, of course, no limit on the number of rough drafts that may be prepared on the way to the final product. It has been said that worthy literary works are not written, they are re-written. Some planning documents may already be in their final form the first time they are formulated, but most will require modifications to one extent or another.

The supervisor should remain mindful that making reasonable changes to an original plan of action does not indicate weakness or indecisiveness. Failure to make *needed* changes does, however, indicate a lack of good judgment.

Once the plan has been refined, clarified, and altered to the satisfaction of the supervisor-planner, the next step calls for communicating the plan's elements to those who will enact it. If the plan involves, say, one team of patrol officers assigned to burglary surveillance, then those officers must be advised of what is expected of them. In order to be really effective, those affected by the plan should be told of the reasons for its implementation, what is expected of each of them, and what the expected results are to be. Their ideas on how to make it better are also needed, and should be solicited.

If the plan involves a change in dispatching procedures, then the communications personnel, the street officers, and their leaders must be informed as to the "whys" and "hows" of the planning effort. Everyone involved must know how it will affect his or her way of conducting operations. Once more, employee input is required.

Communication or publication of the plan to be enacted can be either a very complex undertaking or the height of simplicity. Factors affecting the amount of effort required to pass the word include the complexity of the plan itself and the number of people whose actions will be affected by it. An even minor change in the sort of paperwork completed for an arrest probably will impact on records and support personnel as well as the officers who make the arrests and complete the forms. "Spreading the word" here may require written instructions in order to reach all departments and personnel.

On the other hand, a plan for altering the routine maintenance schedule for patrol vehicles may involve notifying only the concerned shop foreman. In this scenario, the shop foreman has almost certainly been involved as a part of the planning effort from the very start.

The plan–simple or complex–has now been placed into operation, though the process is still not complete. In order to be most useful, any planning effort must make provision for evaluation and critique of the plan once it is put into action. It's one thing to devise and enact a scheme for solving a police problem; it's quite another to find out if the plan is actually meeting its objective.

There are other questions to be answered about any activated plan, in addition to the "Does it work?" query:

1. Does the change in operations or procedures create new, unanticipated difficulties?
2. Does it create new "people problems" while solving other problems anticipated by the plan? For example, a new work schedule eases deployment strains but puts new burdens on the officers' family lives.
3. Is the plan only partially successful? Could it be improved through further change?

The last query is an important one. The planner must examine the results–anticipated and otherwise–of his plan once it has been put into operation, particularly if the plan is a complicated one. Unforeseen consequences may show up. While these surprises may not doom the plan's chances for ultimate success, they may require some changes to accommodate them.

It is worth stressing again that only the ignorant planner refuses to change a plan simply because to do so would admit error or some imagined weakness on his part. Not only does the intelligent planner accept change as part of the planning process, he will seek out constructive criticism as well. Faced with solid and convincing evidence of a need for an alteration in the plan, the supervisor will not hesitate to make the needed changes.

Truly competent planning calls for long term as well as immediate evaluation and critique. Granted, it is quite important to watch for immediately apparent difficulties, but it is equally necessary to monitor the plan and its changes for problems that may appear only after weeks, months, or perhaps even years of operation.

A choice example of the value of long-term evaluation can be seen in the continuous monitoring of a new plan to change from a 5 days a week, 8 hours a day work schedule to a 4–10 plan. Immediately following the implementation of such a plan, officer morale undoubtedly will go up. A year or so later, however, the planner may find that officer overtime and sick time have risen, and shift scheduling problems are rampant. Only long-term monitoring of the 4–10 plan will expose problems and allow for the treatment of these difficulties.

WRITING PLAN OBJECTIVES

Every planner should set concrete, tangible objectives in fulfilling his planning responsibilities. Such planning goals and objectives are vital to the successful planner and his work. They also frequently display some common characteristics.

Good Planning Objectives Are Specific. The effective planner spells out the "what" and "when" expectations very clearly. His objectives are constructed in a manner that leaves no room for doubt as to meanings or expectations. These objectives contain no padding or superfluous information. They embody only the information necessary to understand them fully. Putting too much wording into an objective only serves to make it less precise and more prone to misinterpretation.

Good Planning Objectives Are Tangible. Accurate measurement of results is important. If results or outcome cannot be detected and measured, the plan's achievement of its intended goals cannot be known. It is well recognized that law enforcement, by its very nature, deals with many intangibles. Who can measure, for example, exactly how much crime a marked patrol car prevents by its presence in a given area? Yet, a method should be devised that will allow for the identification of some realistic and tangible factors that can be measured in looking at the whole picture. It is possible, for instance, to say if reported crime goes up or down with an additional marked car placed in a given area.

Good Planning Objectives Focus on Results. The intelligent, objective writer does not dwell long on the mechanics aimed at achieving his stated objective. These details are important, and certainly must be mastered if the plan is to be activated properly, but the planning objectives must concentrate on end results: the changes to be brought about by the plan's correct implementation. Outcome is more important than output.

Good Planning Objectives Are Significant. Drawing up unimportant, vague, or otherwise meaningless objectives is a fruitless exercise that wastes everybody's time and accomplishes little good.

A worthwhile planning objective identifies a target that is worthwhile to those engaged in the planning effort. It is important to plan deployment of one's two dozen patrol cars when one has that many cars. Conversely, it is of no value to make plans for the use of one's paper clips when no one has any paper.

Good Planning Objectives Are Clear. The objectives of the plan must be understood by those who are to carry them out. Complex terminology, professional slang, and legalistic jargon often serve to confuse an otherwise clear goal. Language used in a planning objective must be familiar and understandable to all who will need to read or hear it. Acronyms should be utilized only if their meaning is clear to all personnel involved in the operation.

Good Planning Objectives Are Challenging But Not Idealistic. The successful planner sees the way he wants things to be, but he also leaves room in his thoughts for reality. He realizes that he often needs to do the job with less, not greater, resources at hand.

At the same time, the planner does not set objectives that are already achieved, or nearly so. It is wrong to devise a planning objective to meet what is certain to be accomplished anyway. This challenges no one.

The individual police officer works better when challenged and tried. He should be given ample and fair opportunity to apply all of his talents, and perhaps cultivate some new ones. At the same time, planning objectives that have no realistic hope of being met breed frustration and resentment. The unrealistically lofty must be avoided as surely as the ridiculously easy.

PLANNING GOALS FOR EMPLOYEES

One of the police supervisor's vital roles calls for him to continuously evaluate the performance of the employees under his direction. As a part of the total evaluation process, he helps his people set goals and objectives involving changes in their job status, skills, and professional development. He helps them plan intelligently and logically for where they want to be in law enforcement's future.

In planning employee goals and objectives, the supervisor should be mindful of a few simple guidelines which have worked for supervisors many times before. First of all, a well-planned employee objective is specific, concise, and to the point. Lengthy, complex, and involved objectives tend to confuse employee and supervisor alike. Later, trying to determine whether or not such a troublesome objective has been met can cause any number of problems.

Second, planning objectives should include some deadline for the employee to meet as he directs his efforts. An established due date allows the conscientious employee to know exactly how much time he has to accomplish his work. He may then pace himself accordingly.

Third, a good, written employee planning objective generally employs action-oriented verbs. These verbs include words such as increase, gain, develop, broaden, improve, and others in a like vein. These terms may frequently be seen working in concise but clear-cut job objectives:

1. Increase knowledge of crime scene processing techniques.
2. Broaden experience in the field of interviewing skills.
3. Improve abilities in handling accident diagram preparation.
4. Gain additional understanding of hostage negotiation principles and procedures.

Fourth, employee objective planning should permit the establishment of only those objectives that are beneficial to both the police employee and the police agency. Prospective plans of the employee must be consistent with both the larger goals of the organization and the more specific objectives of the employee's own unit or assignment. This does not represent selfishness on the part of the agency and its managers; it's just common sense and a reasonable expectation required of any loyal employee.

It would not, for example, prove beneficial to the organization to promote an employee not yet ready for promotion simply because a promotion was one of the employee's planning objectives. Likewise, the employee would find little benefit in a planning objective that called for him to work more hours for less money.

The planning of employee objectives need not neglect the interests of either employee or employer. Mutually beneficial goals and objectives can be devised that serve both. The agency's efficiency is increased when the patrol officer achieves his objective of receiving additional training in accident investigation. The detective's self-esteem soars at the same time the agency gains from his newly achieved objective of developing refined skills in crime scene photography.

Finally, whenever possible, employee planning objectives should be mutually devised and approved by the employee and supervisor acting as a team. The employee is more likely to work towards the fulfillment of a given plan of action if he agrees that it is a worthwhile and necessary thing to do.

The formulation of mutually acceptable objectives obviously will require considerable direct communication between supervisor and police subordinate. This by itself is beneficial. Understanding for one another's viewpoints should grow as discussion takes place. In the end, such free discussion should make a mutual objective that much easier to construct.

Occasionally, the police supervisor may be required to set a planning objective without the subordinate's concurrence. It would be difficult, for instance, to get an employee to join in the establishment of an objective to "get to work on time" if that employee had steadfastly refused to acknowledge that he had ever been tardy. In such instances, the supervisor must go ahead and set the stated objective and require that it be achieved without the employee's initial agreement. The welfare of the organization as a whole mandates that this bit of arbitrariness be tolerated by all.

Planning useful and realistic objectives for police employees is vital.

It merits the best efforts of police employee and police supervisor alike.

PROJECTS FOR THE BOSS

Every supervisor works for his or her own boss, perhaps several of them. Unless the supervisor is in a very unique situation indeed, he can expect to receive assignments and projects to be completed for the boss. How those assigned duties are carried out can go a long way in determining the supervisor's future in the agency.

Whether it consists of collecting statistics and doing a written analysis of them or organizing resources for the handling of a large protest demonstration, a project handed to a first-line supervisor by his boss almost inevitably requires planning. Just how much planning is required depends largely on the complexity of the assigned task. Getting all the patrol vehicles equipped with new light bars may not be all that complicated; helping plan for a major political party to hold its national convention in town is a whole different story. Whatever the size of the job assigned by the boss, getting it done calls for many of the same "steps to success."

First of all, the planner must understand what is expected of him. Exactly what is to be accomplished? If he is wise he will write down the expectations and any instructions from his boss on how it is to be done. He will need to know what resources are permitted him and which ones are denied, for whatever reason. He also must know the time frame in which he has to accomplish the task. If he's smart, he will ascertain the boss's deadline and then set his own cutoff date well ahead of it. Experience has taught him that he will need time to deal with mistakes and surprises. He also will require some extra time just in case his boss returns the work to him for revision or repair, something he wishes to avoid by doing it right the first time. He will seek to simplify his task by ascertaining from others who have done work previously for the boss just what that individual expects to see in completed staff work. The superior's pet peeves (Example: misspelled words) to be avoided in the final work product also can be identified in this way. The supervisor's goal, of course, is to hand in work that does not need revision but is instead praised for its thoroughness and overall quality.

In order to plan wisely the supervisor must have a crystal clear understanding of what is expected of him. A lot of time and effort will be wasted if he starts a project only to find out halfway through that he is doing something the boss did not request, or requested be done differently. The smart supervisor will ask clarifying questions about any instructions he does not understand. He will look much less foolish for asking questions at the outset than doing the project in the way he *thought* the boss wanted it done, only to find out at the end that he was quite wrong.

In planning to carry out the work his boss has requested, the sharp supervisor likely will outline for himself a plan of attack. He will list the sub-tasks he must accomplish and note the resources he will need to get there. This is an excellent time to identify and secure any help he may require to get the job done. If he needs access to computer assisted dispatch data, for instance, he will identify who can get it for him and when. If he wants to know more about how some other part of the department operates, he will seek out a fellow supervisor or other source there to help him.

Finally, the supervisor will examine his plan critically for errors and omissions. He may ask a peer to take a look at his work with a critical eye, too. Now is the time to find out where additional effort may be needed and arrange to get it done. A plan is only as good as its weakest element, and a good planner seeks a plan without weaknesses.

In law enforcement as in every other field of human endeavor, leaving a good impression on the boss is vital for an employee's future in the organization. Using the elements of effective planning will help the first-line supervisor on his or her way in climbing the organizational ladder. Equally important, good planning will help him or her get the job done better, quicker and easier.

PLANNING PERSONAL PRIORITIES

The vital importance of the supervisor's planning efforts for his employees and the agency has been discussed at length. At the same time, however, the police leader's responsibilities to himself and his own career must not be neglected. After all, he cannot do his best for his department or his people unless he also does right by himself. A healthy personal outlook and a positive job attitude should be the twin products of careful attention to *his* needs, too.

Unless the supervisor knows where he is headed and how he is going to get there, his ultimate value to the agency cannot help but suffer. He needs and must have a keen sense of direction for himself.

The police supervisor must plan for himself at every turn, detour, and pause in his law enforcement career. In fact, truly far-reaching planning should commence even before the police officer attains the rank of supervisor. The officer intent on wearing sergeant's chevrons someday plans how he will prepare himself for the promotional process. Among his preparations, he plans what he will study, how he will go about studying it, and how he will allocate the time necessary for that study. Said another way, *he is engaging in planning.*

The sharp supervisor will plan his time to make the best use of the minutes available to him in each day. Time management skills are to be found in every effective supervisor's tool box. Organizing his day, week or month will make getting things done in the time available considerably easier. The supervisor who plans his time carefully and works to limit the big time-wasters (gossip, socializing on the job, web surfing, needless e-mail or phone conversations) will find that his level of effectiveness as well as his efficiency rises considerably. Hopefully, his boss will notice, too. Good time management and smart organization skills will pay off every time for their police practitioner.

The newly promoted police person can allow no lapse in attention to personal planning. Now, perhaps more than ever, he must outline where he is going and what he wants to accomplish. He must set priorities, establish goals, and tailor objectives to his new assignment. A new patrol sergeant, for example, might prioritize his duties something like this:

1. Learn about my subordinates' strengths, weaknesses, and overall personalities.
2. Learn the mechanics of my job: which forms and reports to complete and how; what do I need to report to my own boss and how do I do it?
3. Learn how I can improve the way I do my job as a supervisor: what training can I get; what can I learn from my fellow supervisors and my bosses?
4. Learn what it will take to master the next step on the organizational ladder: how can I help my boss with his tasks, while

grooming myself for someday assuming greater responsibilities?

Obviously, the actual time required to realize each step of such a plan will vary greatly from person to person and situation to situation, as well as from agency to agency. Many things in addition to the supervisor's own abilities can enter the picture in determining how soon he will advance further, or if he will advance at all. Some of them, such as internal departmental politics, may be frustratingly beyond his ability to alter.

The police supervisor should be realistic in the career plan that he sets for himself. In the agency that promotes a new lieutenant about every three years, it may be not be helpful for a hopeful sergeant to count on promotion a lot sooner.

In the agency that traditionally assigns only senior supervisors to the detective bureau, it is pointless for a rookie sergeant to anticipate an early call to the world of plain clothes. Good supervisors are optimistic when there is some reasonable basis for optimism. They do not, however, expect the sky to rain honey when the outhouse blows up. Idealism is nice, but it must be tempered with a dollop of patience and a stiff dose of reality.

The police supervisor involved in planning his future must not disregard any potential opportunities to broaden his experience, increase his formal knowledge, and expose himself to the thoughts and feelings of other people.

The patrol supervisor may love the street and the challenges it brings. He may want to do nothing but lead a group of uniformed officers. The wise patrol leader knows, however, that a chance at a specialty assignment will be good for him professionally, and with the additional and varied experience in another area now acquired, he may later return to street supervision at an advanced rank or come back as a better patrol sergeant. Whatever the case, he will be better able to do the job because of his newly widened horizons.

The supervisor also should take advantage of any specialized training offered by the agency in the fields of leadership, supervision, or specialized skills of policing. His abilities will hopefully grow in proportion to this increasing body of knowledge that he commands.

College courses pertinent to police management may prove useful. Many police agencies offer monetary benefits or other inducements to their police officers and supervisors who advance their formal educational level. All agencies *should* do so. For the police supervisor, courses in management, business, supervision and administration of justice can prove especially useful.

Finally, the combined knowledge and life experiences of others can prove invaluable to the interested supervisor who knows how to listen. It is not necessary that the supervisor agree with all that he hears; he can learn from the mistakes and shortcomings of others as easily as from their victories and strengths. He is quick to listen, observe, and learn. He is slow to spout off, convict, or moralize concerning his peers.

The effective police planner is a great many things. He is, of necessity, considerate and understanding of others. He appreciates their strengths. He understands their problems and tries to work with them.

SUMMARY

Simultaneously, the supervisor/planner with more than his share of common sense recognizes that he is not of much use to anyone if he does not also take care of his own personal and professional planning. It is when he plans carefully and wisely for himself that he can continue to be of most use to others.

The police supervisor must be an effective planner at several levels. He is careful to craft specific, tangible, clear objectives that focus on results. As a planner, the supervisor helps subordinates formulate their job-related goals and objectives. In doing so he helps them learn to plan well for themselves. In addition, the capable supervisor plans how he will execute a project or assignment for his boss.

The wise supervisor plans for himself, too. Here he does more than plan for the operations of the work day, week or month, as important as those plans may be. He also will plan for his future in law enforcement. He knows that with a carefully thought out action plan for the future he can demonstrate his greatest value to the police organization as he maximizes his own advancement and personal job satisfaction within the agency. That's called planning for success.

POINTS TO REMEMBER

- All supervisors engage in planning activities.
- Planning can be personal, organizational or both.
- The objectives of a plan must be specific, tangible, clear, significant and results-focused.
- Plan objectives should be challenging but not unrealistic.
- Planning goals for employee performance should, where possible, be done with input from the employee.
- The supervisor planning a project or other assignment for his boss has an opportunity to advance his career in the organization.
- Planning for his own development and career is a valid part of the supervisor's overall planning efforts.

Chapter Nine

THE POLICE LEADER AS
A COMMUNICATOR

Unless he or she is asleep or unconscious, every living human being communicates, either intentionally or otherwise. Words are, of course, among the most obvious of communication tools. But human beings communicate almost constantly without uttering or writing a single syllable. Mom communicates with her toddler when she crosses her arms and taps her foot. The female denizen of a singles lounge communicates with the gent at the other end of the bar when she arches an eyebrow and gives him "the look." And the patrol sergeant sends a message loud and clear without ever saying a word when, irritated by the chatter in the back of the roll call room, he stops reading the briefing notes and stares icily at the offenders. In each of these cases, clear communication has occurred.

What is communication? If one may accept at face value that all forms of communication involve an exchange or, at least, a transmission of thoughts, ideas, and/or feelings, then a related concept automatically follows: it is almost impossible *not* to communicate.

With this in mind, it is safe to say that the person doing the communicating must not only concern himself with the message that he wanted and intended to convey, but must be equally concerned with unintentional, supplemental, and perhaps contradictory information or feelings that he puts across, as well.

An example of such communicative confusion is found when the patrol sergeant tells one of his men that it's alright to take a day of sick leave tomorrow, while simultaneously making some facial expression indicative of his inner feelings that the day off is not really a good idea. The patrol officer, understandably, may be left more than a little confused about what the supervisor is really saying to him.

Likewise, the poorly phrased or awkwardly constructed written order or directive may bring about more harm than good due to the confusion it foments. There may be no limit to the grief brought to the message's author and to the agency itself from such an aborted effort at effective communication. If it holds true that effective communication unites the most remote elements and units of an organization, then it is equally correct that poor communication can create disorder and disunity in the various organizational parts.

Good communication between management and supervisor and between supervisor and the supervised is vital to more than just organizational effectiveness and efficiency. Reliable communication helps guarantee the presence of an additional component to overall agency effectiveness: good employee morale.

The department's line-level leaders and the people they lead will be adversely affected if they feel they are being left out of the agency's information flow. It is increasingly difficult to produce a good work product, regardless of what the work entails, if one feels that he is regarded as being unimportant to the organization of which he is a part. Being left out of knowing when one has a right to know breeds a poor attitude with resultant poor work. Once again, communication–poor or good–is the cause or treatment for morale and attitude changes.

Police people are, by nature or training, very curious individuals. They are interested in what's happening around them and do not like to remain unknowing about things or events that may concern them.

It is said that a lack of reliable information and a strong personal interest are the two ingredients necessary for the manufacture and passing of rudely constructed and dubious information: rumor. It would follow logically that the organization or individual supervisor unwilling or unable to communicate honestly, openly, and effectively invites active rumor-mongering.

The intelligent police supervisor recognizes the importance of all varieties of communication and sees the value of the written word as used in its proper place. He realizes the equal worth of the spoken directive, suggestion, or comment as utilized within its own realm. In realizing these things, he seeks to communicate to the very best of his own ability and likewise does everything in his power to facilitate good communication by others–his bosses, peers, and subordinates.

He knows that to do less is to compromise the accomplishments of his department and himself.

In fulfilling his role as an able and reliable communicator, the successful police supervisor recognizes the need to be familiar with the elemental building blocks of good communication skills. Those elements will be discussed next.

ELEMENTS OF GOOD COMMUNICATION

Whether one is communicating orally or in writing, several factors can aid greatly in assuring that the intended message is the one that gets through. These basic elements for good communication include:

Clear message, simplified message, openness, two-way information flow, application of good listening/reading habits, calm approach, and proper timing.

Obviously, there will be some overlapping and intertwining in any discussion of these key elements. It is impossible, for example, to separate totally the communication elements "clear message" and "simplified message." With this in mind, an in-depth examination of each of these elements to good communication skills can begin.

Clear Message

Whether he is writing a formal order or preparing a procedural memorandum, addressing a class of recruits or giving a group of officers directions for an upcoming raid, the police supervisor must be certain that his message of directions, orders, or facts is very clear. If the communicator is conveying the message orally, he can help assure that his point is made by not trying to convey too much too quickly. Remembering that the average person's attention span shrinks proportionately to the complexity of what is listened to, the smart speaker keeps it short whenever he can.

If the information in the message is lengthy and/or complicated, it is generally best to put it in writing. Then those receiving the information can see what is being covered even as it is being read aloud.

A clear message delivered orally will be presented in a quiet atmosphere. The serenity of the surroundings will, of course, be dictated by the situation at hand. It would be unreasonable to expect the special tactics unit supervisor to have the placid surroundings of a convent to brief his people at the scene of a gun battle. Nonetheless the supervisor should use the best resources available to make known his spoken plans. Most of the time, the relative quietness of a squad room or similar facility will be the best place for explaining procedures, discussing plans, or relaying orders and instructions.

If the message is to be in written form, the supervisor should keep the words, sentences, and paragraphs as short as possible for clarity and understanding. No one wants to read an order or procedure that flows on ceaselessly. Likewise, few will strain themselves to untangle the weighty snarls of a super sentence that drones on and on. Clarity is definitely tied to brevity in this respect.

The directive writer also should remain mindful of some unclear and imprecise words and phrases that can trap even the best-intentioned scribe. A few of these fuzzy, vague, misleading enemies include: sometimes, a few, generally, usually and many.

How often is "sometimes"? How many are "a few"? Do "generally" and "usually" mean the same thing? How many is "many"? The questions triggered by the overuse of such imprecise terms can be confusing to the police employee trying to carry out a vague directive. While recognizing that individual situations are unique and require flexibility on the part of the police person, the smart supervisor tries to provide his charges with as concrete a set of guidelines as possible. Of the two sample directives that follow, only the second would be an acceptable means of conveying the message:

1. Unconscious prisoners generally should be examined by medical personnel prior to incarceration.
2. Unconscious prisoners shall be examined by medical personnel prior to incarceration. Where deemed advisable by medical personnel, such prisoners shall be hospitalized rather than jailed.

Simplified Message

Closely allied with message clarity is the importance of a simple, straightforward message. It makes little sense (and makes for even less understanding) for a supervisor to attempt to convey several different and perhaps widely divergent messages at one time. If, for example, it is simultaneously necessary to spread the word on uniform changes, work hour alterations, and the proper booking of juvenile arrestees, each subject can be best served by affording it separate and undivided attention.

One memorandum or directive addressing all three issues would probably be too lengthy and perhaps too complex, as well. Better that three different memos, orders, or directives are prepared, each one authored by someone who knows enough about the subject matter to communicate clearly.

Some supervisors go overboard and furnish so much information that they complicate an otherwise simple message. It is important that subordinates know the reasoning behind their being asked to follow a certain course of action. However, overwhelming them with too much can serve to complicate rather than inform. A simple, direct message about the plan or directive may be accompanied by some background, but it will not dwell upon very minor points or explain itself into tedium.

The common sense supervisor does not utilize communication with others to convince everyone of how clever he is and what wonderfully big words he can use. Rather, his messages—whether spoken or written—get quickly to the point without wasting words to explore trivialities. The messages instead seek to simplify the complex and clarify the muddled.

Openness

For real communication to take place, all of the participants in the information exchange must be attentive and open with one another. The speaker or writer who talks down to his subordinates is very likely to be recognized for what he probably is: a pompous preacher.

While the preacher is addressing his audience, he is sidetracked from totally open communication because he is concentrating on how to make "those dummies" understand and respond in the fashion he wants them to. Meanwhile, his audience is distracted from whatever topic is being addressed by prejudicial feelings against his contemptuous approach. The basic message is bound to suffer in the resultant turmoil of bad attitudes.

If the listener/reader knows the creator of a given communication at all, it is probably impossible not to feel some sort of preconceived notion about the message at hand. This can work for as easily as against the communicator. For instance, any message from a well-liked and trusted leader is probably going to be better received than the same message from an unknown. At least to some extent, the credibility that the communicator enjoys will make the message itself more credible, and perhaps more palatable, as well.

Unfortunately, the reverse is also true: a message from a disliked or distrusted boss may generate derision, even if the news is otherwise favorably regarded by its recipients. Here is yet another reason for a supervisor to build credibility and trust with his subordinates.

Trickery and deception in any sort of communication often will backfire on its originator. Lies and half-truths, including lies by omission, have no place in any communication from a supervisor to his subordinate.

Lying may be more comfortable and cause fewer bad feelings today when the truth would otherwise be unpleasant. Sad experience reveals, however, that most often the truth will surface sometime, as it should. When it finally does, previous lies are most often greeted with harsher feelings than would have resulted from an earlier, honest communication of bad news.

Hidden messages are inherently unfair. Half-truths are cowardly. Outright lies are damnable. Deception with one's fellows is a cardinal sin. In short, anything less than forthright openness and honesty in one's daily interaction with co-workers, bosses, and subordinates is not in the interests of good communication.

Two-Way Information Flow

It is here that face-to-face oral communication surpasses its paper and ink cohort in efficiency and effectiveness. It is impossible to debate with a memorandum or an e-mail; it is not possible to clarify easily the fine points in a printed directive. Personal contact between the message sender and its intended recipient allows for a more meaningful exchange of information and ideas. A written communication cannot be read for its facial expressions and body language.

One of the supervisor's functions is to explain and clarify to his people the instructions and policies that are handed down to him. To some extent, his role here is that of a translator between management and the work force. Genuine, two-way communication permits him to do more than relay and clarify orders and instructions. He also can listen to his employees' ideas and feelings and relay them to his superiors. This sort of two-way communication helps enormously in keeping the peace between labor and management, so long as both continue to operate in good faith.

So, how can the police supervisor bring about this process called two-way communication? For one thing, he always should remain accessible to his people. He also must be sure that his expressed attitude is not of the "I'm too busy" or the "don't bother me now" sort. If he conducts himself like he doesn't want to be bothered, he probably won't be. Communication and morale will suffer in the process.

This is not to say that the police supervisor can never have any uninterrupted time for himself to take care of his own obligations. He can and must have such personal time. He also must reserve time to service his employees' information needs.

The police leader determined to maintain a good information exchange with his subordinates will see to it that he keeps himself informed and knows where to go for facts or explanations when he does not have the answers himself. If an employee gets an "I don't know" from his boss too often, perhaps coupled with an expression or attitude that adds, "and I don't care enough to find out," that employee soon learns to go elsewhere for his answers. Chain of command deteriorates, an informal information system grows (the "rumor mill"), and the unenlightened supervisor's effectiveness declines by leaps and bounds.

The good supervisor cannot afford NOT to care. He must try to obtain the answers desired by his subordinates or lose respect and control in the process. Where there is no pat answer available, or his own superiors decline to give him the facts he needs, he must tactfully pass this along, too. There may be a good reason why the facts he seeks cannot be set forth just now. He must limit himself to reporting what he does know as fact, however little or distasteful that may be. In other words, he must follow the responsible journalist's rule of reporting the facts without editorializing!

Good, two-way communication is also encouraged by the supervisor who asks questions to be sure he is understood. After explaining a particularly complex procedure or operation, he finds it informative to ask a few pointed questions of his audience. "When are you justified in using deadly force?" "How many breaths to chest compressions are there in cardiopulmonary resuscitation?"

Such questions have served as learning gauges and review mechanisms for more than a few police instructors. The queries do not insult anyone's intelligence if those being questioned know in advance that it's done to help them understand and learn, not to embarrass or ridicule them.

Unfortunately, face-to-face contact is not always practical or possible when information is being conveyed. The second-best alternative–the written communication–must then take over as the vehicle carrying the message. While not as effective for two-way communication as the personal encounter, the written message need not fail in its intended purpose of sending information.

A written "letter to the troops," regardless of its form or content, does not have to stand alone. The most skillful supervisors will strive to anticipate the questions or other problems likely to arise from one-way written messages by doing their homework so the answers will be ready if and when queries arise.

The written communication, when used together with an intelligent explanation and the opportunity for discussion, can be very helpful in its own right. It provides a record that can be referred to later on as a source of instructional material for the supervisor wearing his teacher's hat, and even functions as a memory-jogger when used to record goals, objectives, and plans for individual employees or entire work teams. It, too, can be very successfully utilized in two-way communication.

To be useful, the written message must be accompanied by someone who can explain and clarify and discuss where needed. The supervisor can utilize it along with the spoken message in establishing a useful, two-way flow of information and ideas.

The ability to write well is absolutely essential for today's successful law enforcement supervisor. He cannot succeed and advance in his organization without it. A supervisor lacking in writing skills will seek to remedy the problem via practice, thorough proofreading and, perhaps, a writing or grammar class or two. It is *that* critical to his future.

Application of Good Listening/Reading Habits

There is an old saying that it is possible to look without seeing, to listen without hearing. This implies that the senses can be functioning quite well without the mind interpreting their findings. This would appear to apply with equal accuracy to the written or oral communication and its effect on its recipient.

The supervisor must truly listen to what his subordinate is saying to him. This means he does not look blandly (and blindly) at his employee while his mind is somewhere else. It means he does not interrupt his employee while that employee is trying to tell him something. It means he does not provoke an argument in lieu of a reasonable discussion.

The supervisor can and should question and clarify in his own mind exactly what it the speaker is saying. This is necessary for understanding, a prerequisite of good communication. Questioning, however, should be primarily for clarification and should never be utilized as a means of attack on the speaker. By his tone and demeanor, the police leader must convey that he wants his employee to talk freely. Nothing short of honesty and openness on the part of both parties can assure worthwhile results.

The talented listener is patient, does not interrupt, does not start arguments, and maintains a receptive and interested attitude. The skillful reader is no less talented. He learns from what his eyes report to his alert mind.

The written communication deserves at least as much effort and attention as does the spoken word. Many written memoranda, e-mails, directives, orders, and instructions demand more than a single, casual reading. A first reading done to get the general idea and a slower and more careful second one accomplished to bring out the particulars is a good idea. With complex messages, highlighting in color constitutes a technique long favored by students which can be equally helpful to police professionals.

The smart reader is careful to select whatever passages he does not understand and then seeks clarification from the communicator himself, if needed. If there are other written messages that further clarify this one, he should review them for whatever help they might provide. In order to be able to do this, the individual who has learned his bureaucratic survival skills probably will have his own file system for past written communication of significance. Whether the system consists of a tabbed, loose-leaf binder or a computer hard drive, it should be kept up-to-date, well-organized, and conveniently at hand to be consulted as the need arises.

Generally, the larger the organization he is a part of, the greater the individual's need to maintain his own file system of printed material. This rule of thumb holds true for both supervisor and subordinate, although there may be some differences in the kinds of things each may want to retain as resources. For instance, the patrol officer may want to keep a copy of the revised procedures for completing accident reports; the patrol sergeant may find more lasting value in the e-mailed memorandum detailing the proper review and distribution procedure for accident reports.

Calm Approach

Statements made under the color of strong emotions are often regretted later. The wisdom of speaking while in a highly agitated state is open to question. This is especially critical where supervision is concerned.

At the same time, a less than calm attitude on the part of the listener is also harmful to the communicative effort. The point is that all participants to the information exchange must be in control of their feelings for useful communication to take place.

The supervisor seething with anger is probably not going to be really effective if he seeks to correct an errant subordinate while he is still upset. Meanwhile, the supervisor exhibiting a long-suffering, "what is it now?" face to his employee is almost certain to short circuit whatever communication that would otherwise have taken place.

No one likes to talk when a facial expression reveals the listener's fervent desire for the speaker to shut up so that a vehemently opposing view may be launched. *Debating* a valid point is to be encouraged. *Interrupting* the current speaker to inject an opposing reply is rude. Debate and rudeness are not acceptable companions.

Two-way trust and respect are musts for effective communication. Trust means that the listener knows enough about the speaker and his motives to take for granted that the talker sincerely believes his message is honest and worthwhile. This means that the listener is willing to tune in for awhile, even if he initially disagrees with what the talker is saying. The smart listener realizes that, after the whole message is heard and put in its proper context, it may make a lot more sense and may even be agreeable, after all. Trust grows in the process.

Mutual trust allows the speaker to assume that his listener does, after all, have a worthwhile opinion, too. It tells the speaker that his listener deserves the chance to air his own opinion at the proper time and place. This same trust tells the speaker that his listener will not attack him unfairly.

Proper Timing

When a given communication is carried out can be every bit as important as how it is sent. The proper timing of the idea or information exchange can make the difference in the way the message is received by its intended recipient.

A sample situation might serve to illustrate the importance of proper timing in communication. In this scenario, the police supervisor is less than pleased with the way in which Patrol Officer Jones handled an accident investigation. Common sense and a smattering of basic psychology tell the sergeant that the sooner the miscue is corrected, the more likely the patrol officer will mend his ways.

The communication-savvy sergeant knows, however, that this need for immediacy does not mean he should lambast Officer Jones in front of the citizens he is currently meeting with, or in front of his car partner at whatever meeting site the field supervisor has selected.

"Immediate" handling of the problem means that the sergeant waits until he and his subordinate are alone. Then and only then is the message of correction with its attached offer of help delivered. The patrol officer can in this way be set straight and still save face. Proper timing of the correction means that it now has a much better chance of having its intended effect than would have been the case if it had been presented at a time when distracting emotions would have been stirred.

Finding the proper time for a communication of praise is equally critical. Many individuals are genuinely bashful about being praised lavishly in front of their co-workers. The pleasure inherent in being praised by the boss may be offset by the ribbing they will take from their fellow officers if they are made to sound *too* good.

The praise-minded supervisor will have to judge each situation separately, using his knowledge of the personalities of his people in making a decision about when and how much to praise them. One employee may want to hear good words about himself spoken in front of others. Another may prefer a private commendation. It is the supervisor's responsibility to know which approach is best for each of his subordinates. In this way he can see to it that communication takes place at the time it can do the most good.

Written attempts at communication are not exempt from the timeliness requirement, either. The police administrator who elects to issue a hot memorandum demanding more work and increased loyalty from all employees right on the heels of city council's defeat of the proposed pay raise is courting disaster. The best result he can hope for is verbal derision of and resultant noncompliance with his demands. The communicator with his full allotment of common sense does not publish a real zinger when his people are already smarting over some other freshly delivered bad news.

HAZARDS TO GOOD COMMUNICATION

Any listing of the enemies of good communication would have to include the following: **distractions (physical or mental), prejudices, emotional involvement, inappropriate language, and poor attitudes**. Further examination of each will prove useful in avoiding communication breakdowns.

Communication experts spend much of their time in dissecting the corpses of communication enemies. A more profitable approach, and one that will be utilized here, will be to examine these simply named communication problems in the light of common sense.

Distractions

Whether the information being relayed is written or oral, its chances for reaching its intended listener/reader intact are reduced if it is surrounded by other happenings competing for attention. An example may be seen in the supervisor whose intentions to communicate some roll call briefing notes are frustrated by the level of noisy chatter in the room. Here he is dealing with real, physical distractions. Unless he gets the noise under control, his attempts at good communication will be in real trouble.

Distractions do not have to be tangible to be disruptive. An equally disruptive communication failure can occur if any party to the process is distracted by mental efforts in some other direction that the individual has identified as more pressing at the moment.

In other words, if Detective Fudpucker is deeply engrossed in pondering the possibilities of his upcoming date with Dispatcher Diddle, his sergeant's instructions of the moment are not likely to make much of an impression, if they are heard at all. The distraction's value to the message recipient has overcome any other incoming messages for the moment.

All parties to the intended communication owe one another complete dedication to the task at hand. The originator of the message owes his fellow participants a clear and pertinent piece of information. The recipients of that same message owe its author their undivided attention.

Prejudices

If any or all parties to a given communication allow preformed opinions and feelings about either the subject matter or the person doing the communicating to come to the fore, that intended communication will have a hard time getting through. Prejudices may cause the speaker or writer to talk down to his audience. This same type of opinionating may cause members of the audience to ignore what is being directed at them, possibly because the communicator's reputation established earlier is not a good one.

Despite previous experiences, the effective communicator must put aside any negative feelings long enough to hear (or read) the current message through to completion. This does not mean that he must accept it all at face value. But he avoids prejudging the latest communication solely on the basis of prior experience.

No one can deny a subordinate or supervisor his true feelings and beliefs. This is as it should be. At the same time, however, the subordinate or supervisor owes himself and his organization an open and receptive mind to the new message at hand.

Emotional Involvement

It should be no secret to anyone in police work that strong emotions get in the way of logic and reason. While the police person applies this principle to his street work, he should not overlook what it has to tell him about communicating within his own organization, either.

The supervisor who disciplines while still angry is not effective. The words he chooses may sting to the extent that permanent damage is done to the relationship between himself and the subordinate whom he is talking to. The smarter supervisor cools off first, confirms his information, and disciplines later.

Likewise he will try to examine his own motives behind a particularly strong emotion. Is he mad because his subordinate disobeyed a previous instruction, or because he feels his authority is being challenged? Unless he has solid information that the latter view is correct, he should assume that innocent intentions and accidental disobedience were the culprits. A calmer and more tactful approach to the "offender" will be the result of a deliberate removal of emotions from the confrontation. Good communication requires a calm emotional atmosphere.

Inappropriate Language

The police supervisor would not endeavor to explain the facts of life to his twelve-year-old child while utilizing Freudian terminology. Neither would he engage the local minister's wife in a conversation about sexual assault using street slang for the various acts and bodily parts concerned. He also avoids the use of inappropriate language when addressing other members of his organization or the public at large.

Eliminating the use of inappropriate language from his vocabulary goes far deeper for the supervisor than swearing off vulgar words and colorful phrases during polite conversation. Rather, the leader should concern himself with making himself plainly understood in the terms he selects to carry his intended thought, idea, or feeling to his audience.

A good rule of thumb for the communicator might go something like this: BE BRIEF, BE CONCISE, BE GONE. Put another way, whatever gets the message across in as few and as simple words as possible probably does the job best. Complicating a relatively simple issue does not help anyone.

One does not need to employ big words to impress others. The true test of intelligence is found in how well or how poorly one gets his message across to others. The superior officer who deluges his people with torrents of managerial gibberish and technical jargon accomplishes little beyond verifying his employees' doubts about his ability to express himself clearly. Far from instilling in them a reverence for his superior brain, he is probably only confirming their suspicions of his basic insecurity.

The good communicator refrains from talking down to his audience. He knows that it is possible to overexplain a procedure and belabor a point. The truly effective communicator tries to know his audience well enough to adjust his presentation (whether written or oral) to the ill-defined "average" man or woman. While acknowledging that such a creature may not exist, he nonetheless shoots for a median of audience knowledge and comprehension that will help him to be understood by all while boring none. This is a tall order indeed, but it is one worth seeking.

Poor Attitudes

"Your attitude is showing."

This old saying might be a damning indictment of a failed attempt at communication. There are, of course, many ways besides words in which the speaker or listener can notify his counterparts that he disagrees with the message.

Body language is another method of communicating. Crossed legs, folded arms, eyes rolled heavenwards, and other expressions of contempt or impatience can get the notification across as reliably as spoken words. A missed chance at mutually beneficial communication is usually the result of such encounters.

A poor attitude can be related to most any of the enemies of good communication. A poor attitude can arise from one or more parties using inappropriate language, from prejudice, or from a long-standing grudge. It can even grow from too much emotional involvement of any party or all parties regarding the matter at hand. Regardless of the cause, a bad attitude almost always breeds bad results.

Poor attitude can be combated by some self-evident and largely painless remedies: (1) put prejudices to the back of the mind to the fullest extent possible; (2) do not permit emotions to dictate hasty actions or thoughtless words; (3) keep language appropriate to the audience and incident at hand. Although all of these suggestions are easier to set down than live by, all can help neutralize one more opponent of good communication. With this much accomplished, the attitudes of all parties to the communication process cannot help but improve.

BENEFITS OF GOOD COMMUNICATION

There are unquestionably a number of good things that flow naturally from good and effective communication at all levels and in all functions of the police organization. Nowhere are these positive things more evident than in the employee/supervisor relationship.

The supervisor has worked hard to bring about this favorable state of affairs. He has conscientiously avoided disjointed, vague, or ambiguous statements in his messages to his troops. He has been careful to include the source or authority for the directives and procedures he has carried into action. He has avoided the use of unfair value judgments and personal prejudices in all of his communications. He has spoken clearly and calmly in his verbal orders and instructions. He has steered clear of illegibility, padding, and fancy terms in his written messages.

So, what can be expected to result from such efforts on the part of the effective leader and others like him? For one thing, good communication with the supervisor enables all of his subordinates to know exactly what is expected of them. There should be no surprises when the sergeant gives his officer a written, annual performance evaluation. If the two have been communicating well, strong and weak points in performance are known to both and have been discussed before.

Likewise, the communicative supervisor knows well what his people expect of him, in turn. He has, with their aid, identified areas where they feel weak and need help. In an atmosphere of good communication, everyone knows what expectations are placed upon them and by whom they are placed.

In a law enforcement agency where good, two-way communication flourishes, the top brass is aware of the troops' concerns. Where leaders and their subordinates are open and honest with one another, the chief does not have to hunt down Officer Smith to get her opinions on a given issue. Her concerns and feelings on the topic have already been accurately carried up the chain of command by her supervisors.

Good communication happens where there is mutual trust at each level of the organization. A single element where this reliability does not exist will break the whole communicative chain. If the sergeant trusts the patrol officer enough to pass along intact the officer's feelings, that's good. But if the lieutenant who receives the message fails to pass it on to his boss, for whatever reason, the chain is smashed. As a result, understanding among workers and top managers can only suffer. Everyone must cooperate for good communication to exist.

Where good communication is in place, trust grows on all fronts. The officer on the street knows exactly why it is that the chief cannot get him a much-needed raise this year. Where reasons for decisions are given, increased understanding and heightened trust generally follow. The street cop may still disagree with the decision made by the supervisor. At least now, however, he knows that the boss cared enough to take the time and effort needed to explain the reasoning behind the decision.

Also, the trust felt by the leaders of the agency for their people can only grow from knowing why those people acted in a certain way under a certain set of circumstances. Such knowing comes about through the good communication skills of everyone involved. Hence, the taxpayers are the major recipients of additional benefits of good communication in the police agency. The job gets done better, quicker, and with more consistent results. The police employee profits also, as his job is made easier by his knowing what he is expected to do and how to go about doing it.

Finally, good communication within the law enforcement agency allows subordinates and supervisors alike to feel better about themselves, their agency, and each other. A by-product of mutual trust and understanding, this good feeling may be something of an intangible. Rare would be the officer who would say with a straight face: "I feel really good because my agency has good communication." While he may not put it into words, it is still quite possible for that same officer to have good feelings about himself, his peers, and his job, regardless of whether or not he knows from where these feelings emanated. It is enough that employees at all levels feel better. It is not a requirement that each one knows why.

Good communication can and should mean less infighting, fewer bad feelings, reduced misunderstandings, and less employee turnover. These results in themselves are sufficient cause to justify increased and continuing attention to the communication function by every member of the law enforcement organization. The first-line supervisor is not an exception.

WRITTEN VERSUS ORAL COMMUNICATION

It should be kept in mind that the decision to use written or oral means of communicating is not really an either-or situation. Both types of communication have their own particular values and advantages for the police leader.

Oral communication is obviously best in the person-to-person, one-on-one situation. It offers the clear-cut advantage of an opportunity for each participant to gauge the impact of his message on his listener's face. Expressions, gestures, and the whole range of nonverbal mechanisms by which people communicate can be brought into play in this face-to-face exchange.

Oral communication is best in relatively informal situations, even if the number of parties to the communication is expanded from the one-on-one scenario. Even patrol roll call briefings can fall into this category if the number of persons present is not too large.

Word of mouth communication can sometimes be more effective if it is carried out in something other than a "me boss–you subordinate" atmosphere. The "door closed, me behind the desk and you in the chair in front of me" routine can be as solid a barrier to the open flow of communication as a hostile stare or a closed mind. Even if the message flowing from boss to subordinate is a corrective one on this particular occasion, the atmosphere does not have to fit the "formal" tail-chewing image.

When the situation merits it, the "formal" approach can still be used for the hard-to-reach, chronic, or serious problem. In far more numerous situations, however, the more informal surroundings of the coffee shop or the patrol car serve quite nicely. The same message is delivered in the informal setting without the unintended but threatening atmosphere found in the less comfortable environment of the office.

Written communication comes into its own in the realm of record keeping. Written messages bring a greatly increased degree of permanency to any task of communication. If the employee is going to have need to refer back to the details of a particular procedure, then the procedure should be available for his future use. If there is a real need to trace accountability and identify responsibility, the directive that does the tracing and identifying needs to be documented for the record.

Written communication also can serve as a memory refresher from the past and it can allow more thinking time for everyone involved in the communication process. Face-to-face oral exchanges generally require immediate responses. Sometimes this is desirable. For situations that instead demand some time for thought and planning before commitments and actions, the written message with its built-in delay factor is ideal.

Some actions for which the supervisor is responsible require the keeping of written records of what transpired and how. Disciplinary actions such as letters of reprimand or notices of suspension are good examples of this part of a supervisor's job. If these formal actions are questioned later in civil court or elsewhere, the impact made by an existing written record could be huge.

The written comments of the line supervisor are extremely vital in building the case for either praise or correction of the deserving employee. Written documentation of specific acts and events provides the proof so necessary for backing up an employee performance evaluation or a formal supervisory recommendation for action of any sort.

Whether written or oral, formal or relaxed, the communication engaged in by the police supervisor is vital to his ultimate success as a leader. With a good, common sense understanding of communication's elements and potential problems, the supervisor can effectively lead the police personnel under his command. Without such comprehension, he can expect to command little more than the desk or steering wheel in front of him.

SUMMARY

The individual who cannot communicate clearly and openly with his subordinates and superiors will not succeed as a police supervisor. It really is as simple as that.

Good communicators must understand others and be understood easily by them, both orally and in writing. They avoid such enemies to effective communication as distractions, prejudices, emotions, inappropriate language and difficult attitudes. Instead they communicate effectively with the sharing of information and ideas.

The intelligent police leader uses effective communication to help improve the efficiency and impact of the organization of which he is a part. He knows that an agency where ideas and information flow freely and accurately is an organization of contributing, trusting and reasonably content employees. He knows, too, that by being a good communicator he can play a major role in making that positive scenario a reality.

POINTS TO REMEMBER

- It is virtually impossible NOT to communicate.
- Good communication requires the full attention of the message sender and receiver.
- Good communication must be clear, simple, open and allow for two-way information exchange.
- A good communicator will develop excellent listening as well as reading habits.
- The ability to write well is absolutely mandatory for a supervisor.
- To be effective, communication must be calm and unemotional.
- Timing is important for effective communication.
- Enemies of effective communication include distractions, prejudices, emotional involvement, inappropriate language and poor attitudes.
- Everyone benefits from good communication.
- Depending on the situation, either oral or written communication may be more effective than the other.

Chapter Ten

THE POLICE LEADER AS A COUNSELOR

Among his duties, the police supervisor is assigned the task of help-ing his employees to recognize and fulfill their potential as pro-fessionals in a difficult field of endeavor. One way in which the super-visor carries out this obligation is through providing a patient ear and an alert eye for detecting potential problems and addressing them with the concerned employee before they get out of hand.

Employee counseling is one way in which the supervisor works to ease the extra burdens placed on his people by the strains of work demands or personal crises. By sharing the benefits of his life experi-ence, training, and fact-based opinions, the leader helps his employees attempt their own solution to a vexing problem. The concerned police supervisor will help both his employee and his organization through timely intervention, when necessary.

Instances will occur in which the supervisor has little choice but to intervene in employee behavior. A sample situation may be seen in the deliberate violation of a departmental rule or directive by an employee under his command. Another situation requiring immediate counseling intervention may be found in the case of the police officer so troubled by a personal problem that his preoccupation with it is exposing him to additional danger on the job.

Not all situations, however, will be so obvious or so pressing as to require instant intervention by the police supervisor. In the borderline situation in which the employee is not sure if he really wants to bring his problem to anyone's attention, the accessibility and reputation of the supervisor can make all the difference in whether or not the prob-lem is brought to light. An aloof, uninterested, and seemingly uncar-ing boss is not likely to be asked for help or guidance. A chance to address a developing problem will have been missed.

On the other hand, a supervisor with an established, deserved reputation as a sensitive and caring human being likely will have a chance to intervene while there is yet time to prevent more serious difficulties. If his employees rely upon his good common sense and proven sound advice, he probably will be asked to help them with their fears, feelings, and worries.

Before the supervisor can help his people through counseling, he must first recognize the existence of a developing problem. There are some recognizable signs, symptoms, and situational factors that can help the supervisor do this. A look at some of those warning flags is next.

IDENTIFYING PERSONAL PROBLEMS

In the most ideal of worlds, the problem-laden employee comes to his boss and delivers himself of a well-thought-out but devastatingly tragic tale of woe. In this best of all possible worlds, the Yoda-like supervisor dispenses advice and soon has the eagerly cooperative employee back on his feet again. Good has triumphed over evil, the sun is in the sky, and the amazingly talented supervisor has saved yet another police soul from damnation.

If only the real world was so cut and dried for the police supervisor. The experienced police leader knows that only sometimes does the troubled employee place his problems voluntarily under the scrutiny of his boss. Much more frequently, it is the supervisor who must inquire diligently, probe gently, and explore thoughtfully the words and actions of a subordinate who may be signaling that he is in need of help.

There are a number of things that can cause problems for the police employee. Some of them can affect any member of the work world, whether that member is a cop or a candlestick maker. Yet other problems are more unique to police work and are seldom experienced by the rest of working society.

Difficulties peculiar to policing with its attendant hazards include family problems caused by bizarre work hours and days off. Less than outstanding working conditions may enter into the picture, as well. The young man or woman from a rural or suburban background thrown suddenly into core city patrol duties may find his or her reactions to be puzzling and troubling.

Scheduling changes can bring difficulties for police employees, too. In a department that rotates its work shifts periodically, the officer who enjoyed weekends off may now find Tuesday and Wednesday considerably less desirable as days away from the job. Routine schedule changes also may cause troubles for the employee who sees himself a day person yet finds himself working the all-night watch.

Unanticipated changes in the work schedule, particularly those in which the employee has no real voice, will bring about even greater distress. Anything resembling a normal, off-duty social life may suddenly vanish for the police person.

Changes in laws or court decisions that the police employee sees as against the interests of law enforcement also can cause unhappiness. An attitude of "if the public doesn't care, why should I?" may eventually pervade his thinking, and his morale may suffer gravely. It is easy to tell an officer not to let such things bother him, but it is quite something else for him to put such good advice into action.

Problems growing directly out of specific, job-related incidents may trouble employees to no end. Peer pressure is extremely influential in the world of the working cop, and the plainly unhappy officer may be troubled by whether or not his peers think he is tough enough, or brave enough, or smart enough in a given incident.

The officer may play a specific incident over and over in his mind, all the while attempting to convince himself that what he did was logical, proper, and otherwise the right thing to do. Particularly if the employee is new at his job, he may be disturbed over some gruesome scene, an especially violent crime, or an unusually pathetic victim or situation.

Frustrations originating from the internal workings of the police agency also may be bothering the employee. He may feel he was disciplined unfairly, criticized unjustly, or wrongly passed over for a promotion or special assignment.

Although bureaucratic intrigue and political infighting are by no means the exclusive properties of law enforcement agencies, the honest and intelligent police employee may find the detrimental effects resulting from such maneuverings to be particularly distasteful and frustrating. In a job where meritorious performance should be rewarded without fail, he may sometimes see blind obedience as the best key to advancement. Where such a situation is permitted to exist, employee problems are guaranteed to arise.

Situational factors that can affect all working people regardless of their trade can wreak havoc with police personnel, as well. Organizational changes in staffing levels or policy can cause uncertainty and distress. Familiarity is comfortable; change can breed uncertainty and worry, whether warranted or not. Security is important to just about everyone, and the police worker is no exception to this.

When staffing level changes are a part of the organizational shuffling, questions may arise: Will I be laid off? Will I lose my status and position? Will I get a new boss? Can I work for my new boss? What kind of work will I be doing? All of these questions and a myriad of others can trouble the employee faced with a change in the shape and makeup of his work world. Getting answers to the questions will be an important priority for him. Some queries will mean more to him than others, but all may distract him until the uncertainties are satisfactorily resolved.

Financial disasters also can unsettle the most stable of employees. Annual budget battles and salary adjustments become all important to the man or woman who is just making ends meet. Increasingly today, that man or woman straddling the line of economic survival is becoming more the norm than the exception.

There are a lot of difficulties that can beset police personnel. How can the supervisor know when his employee is afflicted by one or more of them? Work problems, like illnesses, are attended by symptoms. They often display "early warning signs" if one knows what he is looking for. While these signs that something has gone wrong will vary in intensity and visibility from one person to another, there are nevertheless indicators that the observant supervisor can anticipate.

Some of the most readily apparent changes in the troubled employee may be actual alterations in physical appearance. The employee who has always dressed neatly and showed great care in personal appearance may start to arrive at work poorly dressed and sloppily groomed. This may only be a one-time problem with the individual who was perhaps without sleep last night. Or it may be a symptom of a serious personal problem. The supervisor will want to learn which is the case. Physical ills needing attention can, of course, produce similar signs.

Personality or mood changes are perhaps even more important than physical appearance as indicators of problems inside. The always jovial employee who is suddenly the quietest guy on the watch may have a big problem. The team "nice guy" who is suddenly the unit agitator may have something really serious gnawing at him. The talkative optimist who has become the moody loner of late may be equally in trouble with himself.

The problems involved with these troubled individuals may not be major ones, as viewed by an outsider. The boss must keep in mind, however, that the issue as viewed by the person closest to it may seem hopeless or of major crisis proportions.

Other indicators may include the abuse of sick leave. The always healthy officer may begin using his accrued sick time as rapidly as it accumulates. The dispatcher who has always been punctual is suddenly tardy on a regular basis.

Being the last to arrive and the first to leave work may be merely an unfortunate work habit. If it develops in an employee who previously showed no such tendencies, it may betray a newly developed problem. Some inquiry is clearly in order.

A previously devoted employee now taking up more and more company time with personal errands and private business may be displaying indications of a serious problem. Perhaps some really pressing personal problems are at hand. Perhaps the employee is trying to jam too much into too few hours, or maybe he feels he is being cheated and is getting back at the employer by using company time for personal business. Regardless, the supervisor is obligated to don his counselor hat and find out what is going on.

The alert supervisor also should be on the watch for the normally well-accepted employee who is, without apparent reason, now being avoided by his peers. Perhaps an argument has brought about some temporarily scorched feelings and the whole thing will pass. On the other hand, maybe the ostracized employee is displaying enough of the troublesome symptoms described earlier to have made himself unpleasant company for his co-workers. The problem could be a serious one. Regardless of what it is, the police leader will find it necessary to learn what the trouble is and what kind of intervention is required.

The employee who is showing up for work with bloodshot eyes, flushed face, and the smell of either alcohol or strong breath purifiers about him may have a really serious drinking problem. The presence of other "hangover" symptoms such as body tremors or overreaction to loud noises and bright lights also may be telltale signs that the individual is afflicted with the effects of alcoholism.

The police employee's alcohol problem may have developed independently of his other difficulties, or it may have developed at least partially because of them. To escape stress and its attached bad feelings, police people, like so many others, sometimes find themselves drinking more and more alcohol. Immediate intervention is required if the police employee is to arrest the progressively damaging effects of true alcoholism. Again, the supervisor's early recognition of a problem and his reaction to it are critical.

Any gross change in an employee's work performance or attitude should serve as an indication that all is not well. The skilled accident investigator who does not like working accidents anymore may just be ready for a career or assignment change. Then again, he may be evidencing the signs of a devastating and distracting personal crisis. The diligent supervisor will try to find out which is the case. The agency's effectiveness and efficiency and, more important, his subordinate's well being mandate the supervisor's careful and tactful inquiry and intervention.

How should one get involved in this problem solving? The well-meaning supervisor intent upon helping will need to develop a few crisis intervention skills.

PROBLEM-SOLVING TECHNIQUES

Detecting the existence of a problem is the first step towards resolving it. Determining the nature of the problem should be the next logical step towards a solution. The supervisor's most reliable ally in this effort is a direct and forthright approach to the troubled employee. When privacy is the rule, and work interruptions are at an absolute minimum, the supervisor may bring up the issue in a thoughtful, calm manner: "It's obvious that something is bothering you, and I'd like to help," or something along these lines.

The individual supervisor obviously will want to choose his own words and design his own approach. The key is to express a sincere concern and a real desire to help. It is important that the employee realize that the boss is truly interested in the difficulty his subordinate is experiencing. The supervisor must never portray himself as interested only in fixing the disruption caused by the employee's difficulties.

It is possible that the employee will deny or, at least, play down the existence of any difficulties. The supervisor must persist without being antagonistic. Again, he does not accuse but merely points up the signs of a problem. It may even prove necessary to drop the delicate discussion at this point, only to return to it at the next logical time, such as when the problem's symptoms become evident again.

The seriousness of the apparent problem and the potential for a real disaster from allowing it to persist will determine whether or not the supervisor can permit a waiting period before continuing the discussion. An employee who is signaling a problem by coming to work intoxicated requires immediate inquiry and action, whether the employee is cooperative or not. On the other hand, a potential problem indicated by a moody employee can be approached again later if the first efforts at inquiry and intervention are rebuffed.

It has been suggested that an employee cannot begin to solve his problems until he is willing to "own up" to them or accept them as real and legitimate. While it is desirable that the employee concede that a problem does exist, and then assist in a mutual effort of further defining it, this is not mandatory in order for intervention to commence. Recognizing man's defense mechanisms for the powerful forces that they are, the wise police supervisor will realize that he cannot always expect an employee to agree on the identity of a problem or even acknowledge its existence.

The leader skilled in the application of good common sense knows that he often must proceed to address the difficulty, whether the employee admits its existence or not. He cites the evidence establishing the existence of the problem, expresses a sincere desire to help, and then communicates a clear indication of the changes that he expects to see occur. After this, he initiates follow-up to see if the needed changes actually occur and are continued.

The police supervisor may need to know more about an employee's past than can be revealed in a conversation with the employee. A thorough "research" effort on the supervisor's part can sometimes shed additional light on the situation. Often, the employee's personnel file can provide some insight into the past. Job performance evaluations by previous supervisors and past entries in employee logs can reveal hints of previous difficulties of a similar nature.

Previous supervisors should never be forgotten as potential reservoirs of useful facts. Many personal problems occur more than one time only. It is quite possible that an earlier boss had some concerns, too. What was said and done about the earlier difficulties can be useful knowledge if problems reappear.

The troubled employee's peers often know what is going on before the supervisor does. This presents a very delicate situation. A supervisor who talks openly about an employee's perceived problems among the employee's peers is asking for trouble. Both his subordinate's reputation and his own credibility are in danger of severe damage by such unthinking behavior.

Any mention of an employee's apparent difficulties must be made delicately in an atmosphere of "I wonder what's bothering Joe and what can we do to help?" If an answer is not forthcoming from one of Joe's pals, the subject should be dropped for a time. No supervisor will succeed as a counselor if he creates the impression that he is trying to make subordinates inform on their peers.

There are still other techniques of proven usefulness for interviewing the distressed employee. First of all, it is vital for the supervisor to remember that an overly formal approach can create communication difficulties at the outset. Physical barriers seem to create equally real obstacles to communication. For this reason, two chairs not separated by a desk or table and relatively near each other can be much more comfortable and effective for a counseling session than the old "boss and flunky" furniture arrangement. Relative informality can be helpful to a successful counseling effort.

The effective counselor pays attention to what his employee is saying, even if he thinks he has heard it all before. He gets to the point of the session without clouding the air with aimless small talk and forced banter. The employee knows, or at least suspects, the reason for the conversation with the boss. An unnatural attempt at natural conversation will probably fool no one, so the honest counselor comes to the point after some initial, brief pleasantries.

Excellent listening skills are a must for the supervisor who intends to succeed as a counselor. That means he finds a quiet spot and then listens intently to what the employee is saying. He does not interrupt. He nods in the affirmative from time to time to indicate understanding and encourage the speaker to continue. He LOOKS and acts like he is listening. He asks brief questions as necessary to clarify points, but he avoids pronouncements and judgmental comments.

The attentive supervisor maintains eye contact with the speaker as much as is comfortable for them both and avoids facial expressions or body language displaying disbelief, disapproval or shock. The idea is to keep the employee talking until he or she feels more at ease. Even when the speaker appears done it is oftentimes a good idea to remain silent for a bit in case the employee is searching for thoughts or words and intends to resume speaking shortly. Listening cannot and must not be rushed.

The skilled counselor sticks as much as possible with the issue at hand. This is no time for "garbage bagging"–the process of dredging up all past grievances and alleged wrongs from day one. While it is extremely important to let the employee continue once he starts talking, it is no less vital to bring him gently back to the subject if he wanders too far afield. It is entirely logical that he may wander in this manner. As thoughts come to him, other things, seemingly only distantly related, may come to mind also. Getting the talker back on track often can be accomplished with a few words as a gentle reminder "You were saying that. . . .")

It is important that the supervisor enter the conversation with his subordinate with an open mind. It is natural to have some preconceived ideas about the problem and the person who has it. It is only when these notions and ideas cloud good and objective judgment that a miscarriage of supervisory responsibilities is possible.

The counselor should allow plenty of time for the discussion. He does not distract from the session by looking at his watch or fidgeting nervously. He must instead strive to communicate to his subordinate that the issue is just as vital to him as it is to its owner. The skilled police counselor also offers to make a future appointment for further discussion if time runs short in the present effort.

The police supervisor who has mastered the art of empathetic counseling knows that he must guard the privacy of his employee's personal troubles. If the employee decides to make his plight known to others, so be it. That is his decision. It is not the supervisor's place to operate a broadcast service for him, however. It is no secret that a supervisor who cannot keep a reasonable confidence soon becomes a supervisor in whom subordinates have no trust and little confidence.

Along the same lines, a good counselor does not compare his employee's problems to those of other people known by employee and supervisor alike. Comparing the employee's problem to someone else's for the purpose of belittling the seriousness of the current difficulty is unwise. It must be remembered that, to the owner of the current problem, no one else's difficulty has ever been greater or more important. The problem is very big to him, and he expects his listener to regard it accordingly.

The supervisor/counselor recalls and utilizes what he learned as a fair and effective disciplinarian: one does not criticize or attack an individual; one criticizes, in a constructive manner, that individual's behavior or actions. The person himself is not to be seen as bad or messed up, though his actions may be either or both. Attacks on behavior should be constructive. Attacks on people accomplish little good and are remembered for a very long time, often with much bitterness.

It is important to bring a counseling session to a logical, hopefully positive, conclusion. It is not necessary that all problems be solved prior to the session's end. It is very helpful, however, if both parties to the discussion can at least agree to what has been accomplished so far, and what the next reasonable steps should be.

The counselor should not expect too much too soon, particularly when the problems being confronted are of a long-standing and personal nature. If the problem was a long time building, it is unlikely that it will be solved overnight. When a given topic is one that is difficult to discuss, the supervisor should be content if a first meeting just brings a mutual agreement that a problem *does* exist. Additional sessions can explore the details of the issue and any corrective measures that are needed.

There is an additional consideration that the supervisor-counselor must keep in mind, regardless of the nature of the problem faced by his employee. If the difficulty distracts significantly from the employee's ability to do his job properly and safely, a temporary relief from duty will be required. At this point the supervisor will brief his chain of command on the situation and, where necessary, secure the involvement and advice of his agency's Human Resources experts.

SOURCES OF ASSISTANCE

Just what kind of help is available for the police officer with a problem? Perhaps even more vital, what sort of long-term or continuing assistance can the concerned supervisor call upon in aiding his troubled employee?

Regardless of the supervisor's field of endeavor, any counselor is dependent for ultimate success upon obtaining sources of professional assistance to supplement his initial efforts at solving major problems. Many personal difficulties confronting the police employee in contemporary society require more professional expertise for their successful resolution than the best-intentioned police leader can hope to provide. While police people do a great deal of counseling in their work, they are generally not highly trained counselors by profession. Thus arises the need for some additional resources outside of policing itself.

First, the police supervisor must be able to recognize when his own efforts require some professional backup. Alcoholism is one such problem mandating skillful, outside help. Serious behavioral disorders hinting at mental illness are some others. There are additional, perhaps less dramatic, difficulties that may also require outside aid.

When the supervisor/counselor recognizes that a problem is so deeply seated, so long-standing, or so self-destructive as to demand immediate, highly skilled intervention, he undertakes another of his truly difficult roles: the task of showing his employee the wisdom of seeking additional aid.

This task may not be easy, particularly if the employee has trouble accepting the reality of there being a problem in the first place. The possible consequences of not obtaining effective help demand that this be done, all the same. Persuasion, argument, and logic may all be used as tools in convincing the employee to seek help.

Police people are an independent and proud lot. They keep to their own kind, probably too much. Sometimes, they steadfastly view that which they identify as being from the "outside" as being unrelated to them. Likewise, police people are sometimes reluctant to expose their problems and shortcomings to an outside world they are not really sure understands them.

Whether on an agency-wide or very personal level, police officers sometimes see problems as something others may use against them. This general mistrust unfortunately makes them reluctant to seek needed outside help, particularly at a very personal level.

The police supervisor must fully utilize his reasoning abilities and call upon the relationship of mutual trust that he has previously established with his subordinate in convincing him to accept professional assistance. The old "you'd want a doctor if your leg was broken" logic is not out of place here. Professional sources of help for problem solving are available. The officer with an alcohol problem may have several avenues of aid open to him. Alcoholics Anonymous is national in scope and has established a reputation over the years for both compassion and effectiveness. Substance abuse counselors are also available, especially in urban areas. Private physicians and HMOs can help, as well.

Now properly identified as a real disease, alcoholism does not lack for treatment programs to combat its effects. A little searching by the supervisor could help a subordinate locate a treatment program best suited for him. The local United Way offices generally provide a good directory of resources and services available in the area. Where available, Employee Assistance Plans (EAPs) can do the same.

As employers become increasingly aware of the dollar losses added to the human misery brought about by alcoholism, many are including alcoholism counseling in the fringe benefits available to their workers. The resourceful supervisor will inquire within his agency as to what it offers for solving an employee's problems—alcohol-induced or otherwise.

Job-related discord is present in too many police marriages today. On the positive side, there are indications that today's police men and women are willing to accept outside advice and counseling when the marital road gets rocky. This is a healthy sign. But when the employee refuses to recognize the need for outside aid in a deteriorating marriage, then it may be the supervisor's job to discreetly intervene in an attempt to salvage a good employee. Obviously, the supervisor is operating on grounds of suggestion, not orders. Nonetheless, a sincere and well-intentioned effort to point an embattled employee in the direction of professional counseling may prove to be what is needed to help him or her overcome a personal crisis. The attempt is certainly worthwhile if it means a chance for a good employee to remain in law enforcement, and a marriage.

As in so many of his tasks, the police leader has responsibilities to the public, the agency, and the employee when it comes to the topic of mental health in his subordinates. It has been said that everyone is somewhat mentally ill in one fashion or another, at one time or another. In the public safety field, however, the requirement of consistently logical and sound mental behavior is absolute. Society cannot permit illogical, irrational, or grossly unpredictable behavior on the part of its agents assigned to maintaining order, particularly when they have ultimate life-and-death authority over others.

The police supervisor cannot permit unrealistic or bizarre behavior on the part of police officers to go unreported up the chain of command. Extreme incidents of irrational conduct require an immediate relief from duty and a prompt and thorough inquiry into the problem. Such inquiry may, in extreme cases, require that the troubled employee be disarmed and ordered to seek a mental health evaluation at the agency's expense.

Fortunately, most mental health problems handled by the police supervisor are not so grave, perhaps because they are appropriately detected, discussed and treated early. Again, the importance of a line supervisor knowing his people well is stressed. Only through such knowledge can he detect significant changes in employee behavior which may herald more drastic things to come.

The seriously troubled employee, the depressed officer, the individual who is seeing things in a way that distorts reality, all of these people may require a quick referral to professional help. The supervisor will now be faced with the task of finding the best source of mental health counseling available for the employee in need. In an urban area, a city mental health agency is often available. In more rural settings, the county often assumes this service responsibility. The employee's own physician can probably provide both initial consultation and eventual referral services. If the police agency itself retains a physician or psychologist, he or she ought to be able to provide the same consultation and referral service.

Once again, the supervisor should ask his employer to ascertain if employees' stress-related problems are covered as part of a benefit or insurance plan. Especially in larger departments, police agencies themselves sometimes offer psychological counseling services through a departmental professional or Employee Assistance Program hired to tend to the mental health needs of police employees. Such agencies are recognizing their responsibility to treat the stress that they may have helped to create.

Whatever the source of help chosen, the police supervisor may be able to provide the professional counselor with some insight into the problem. Given with the permission of the employee concerned, this information could help the professional in his efforts to isolate, identify, and ultimately treat the troubles of the police employee. In providing this help to the professional, the conscientious supervisor will have fulfilled yet another of his obligations to his multiple masters: employee, agency, and public.

COUNSELOR-COUNSELED RELATIONSHIP

A particularly nasty, if effective, military drill instructor used to conclude his introductory speech to his terrified enlistees by reminding them that, for at least awhile, he was to be their "mama, papa, and best girl, all rolled into one." This cleaned-up version of his pronouncement was pretty accurate as far as the green troops were concerned. He was, in fact, just about everything to them. He dictated when they would speak, eat, sleep, and relieve themselves. He would help them with their problems, generally at the expense of a severe tongue lashing.

The police supervisor is not a drill instructor. He can teach his people and he can support them. He can correct them and he can counsel them. But he cannot possibly solve all of their problems for them, and he cannot think for them. At some point, the realistic police leader must recognize that he has done everything he can for his employee, whether through counseling or otherwise. Given that help, it is then up to the employee to make his own way. In the final analysis, the problem remains the property of the employee.

The relationship between counselor and counseled should be one of mutual honesty and frankness. The problem-solving session is no place to put on fronts or false faces. Openness and truthfulness are the keys to any successful attempt at solving difficulties, whether personal or professional in nature.

In addition to honesty in all aspects of the counseling effort, the supervisor owes his employee confidentiality in the counseling relationship. While the supervisor can never give advance promises of guaranteed confidentiality without knowing what the problem is, once he is satisfied that illegal or improper conduct is not the subject under discussion, he should give his promise of confidentiality without reserve.

For his part, the counseled employee must give his most sincere efforts at correcting the difficulty. Nothing less will suffice.

Just plain common sense dictates that the police supervisor will give his best to the subordinates he serves. He will do everything that ethics and legality will allow in seeking to find help for a troubled employee. Then, if he is smart, he will be satisfied that he has done his best and will feel good about it.

The supervisor should remain mindful that his employees' successes and failures are not automatically his own. It is quite possible for them to succeed without or even in spite of him. Likewise, their failures and difficulties are not his, and may, in fact, have absolutely nothing to do with him. It is even possible that an employee's difficulties may have occurred because the supervisor's advice was ignored or forgotten in the first place.

The police supervisor, unlike the highly opinionated drill instructor, is not the whole world to his troops, either. He cannot rightfully claim too much credit for their successes. Nor should he lay awake at night castigating himself for their occasional disasters.

Special concerns may arise in counseling special groups or individuals. A young supervisor may be uneasy counseling a veteran officer of considerably more years experience. The problem should not be an insurmountable one, however.

Regardless of relative ages, experience, or eye color, the supervisor IS the supervisor and must fulfill his role as such. The veteran's added time may prove beneficial to the counseling effort in that experience can be a good teacher of the advantages found in sound procedures and good work. Whatever the situation in reality, the effective leader cannot be intimidated from performing his counseling or other responsibilities through fear of reproach or derision from the vet. A good command of self-confidence as well as a firm application of common sense can do wonders here.

Counseling members of the opposite sex also can pose special concerns. A police officer of many years experience once lamented how nice it would be if human beings could regard sexual matters with the same detachment with which they view many other bodily functions. Practically speaking, however, human physical and mental factors make this prospect unlikely.

The fact remains that on-the-job relationships of the two sexes are important ones, but are also ones that can sometimes lead to misunderstanding, confusion, or outright abuse. Recent years have seen increased numbers of complaints of sexual harassment by peers or supervisors from women who have joined the work force in larger numbers. A few of the complaints may be the result of hypersensitivity on the part of individuals who are *expecting* abuses to occur. Most are, however, legitimate complaints of women who have been exploited by their male co-workers and bosses.

The police supervisor's cardinal rule in his or her dealings with a subordinate of the opposite sex should be *equality* in all things. That is, the difference in gender should not result in a given individual receiving special treatment or unwanted attentions from the supervisor.

The wise supervisor realizes that his relationship with his subordinates and others can suffer just as much from perceived acts of sexual discrimination or harassment as from the real thing. Consequently, the supervisor strives to avoid even the appearance of sexual misconduct in his dealings with subordinates.

The supervisor has probably learned from firsthand experience just how damaging misperceptions of supervisory intent can be, even when the misbehavior was actually nonexistent. A case in point may be seen in a true situation where a patrol sergeant, who had three rookie officers assigned to his unit, spent extra time and effort with each new officer in an attempt to help them adjust to their new responsibilities. One of the officers was female. The supervisor, believing that she might need extra encouragement and aid in a still largely male profession, spent even more time with her than with her novice cohorts. The added attention was misinterpreted by the young woman, who assumed that the extra attention was sexual rather than professional in nature, even though there had been no sexual overtones attached.

The female rookie became uncomfortable and confused. She did not express this discomfort to her supervisor, but she eventually communicated her fears to her co-workers, and word of her plight got back to her sergeant—the source of her discomfort. The difficult situation was finally corrected only by the sergeant and officer sitting down with the unit commander to clear the air. The problem was solved, but only at the expense of some unpleasant moments for all concerned.

If a lesson for the supervisor/counselor is to be learned from such an experience, the lesson might be that the supervisor must be cautious as well as sensitive in his dealings with an employee of the opposite sex. Particularly if employee problems of a personal nature are to be discussed at a counseling session, it might be a good idea to have another supervisor present during the meeting.

But the police leader must do much more than avoid even the appearance of engaging in sexually harassing behavior himself. He must see to it that the workplace remains free of its influence. He often will find that his employer has assisted him by providing a definition of just what constitutes sexual harassment. Frequently the definition is found in an employee handbook issued to all personnel and may be displayed in poster form, as well. It might look like this:

***Sexual harassment* refers to any unwelcome sexual attention, sexual advances, requests for sexual favors and other verbal, visual, or physical conduct of a sexual nature when:**

- **Submission to such conduct is made either explicitly or implicitly a term or condition of an individual's employment; or**
- **Submission or rejection of such conduct by an individual is used as the basis for employment decisions affecting such individual; or**
- **Such conduct has the purpose or effect of unreasonably interfering with an individual's work performance; or**
- **Such conduct has the purpose or effect of creating an intimidating, hostile, or offensive work environment.**

It is fairly easy to discern misbehavior in conduct in which one employee demands or attempts to forcibly obtain sexual favors from another. Stationhouse horseplay in which employees grab or touch others' sexual regions is also a "no brainer" which any supervisor should recognize as conduct which must be stopped. (It goes almost without saying that the supervisor himself must NEVER be a participant in such juvenile conduct.) Harder to detect is conduct which is less overt but nonetheless contributes over time to a general atmosphere in which the victim employee or employees find it difficult to work. Such an atmosphere might be found where employees are routinely engaging in obscene, sexually demeaning, harassing remarks or actions to one another to the discomfort of one or more of the group. And while sexual harassment is frequently viewed as something a male commits against a female, any combination of genders can be part of sexual harassment. In other words, a male can sexually harass another male, a female can sexually harass another female, or a female can sexually harass a male. The conduct is unacceptable no matter who commits it. In each case it is the line supervisor's job to stop it as soon as he becomes aware of its occurrence. That awareness may come from his own observations or the complaint of a victim. As he assures the aggrieved party that he will stop the misconduct and instigate an inquiry into it, the supervisor also must assure the complainant that he or she will not be punished, formally or informally, for bringing the issue to official attention.

The key reason that the supervisor must not tolerate sexual harassment in the workplace is a humane one: it is simply wrong and unethical to permit another human being to be treated in such a manner. Beyond that, permitting sexual harassment eventually will damage the law enforcement organization and destroy the reputation its members enjoy in the community. But if the supervisor needs a bit more selfish reason to root out sexual harassment where it exists, here it is: participating in sexual harassment or allowing it to exist unopposed is practically guaranteed to bite the leader who permits it to flourish under his or her nose. That could result in the supervisor getting fired, becoming the subject of a civil lawsuit, or even finding himself the subject of criminal charges. Sexual harassment is viewed that seriously in today's America, as it well should be.

The supervisor-counselor also may be called upon to display mentoring skills. Mentoring requires a bit more than role-modeling, as vital as that function is. A mentor helps prepare a subordinate for a new role. In many cases, it may be the supervisor's own job that the subordinate is being groomed to assume at some point in the future.

Mentoring has long been practiced in the private sector. More recently law enforcement supervisors and managers have come to see the practical value in actively preparing a subordinate to assume greater responsibilities. This the leader does by showing the employee how the boss's tasks are carried out. It is also accomplished by allowing the employee to execute those tasks himself under the critical eye of the supervisor. On some occasions the subordinate will be coached and evaluated as he serves in the role of an acting supervisor. Coaching and mentoring go hand in hand.

Attitudes are, of course, as important as technical skills in the mentoring process. Here the mentor models for his subordinate the demeanor and mindset of a successful leader. In addition to showing the subordinate *what* he does and *how* he does it, the supervisor-mentor also explains *why* a given action or response is the appropriate one. It is all a part of being a good mentor or coach for a promising, future police leader.

SUMMARY

The police supervisor's role as a counselor and advisor is as delicate as it is vital to the employee, agency, and public. It is one that cannot be shirked except at great risk of neglecting supervisory responsibility.

The role is not one that can, in good faith, be left to another supervisor or the next person up the chain of command. It is only through accepting his sometimes uncomfortable but always necessary twin roles as problem solver and resource person that the leader-counselor can live up to the trust placed in him.

POINTS TO REMEMBER

- The supervisor's job includes watching for indicators of significant personal problems among his subordinates.
- Employees' problems can range in origin from the workplace to personal life.
- Marital difficulties trouble more than a few law enforcement employees.
- Alcoholism presents a serious and frequently-encountered problem in today's society.
- The supervisor's intervention efforts may result in very uncomfortable moments for both him and his subordinate.
- There are professional sources of help to which a supervisor may refer a troubled employee.
- An earned reputation for trust established earlier will help the supervisor intervene with a troubled employee.
- Sexual harassment represents a real and serious form of workplace misconduct that cannot be allowed to exist.
- Counseling employees of the opposite gender is a task that merits the supervisor's utmost skills and professionalism.

Chapter Eleven

THE POLICE LEADER AS A MANAGER

He directs. He controls. He coordinates. All of these phrases have been used to describe the role of the manager in a police agency. All are functions that the first-line supervisor participates in as a part of management. How, then, is the police sergeant in a quasi-military organization different from and similar to the mid-level manager, such as a commander or lieutenant, in management functions and responsibilities?

One obvious difference lies in the level of the organization at which the leader engages in tasks of direction, control, and coordination. The primary supervisor or sergeant must concern himself with the daily, practical problems of the working police unit. He must answer his employees' requests for advice or information; he handles pressing personnel problems; and he sees to it that the objectives of the agency are translated into concrete action at the actual service delivery level.

The mid-level manager concerns himself with some of these practical matters, but with other things, as well. The mid-manager considers the coordination of a number of smaller units in the overall scheme of the organization, and he sees to it that one group of people is not working at cross purposes to some other departmental entity. He attempts to view his own role as being a part of the bigger picture involving the entire police organization.

The first-line supervisor shares his superior's concerns for getting the agency's jobs done and done well: he works to keep channels of communication open not only laterally but up and down the chain of command. He shares the mid-manager's concern for the securing of skilled services from both personnel and equipment. He inspects and evaluates in an attempt to use resources as efficiently as possible. And he rewards, corrects, and counsels as he strives to obtain maximum effectiveness in all things.

The supervisor assists the mid-level manager by recommending his people for awards, recognition, and other incentives. He also participates fully in the formal disciplinary process when it must be invoked to preserve the integrity and credibility of individual employees or the agency as a whole.

As he directs, controls, and coordinates, the supervisor serves as a manager in every sense of the term. He also engages in various planning activities, whether at the team, section, or department level. He organizes and assembles resources. In some agencies, he may participate in the budgeting process.

This hybrid creature called a supervisor is quite certainly a part of management in addition to the other memberships he maintains in the police organization. As such, he faces other duties, too. What are they?

THE MANAGEMENT ROLE

It is possible to get more specific about the contemporary manager's job than just to say that he directs, controls, and coordinates. When the first-line supervisor is fulfilling his obligations as a manager, he is engaging in some of these "more specific" activities. Any thorough discussion of these activities should include the following:

Interagency Liaison

The police manager carries out day-to-day contacts with his counterparts from other agencies within the criminal justice system. One of these contacts might be an informal cup of coffee with another street sergeant from the neighboring jurisdiction. Another might call for a lunch meeting with a representative from the district attorney's office. Whatever the situation, the supervisor is a representative of his agency and must conduct himself accordingly.

Hopefully, the supervisor representing his department as a delegate to a policymaking body has been thoroughly briefed in advance as to his agency's position on an issue. He must remain alert not to commit his agency and its resources to a project or program without knowing in advance if the commitment is an acceptable one to the department's leadership.

Personnel Matters

The first-line supervisor should be involved in decisions affecting his unit's personnel. He should have a big voice in hiring and firing discussions. He should participate in decisions to grant merit awards, pay bonuses, and special recognition. He must figure directly in any matters pertaining to the discipline of his subordinates.

The manager devotes a great deal of his time to both the prevention and treatment of personnel problems. For example, he may work to help prevent difficulties through his recommendations on a just employee pay plan, or he may combat already-developed problems through his membership on a disciplinary review board or employee grievance committee.

Role Model

The supervisor in his capacity as a manager serves as a role model for his subordinates. This responsibility extends further than giving an example of how to dress for work and how to clean a weapon, although such tasks also may be quite appropriate for police supervisors in many job descriptions.

The supervisor also helps in setting the mood of the work group. It is amazing how many gruff, abrupt employees have gruff, abrupt bosses. Fortunately, the opposite also appears to be true much of the time. A boss who creates a pleasant, healthy job atmosphere has employees who are easy to work with and who generally display an equally healthy outlook.

The supervisor/manager does not have to be an adherent of the "let's have a picnic" school of management in order to have a group of reasonably content employees. A little fairness, good temperament, sound judgment, and a liberal application of plain old common sense can achieve remarkable results as morale builders and mood setters.

Information Transmitter and Relay

The effective manager utilizes information best when he relays it to those who will use it. This means that not only does he relay the pronouncements of the "Big Boss" to the people who will get the job done, but that the manager makes the chain of command function more smoothly by passing along the concerns of subordinates to the higher-ups who need to hear them.

As an information carrier, the manager ascertains that the message he is passing along gets to where it is going with nothing added, deleted, or distorted. It is fine for him to provide his own opinions when asked, but he must refrain from editorializing when it is not appropriate.

Interpretation and Clarification

On occasion, the police manager will find that a piece of information he has received for forwarding from either end of the chain of command is too incomplete, confusing, or unclear for it to be understood at the other end. It is a good rule of thumb that if the supervisor cannot understand it, others will have difficulty with it, as well. Faced with such a hazy message, the alert manager will seek clarification at the source before passing the information along.

The manager probably would find it relatively painless to go to his subordinates for a clarification of their thoughts or concerns. It may be more difficult for him to ask the boss for additional details of an otherwise obscure message. Nonetheless, the clarification must be obtained.

Quality Control

The manager also serves as a quality control inspector for the people who employ him. His inspectional duties may include spot checks of incoming investigative reports in the detective division. If he is assigned to patrol, the manager may find himself checking the quality of summonses issued by his traffic officers. If he is a manager in the narcotics unit, he may become involved in a periodic accounting of the disbursement of "buy" money.

Personnel concerns also fall within the inspectional responsibilities of the police manager. For example, the review of officers' probable cause for arrests may be a key function of the supervisor/manager. This job, too, is a sort of quality check.

General Supervision

In addition to his assorted specialty tasks, the manager often carries out the daily functions of a first-line supervisor, too. The extent to which the manager becomes involved in these tasks will vary widely from one agency to another. Depending upon his place within the organization, he may find himself reviewing crime reports, looking at investigators' lead sheets, or directing operations at a major crime scene or other significant event.

The police leader is not permitted the questionable luxury of isolating himself within the role of a desk-bound manager. Only in large police organizations can the practice of totally removing a supervisor from the more traditional duties of policing take place. Elsewhere, the office manager of today may find himself thrown into field application of his leadership skills tomorrow.

The police supervisor must "keep a hand in" insofar as the practicalities of his profession are concerned. While this fact of managerial life may temporarily distract him from attending to his other activities, he will benefit in the end from his continuing contact with the basic elements of the police task.

Information Source

The skilled and experienced police manager is a resource person for those beside him, above him, and below him in the chain of command. His previous job experiences have prepared him for the questions and problems of his fellow managers. He can furnish them with advice on how he handled a situation similar to the one besieging them now. The situation may involve a disciplinary action, an internal investigation, or some other special assignment or detail. He has been there before and can help others now.

The supervisor/manager's bosses may wish to mine his wide array of knowledge. Questions on how a given procedure is performed in the field, how the troops are feeling about some issue, or how a departmental policy might be altered in view of new practical experience are all valid topics for application of the supervisor's personal knowledge.

The supervisor's subordinates will call upon his job knowledge and expertise more than any other single group of people. Not only *how* a certain task is to be executed but also the *rationale* behind doing it this way may be questions needing answered. Today's police officers are unwilling to be driven rather than led. They are intelligent. They want to know the thinking behind a practice, procedure, or policy. They are capable of thinking and questioning for themselves. This is good. The manager cannot afford to be without accurate replies for his subordinates' earnest inquiries.

Special Assignments

As yet another of a manager's duties, the supervisor may be called upon to execute projects of research and development, budgeting and finance, or investigation and reporting. While handling a special detail for his superior, the supervisor may find himself exploring an area of administrative functioning not previously experienced. He may hate math but find himself tied up in the annual budgeting process. He may dislike writing assignments yet be deeply engrossed in the preparation of the annual report on the department's activities.

Whatever his initial reactions to his assignment, the supervisor with an eye on the future does not whimper. Although it may mean a period of temporary discomfort or added stress, he knows that it will, in the long run, aid in his career development and total job knowledge.

The expanded experience the supervisor gains from exercising his managerial skills will make him a better candidate for promotion, if that is his eventual goal. Perhaps even more important, the expanded versatility will make him feel better about himself.

Community Relations

The supervisor should view himself as a representative of his agency. He is a visible representative of its goals, objectives and practices as these things relate to the public at large. While the supervisor, like his subordinate, has always been an ambassador of his agency, he may find his community relations role broadened by assignment to specific projects or programs. The supervisor/manager must be capable of preparing himself for the public presentation of crime prevention or public education topics ranging from child abuse to bicycle safety. As a recognized leader in the police agency, he will be looked upon by many as an authoritative source on a multitude of subjects.

As a police representative to the community, the police supervisor will find his manager's role includes the task of translator and, sometimes, defender of police actions and methods to a concerned public. In properly handling his educational tasks, he will aid his fellow officers, himself, and those who help pay his salary in reaching mutually increased trust and understanding.

HANDLING SPECIALIZED TASKS

It has been noted that the supervisor may be called upon to handle what might be termed "specialized tasks." Such a phrase can cover a broad range of responsibilities, and the manager must adequately address all of them.

Much of the specialized work done by the police supervisor serving in a managerial capacity will be reduced to written form. When this written work is done completely and adequately, the person to whom it is submitted should have little more to do than read it and approve or disapprove the final product.

The supervisor/manager attacking a special project should first obtain several key pieces of information from the person assigning the task. To do the job well, the supervisor needs to know the identity of any problem involved and learn as much about it as possible at the outset. If, for instance, the supervisor has been given the task of researching the requirements for changing the department's off-duty employment policy, he will need to know more about the scope of his own role in the project. Will he be researching employee attitudes on the issue? Will he be checking into needed changes in the agency's insurance coverage? Will he be involved in surveying the need for a policy change? Will he be expected to make recommendations for formal policy changes or just present the facts for decisions by others? All of the supervisor's questions need to be answered early if the job is to be a complete one. His boss may give him some of the answers at the outset. The supervisor must not hesitate to ask if he has a question.

Any time limits within which he must work must be identified. Will interim progress reports be required? Time constraints must be known if the supervisor is to pace his work properly and not end up in a rush effort at the last moment.

With his early questions answered and the scope and objectives of his work set before him, the supervisor can begin gathering information needed to complete the quest. Enough research must be done to fully define the problem, and enough information must be collected to back the findings and/or recommendations he develops.

Many of these special assignments will culminate in written report or memorandum format, as opposed to an oral briefing. A written presentation makes it much easier if the final work product is to be reviewed by several individuals at different times and places.

The body of the presentation itself should be as compact and concise as possible. This is not the place for great detail, though attachments or appendices can explore minute points, where appropriate. In this way, the reader is not forced to slice through a forest of perhaps tedious facts to get at the main problems, points, and proposed solutions. If the reader wants specifics, they may be found at the end of the presentation.

For the sake of consistency, the supervisor preparing a written version of his work should follow a standard format. The problem-oriented project might be laid out in six sections: (**1**) **statement of the problem; (2) background information; (3) recommended action or proposed solution; (4) alternatives; (5) action or approval section; and (6) attachments or appendices.**

The supervisor/manager may wish to rearrange the sections, add some of his own choosing, or delete others. All sections will not be applicable to every situation. However he decides to arrange or use them, these sections do cover points that should be addressed.

"Statement of the problem," for example, should attempt to identify what the problem really is, why some sort of action is necessary, and what issues are being addressed. If a policy or procedure already exists in this area, the section should include why a change is indicated.

The supervisor's segment on **"background information"** may be the lengthiest part of the composition. In this section, he will attempt to give his reading audience an appreciation of all of the important information relevant to the issue. Financial and manpower considerations involved may be among the key resources discussed here. Persons, places and things involved should be identified in this segment. Past events or situations that may have bearing on the current situation should be noted. The reader should be brought up to date as far as the known facts will allow.

This background section can make use of the "who, what, when, where, why, and how" formula of writing. All of these topics need to be covered in giving a solid background to those who must deal with the problem or assignment.

The **"recommended action or proposed solution"** category allows the manager to set forth his conclusions as to any needed actions or repairs. Here he also states his reasons for the options or solutions that he has suggested. If a timetable for implementation of his proposal is required, he states that, too.

In advancing his suggestions and recommendations, the manager remains mindful of the very real limitations placed upon him and the agency in such areas as funding, manpower, and other resources. The realities of life are not placed entirely out of mind, either. A tongue-in-cheek example: A proposal to improve a pitiful court conviction rate by impeaching the local judge is probably not realistic.

"Alternatives" may not be a category that all managers will want to use. Those who do elect to utilize it often list other possible solutions or responses to the problem or situation. These may range from a recommendation to continue with the present policy or procedure to suggestions for radical changes in the way things are done. Some supervisors attach to each listed alternative the reasons why it was not the one recommended by the writer.

The **"action or approval"** section allows the reviewers up the chain of command to indicate personal feelings and preferences about the supervisor's assessment and suggestions. In some agencies, this response may take the "approved or disapproved" approach. Other departments may solicit general comments from readers. Some departments dictate that chain of command comments go into the report itself. Others require the attachment of a separate page. The supervisor should be aware of his agency's preferred format for this work.

"Attachments or appendices" are self-explanatory. Any lengthy, involved material inappropriate for the main body of the document should go here as supportive evidence or explanation. Related articles of interest or tables of figures could be placed here.

The manager should not feel obliged to put something here just to lengthen his presentation. A study of a financial problem might call for several supportive tables and charts. On the other hand, a piece of work covering an opinion issue might warrant little or nothing as back-up. Not every written presentation will require this ending section.

By the time his work is completed on the assignment, the supervisor functioning in his manager's role should have covered three vital areas of concern. First, he has conducted a study of the situation or problem. Second, he has presented a solution or recommended a change and has backed up the proposal with facts. Third, he has submitted the work for review and action by his boss.

The police supervisor should remain mindful that since he does not like to receive poor or incomplete work from a subordinate, it is reasonable to assume that *his* boss does not care for it, either. Before submitting any completed project or presentation to the next person up the chain, the supervisor should query himself: Is this finished? If I were required to make a critical decision on the facts contained here, would I have enough to make an intelligent choice? Am I setting up my boss, or am I giving him what he needs to act wisely and decisively?

If the supervisor is not fully satisfied with the responses from his own questions, chances are that the work is not yet done. A little more research, a bit more thought, a tad more effort may be needed. Rough drafts and working copies are fine for their limited purposes, but the end product should look like neither.

THE FINISHED PRODUCT

Keeping in mind the points discussed earlier, a look at some practical examples of work submitted by the police supervisor/manager should be of use. Work submitted by the manager can range from a quickly and relatively easily prepared inquiry to a time-consuming, exhaustive study.

The supervisor might be assigned the relatively simple task of administratively investigating a minor accident involving a police vehicle. Here, the supervisor's concerns should be quite clear: he must conduct a thorough field investigation. The set of facts from which he will write his report or memorandum must be accurate and complete. To be sure of accuracy, he will check and re-check them. He may want to interview the persons having facts relevant to the incident. He will review and obtain copies of any documents pertinent to the occurrence.

The sharp supervisor will avoid putting unnecessary words in the written report that he submits. A brief, concise document may result from a fairly extensive investigation. In the minor situation being dealt with in the following example, the inquiring supervisor's final report may be quite short, yet complete. Note that in this case the supervisor did not find it necessary to use the categories or subsections previously described.

MEMORANDUM

TO: B. D. Glasscock, Sergeant
             Watch Three
             Field Operations Bureau
FROM: B. J. Smith, Corporal
             Watch Three
             Field Operations Bureau
DATE: July 14, 2009
SUBJECT: Investigation of Patrol Car Accident

At 2242 hours this date, reporting officer was serving as acting sergeant on Watch Three when a radio call was received from Agent Jones (3A23) advising that he had been in a minor automobile accident on the parking lot of the "Ground Round Restaurant," 1215 N. Wadsworth.

This officer responded there and observed two new creases in the right-side front and rear doors of patrol car number 36. Agent Jones advised me that he had been looking for suspicious persons in the area. As he was driving around the rear of the restaurant with his headlights out, he saw a small concrete pylon protruding from the pavement in the parking lot but was unable to avoid striking it as he passed by. He estimated that he was moving at about 10 miles per hour when the right side of the car struck the pylon.

This officer noted that the concrete pylon was about 20 inches high with electrical conduit sticking out of its top, making its total height 30 inches above the ground. The structure was 36 inches in diameter and was of a dark gray color. I noted that the pylon was located in a dark area of the lot. There was no direct lighting within 150 feet of the location.

This officer found that the pylon was nearly invisible from a vehicle operated without headlights. The structure was easily seen when the lights were illuminated.

Reporting officer took photos of the scene and the damaged patrol car. Agent Klutz filled out an accident report.

This completed effort is fairly brief, yet it accomplishes its goal. It lets the sector commander know how the damage to the department's equipment took place. It notes how the damage might have been prevented. Further action will be the province of the boss.

Other specialized assignments may require more research and analysis by the supervisor/manager. Excessive paperwork–the eternal nemesis of the police officer–makes an excellent example of a growing problem skillfully and constructively examined by a thoughtful supervisor:

MEMORANDUM

TO: R.E. Armstrong, Lieutenant
         Watch One
         Patrol Division
FROM: L.T. Gray, Sergeant
         Watch One
         Patrol Division
DATE: August 11, 2009
SUBJECT: Reduction in Paperwork for Patrol Officers

PROBLEM:

An even cursory examination of the time spent by patrol officers in the completion of various types of written reports reveals that an inordinate amount of resources are being expended in written efforts.

BACKGROUND:

Normal attrition of the patrol force coupled with the lack of any new patrol personnel have contributed to a serious problem in having field units available to answer priority calls during peak "calls for service" periods. On Watch One during the current watch rotation, a lack of available units has more than once required the patrol division to seek supplemental manpower from other divisions in the agency.

Much officer time is currently being consumed by very lengthy and sometimes repetitious written reports. Often, it appears that information is being recorded in great detail that has no further use to either this department or an outside agency.

In addition, the considerable amount of time being devoted to paperwork is harming the morale of some aggressive, intelligent police officers who may feel that their talents are being diverted from "real police work." Such an attitude would appear to be common, judging from overheard comments and complaints. There also appears to be some feeling that patrol officers are gathering reams of data to support an informational processing function that should be supporting them, not the other way around.

RECOMMENDED ACTION:

An immediate, serious, and concentrated effort must be made to review all types of written reports completed by patrol officers, with an eye towards eliminating as much unnecessary paperwork as possible. It is vital that this effort be a timely one. It must not become mired in endless rounds of committee meetings, task force groups, and special project appointments. For maximum effectiveness, changes must be quick and real. No reporting system or individual report should be immune from this examination.

Although patrol officer representation is necessary in any attempt at reducing paperwork, it is imperative that patrol deployment not be further decimated by pulling field officers and supervisors into lengthy and frequent meetings for this effort. I instead recommend that a short-term committee of police employees be formed and directed to submit recommendations within 90 days.

As a starting point, the writer has attached an appendix listing some possible areas to be explored for the reduction of patrol officers' paperwork time.

ALTERNATIVES:

1. Continue using the current reporting system without modification.
2. Abandon the state's reporting system with its required forms and format in favor of a new, abbreviated reporting format of this department's own design. The department would assume the costs involved in placing the new system into operation.

ACTION:

Recommended	Date	Not Recommended
R.E. Armstrong, Lt.		R.E. Armstrong, Lt.
Approved	Date	Disapproved
S.K. Smith, Capt.		S.K. Smith, Capt.
Patrol Commander		Patrol Commander

APPENDIX:

Suggested targets for reporting procedure revision:

1. *Arrest reports on traffic-related offenses.*
   The narrative for DUI, DUS, and other traffic-related arrests result-ing in physical custody could be handled by a single "Custody One" sheet plus good notes on the summons and complaint form itself. Supplemental pages could then be eliminated.
2. *Shoplifting arrest reports.*
   The narrative might be further reduced by referring the reader to wit-ness statements, which we would require store security personnel to complete on shoplifters they take into custody and hold for our officers.
3. *Minor penal offenses.*
   Custody reports for minor violations of penal laws could be elimi-nated. Narrative for the arrest report could be handled in the notes section on the back of the penal summons and complaint form. Offenses for which this procedure might apply include: noise ordi-nance violations, littering, and curfew violations.

The supervisor also could have included his suggested "targets for revision" in his RECOMMENDED ACTION section.

The supervisor in this example has gone to the trouble of proposing some concrete, specific actions to combat a problem that virtually everyone complains about but few act positively upon. The marked difference between him and the others is his willingness to expend some personal energy in an effort to do something about the paper dis-aster. He has at least set the administrative ball rolling in an attempt to get some favorable results and has indicated his willingness to help. Now, the decision to act or continue to tolerate the *status quo* lies with others above him. He has set himself apart as a doer rather than a chronic complainer.

The special activities and projects that a police manager can be drawn into are virtually limitless in number and variety. Tasks assigned can range from the evaluation of a new piece of equipment being considered for purchase to review of a tactical operation that has just ended. Both assignments can be very important to the well-being of the police organization and its members.

One kind of sensitive and special assignment that may fall to the supervisor/manager is the "after action" critique of a police tactical operation. The preparation and review of this report is extremely important to the healthy police agency. Properly handled, the critical review allows personnel to look as objectively as possible at their handling of a recent major event, ranging from a multiple-homicide investigation to a natural disaster response. In this way, individual and agency-wide strengths and weaknesses can be identified and, where necessary, acted upon.

Most police agencies have a review procedure which is activated following each instance of shots fired by law enforcement personnel. Such inquiries must be thorough, competently done, and promptly completed so as to answer the questions and concerns of other officers, the public, and the press.

The supervisor, serving in another of his managerial roles as investigator, may play an integral part in the pursuit and completion of this necessary inquiry. The internal investigation of a police-involved shooting or other use of deadly force should evoke the same, careful attention to detail which the supervisor would apply to any other of his tasks. Cautious focus upon the shooting scene itself, the collection and documentation of pertinent evidence, painstaking interview, and thoughtful analysis of the facts must precede an equally careful effort at preparing the report.

In the preparation of the final written accounting, the manager's most useful tools will be the rewrite and the revision. Anxious not to bore with trivialities, neither does the conscientious writer want to leave pressing questions unanswered. Unanswered questions betray a less than complete investigation.

One supervisor summarized the results of a shooting inquiry in which he was the coordinator of the investigation in a concise, complete fashion:

INVESTIGATION REPORT

SUBJECT: Employee-involved shooting
DATE: September 8, 2009
            Case #09-15932

Synopsis

At 1540 hours, September 5, 2009 David Smith and Jerry Dykes entered the Holiday Drugstore at 955 Sheridan Boulevard. Dykes remained by the front door and Smith went to the drug counter where he robbed the pharmacist by pointing a small automatic pistol and saying "Give me all your drugs . . . make it snappy." An employee activated a silent alarm.

Smith and Dykes ran out of the store with a sack of narcotics and ran behind the building, and the employees lost sight of them.

Deputies Kenneth Jones and Richard Bailey were at Quitman and Colfax Avenue when they heard the broadcast alarm and they drove into the area of the store. In the meantime, Deputy Stieren had arrived on scene and began broadcasting a description of the clothing worn by the robbers. Unique to the description was that one of the robbers was wearing a bright blue headband.

As Deputies Jones and Bailey neared the scene, they passed a blue Dodge going away from the scene rapidly. The driver was wearing a blue headband. The Dodge ran a stop sign at Ninth and Sheridan and the deputies began a pursuit. Bailey was driving the unmarked car with a siren under the hood and red lights behind the grill. The emergency equipment was activated, but the Dodge failed to yield.

Jones and Bailey chased the Dodge south on Sheridan to the service road of Sixth Avenue. Only Dykes could be seen in the car until it entered the service road; at this time, Smith sat up in the back seat of the Dodge and looked back at the pursuing deputies. Deputy Jones could see a short-barreled pistol in the right hand of Smith. The pursuit was now proceeding at 50 to 60 miles per hour.

In the 6800 block of the Sixth Avenue service road, Smith threw a tan sack out of the window. It was later recovered and found to contain the drugs taken in the robbery. As the pursuit neared Sixth and Crescent Lane, Smith displayed his pistol again and pointed it at the pursuing police car. The Dodge turned north on Crescent and Smith was leaning out of the right rear window pointing the gun at the deputies. At this time, while still on the service road but turning onto Crescent, Deputy Jones fired two shots from his 9mm pistol. Afterwards, he stated that he intended to kill or wound Smith to prevent him from firing on the officers. Smith ducked down in the seat at this time, and both shots missed the fleeing car.

Approximately 100 yards further North on Crescent, Dykes lost control of the car and it crashed into a parked vehicle. Both Dykes and Smith were seized by Deputies Jones and Bailey without incident. There were no injuries to anyone.

Smith and Dykes will be charged with aggravated robbery, first-degree assault, and violent crime. Both men were found to have extensive criminal records, with Dykes having a conviction for murder in

California.

Two handguns were recovered from the Dodge: a .25 caliber pistol was found in the front seat, and a .38 caliber revolver was found in the back seat. The guns were fully loaded, although they apparently had not been fired during the pursuit.

A fragment of a bullet was retrieved from the pavement at Sixth and Crescent. No other traces of the two rounds fired by Deputy Jones were discovered.

Facts and Circumstances of Shooting Justification

1. Deputy Jones, at the time of the shooting, believed Smith to have participated in the robbery of a drugstore.
2. Deputy Jones, at the time he fired, observed Smith with a handgun and believed that he was about to fire or had already fired at the deputies. Deputy Jones observed this from about 60 feet away, by his estimation.
3. When Deputy Jones fired, he intended to kill or seriously wound Smith.
4. Deputy Jones stated that he was not shooting at the fleeing car or its tires but directly at Smith.
5. Prior to the time that Deputy Jones fired, Smith had displayed a weapon in the direction of the deputies.
6. The shooting occurred in a residential area in which no other vehicles were traveling at that time. No pedestrians were noted in the area, either. The line of fire at the time of the shooting was free of innocent bystanders.

Findings Pertinent to Policies, Procedures, and Laws

1. All radio traffic during the pursuit was carried out in accordance with established procedures.
2. The pursuit was reasonably safe while on the Sixth Avenue service road. The use of an unmarked vehicle and limited emergency equipment would have called for the pursuit to be stopped if heavily traveled streets had become involved.
3. Deputy Jones was using a temporary issue sidearm while his weapon was being repaired and he had not fired it before.
4. Official department issue rounds were fired from the deputy's weapon.
5. No one was hit by the rounds fired by the deputy.

Conclusion

Based upon the foregoing facts and circumstances, the firearm discharge by Deputy Kenneth Jones was justified.

Submitted by: <u>Wallace</u> <u>Weasel,</u> <u>Sergeant</u> <u>#0306</u>

The supervisor in this case has prepared a report that accurately reflects the work done by other investigators, in addition to himself. He has furnished transcripts of the actual interviews, which are available as appendices if anyone wishes to refer to them. The dozens of pages of police reports pertaining to the incident are there, too, as are lists of physical evidence recovered relative to the crime and subsequent shooting.

It is important to note that none of these supporting documents take up the reader's time. A summary tells him what he needs to know, quickly and concisely. The details may be found elsewhere, if someone wishes to examine them. The police executive, attorney, or investigator wanting to get to the heart of the matter as quickly as possible can do so without undue distraction or delay. In this key aspect alone, the report as presented is quite effective as an "Executive Summary."

The successful completion of special assignments and details of varying designs and complexities is clearly part of the supervisor's job life. The increasing frequency with which the line supervisor may be asked to participate in handling these responsibilities indicates a positive trend in American policing institutions. On a larger scale, the manner in which changes of all kinds have come to affect police supervisors and the personnel they lead is a topic warranting further discussion.

ATTITUDE TOWARDS CHANGE

Change is inevitable.

Human beings grouped into work organizations have long appeared resistant in varying degrees to change, or at least to its effects upon them. The human animal, generally speaking, appears relatively content within the security of the known and familiar. Often it seems to take the known and familiar becoming downright uncomfortable or inconvenient to motivate any real interest in change.

Policing has been accused of being a field particularly resistant to change. Beat cops and chiefs alike have been labeled (sometimes quite accurately) as being too much at ease with the tried, if not true, way of doing things.

Police leaders over the past decade have bolstered the role of change in law enforcement. A sincere interest in helping professionalize law enforcement has helped the cause, as have some critical court decisions, particularly at the federal court level. Law enforcement clearly is changing.

Change has not always come easy to officers and agencies satisfied with the comfortable familiarity of old ways. The officer on the street, perhaps aware of his supervisor's resentment at having to alter old ways of thinking and acting, has found it easier to resist change himself. Change is slowed, progress is delayed, and the overall efficiency and effectiveness of the officer and his agency may thus suffer. Strident protest and dissent are understandable, but little good is accomplished if the required change is a good one that is going to have to be implemented eventually.

Change merely for the sake of change is as unacceptable in policing as it is in any other area of human endeavor. It is patently absurd and criminally wasteful to alter an effective way of doing things just so someone can say that things are being done differently now. The supervisor intent upon climbing the bureaucratic ladder by looking for things to change without any real reason other than the attention it might bring him should be made to fall on his own felt tip pen! That is not the sort of change that intelligent police supervisors should be promoting.

Rather, the sensible police leader is constantly looking for ways in which he might alter his unit or department to get the job done better, quicker, more accurately. Where he finds need and room for such a change, he becomes a salesperson for it to both his supervisors and his subordinates. His superiors must be "sold" if they are to be moved into authorizing a major change. The subordinates must understand and approve of it if the work is to be done without unnecessary strife and resentment.

The supervisor should remember that he must often convince many people besides himself that a proposed alteration will be beneficial and worth the effort expended on it. He does this by first getting his own facts straight and then by presenting them logically and clearly.

There is nothing inherently wrong about a "what's in it for me" attitude on the part of his audience. It is logical and desirable for an employee to have a personal stake in what he is doing on the job and why he is doing it. The insightful supervisor anticipates this line of thought and tailors his presentation for it. There are, of course, any number of topics that are dear to the police officer's heart. Truthfully addressing any one of them practically guarantees that the proposed change will be accepted with ease:

1. The change will make the job easier.
2. The change will make the job safer.
3. The change will get the work done faster.
4. The change will make the work environment more comfortable.

Proposed change from some other source presents a slightly different prospect for the police supervisor. It may be easier to argue for one's own "baby" than to unswervingly support someone else's. Nonetheless, the ethical supervisor will enthusiastically back logical and needed change, even if he is not its author.

Confronted with a change in policy or procedure, the supervisor reviews it for completeness and clarity before he passes it on to others. If there are additional points to be made or questions to be answered, now is the time to get the needed answers from those who should have them. The boss who anticipates the questions and concerns of his people and gets the responses for them now will save time and, possibly, grief later on.

It is the police leader's responsibility to set forth his reservations concerning proposed changes. At the same time, it is also his duty to see to it that his supervisory effectiveness and management's overall control of the agency are not damaged by a public debate over a proposed change. The wise leader knows where, when, and how to conduct his arguments. In front of the troops or after the change has already been made are not the proper arenas for dramatics.

SUMMARY

In serving in his manager's role, the police supervisor is not doing anything all that different from what he does daily as a front-line leader of police personnel. He is still directing, controlling, and coordinating activities in which people and things get the job done as well as possible. He is still giving direction and purpose to the efforts of others. He is assisting them where they are weak or need the guidance of his experience. He is correcting or commending them for performances significantly below or above his expectations.

Some of the experts on management make rather much of the difference between front-line supervisors and their bosses, the mid-level managers. There are differences, true enough. The middle managers are generally seen as less involved in practical aspects of policing and more concerned with the development of policy and procedure. However, the police organization that excludes its line supervisors from the exercise of their managerial skills in such areas as the creation of policy and procedure does so at its own peril. Law enforcement agencies that have allowed and encouraged contributions from their street-level supervisors have not infrequently been pleased with the pragmatic influences these people have brought to the final work product: service to the public.

Granted, the police supervisor's role should remain one which involves him in the frontline application and implementation of agency policy and procedure. This task, too, is a part of his managerial responsibilities, and it generally must take precedence over any other duties. Just the same, to bar the supervisor from participating in the development of the guidelines that he will later implement will reduce the agency's effectiveness at the same time it hurts the morale and career development of a key member of the management team. Such waste must not be allowed to occur.

POINTS TO REMEMBER

- The first-line supervisor is a part of management.
- The manager must serve as a positive role model.
- A good manager relays, transmits and clarifies information and opinions.
- The manager is also a supervisor who participates in quality control.
- In his manager's role, the supervisor should expect to complete inquiries and investigations and reduce his findings to writing.

- A manager absolutely must be able to write clearly.
- As a manager, the supervisor should be prepared to make recommendations for personnel actions as well as changes in policies and procedures.
- The manager must accept change and be prepared to explain and support it to his subordinates.

Chapter Twelve

THE POLICE LEADER AS A
COMPLAINT PROCESSOR

The citizen who feels he has been mistreated by a police officer. . . . The police officer who feels that the department is mistreating him. . . . The police supervisor who feels that improper actions have been taken by a police employee. . . . The police union that feels one of its members is being picked on by management. . . . What do all these individuals and organizations have in common? For one thing, all of them are concerned that someone is being treated improperly at the hands of some member or element of the police organization. All want some kind of action, satisfaction, or redress of real or perceived grievances.

Second, all of the above eventually may reach a police supervisor in an attempt to find help in resolving the difficulties. The citizen with an allegation of misconduct by police personnel will need to find someone "in authority" within the police organization to whom he can make his complaint. The police employee who thinks that his own organization is treating him unfairly will want to start his own grievance proceedings within that organization. His immediate supervisor will probably be the first person to hear the details of the argument.

The fellow supervisor who has a beef about how things are going within another unit of the agency may seek out one of his peers to make his feelings known. Unless the problem is a result of an ongoing emergency that requires immediate corrective action, the displeased supervisor will be wise to wait until a supervisor of the offending unit is available to him for an accurate and first-hand relay of the problem as he sees it. It will then be the fellow supervisor's job to listen to the complaint and try to resolve it fairly, promptly, and with any needed changes accomplished.

Finally, the line supervisor sometimes will be the first to hear of a formal grievance or complaint by a police employees' union or association regarding alleged mistreatment of one of its members. Here the supervisor's role may be that of a careful reporter. He may be called upon to assist the labor organization in gaining access to the formal grievance mechanism of the police agency.

On another occasion, the supervisor may be able to help settle an issue of interest to a police labor group by providing facts of his own finding to management and union alike. This way the issue may be resolved with no further action necessary.

In yet another scenario, a final resolution of a particularly sticky employee/management tiff may see the supervisor giving testimony before a formal grievance hearing board or similar body. Both his memory and his sense for fair play may be called upon at such times.

There are several ways in which the police supervisor can find himself involved to receive, investigate, and/or report upon a complaint from somebody. The good attitudes, skills, and concerns he must exercise in serving in his capacity as complaint processor are the subject of this chapter.

ALLEGATIONS OF MISCONDUCT

The citizen who wants to complain about the police car he saw speeding and the resident who desires to make his feelings known about the "unjustified beating" he received at the hands of a police officer have something in common: They are both unhappy about what they perceive as improper and perhaps illegal conduct by public servants. They both want their questions answered and some sort of corrective action taken. Though they may vary greatly in the degree to which they are upset and personally offended, they will both require the intervention and action of a supervisory member of the police organization.

The manner in which the supervisor reacts to the complainant, pursues a fair and thorough inquiry and arrives at concrete results can have a great deal to do with the future attitude and well-being of the complainant, the concerned employees, and the police organization as a whole.

Police agencies examine complaints against their personnel, procedures, and policies for several good reasons: (1) to protect the public
from actual police misconduct; (2) to protect police employees from
unjust accusations and the undeserved reputations that can go with
them; (3) to detect and correct improper or inadequate operating procedures or policies; and (4) to protect the credibility and integrity of
the police agency.

Good selection and training can go a long way towards preventing
many of the problems and abuses often connected with police corruption, incompetency, or misuse of authority. Intelligent, ethical, and
fair first-line supervisors can do much to arrest such difficulties, too.

Legitimate complaints and inquiries from the public must be
received and processed by the police supervisor. Some police agencies
differentiate between the handling of the apparently minor allegation
of improper police action and the processing of the serious accusation
of wrongdoing. A complaint of speeding by a patrol officer might be
one end of such a scale, with an alleged criminal act, such as robbery,
at the other. These agencies generally allow the supervisor receiving
the "minor" complaint or question to handle the reception of the information, the investigation of the facts of the incident, and the reporting
on the findings of the inquiry. Any necessary, minor corrective action,
such as employee counseling, is also handled by the line supervisor.
Whether the complaint is serious or trivial, the complainant must be
notified of the results of the inquiry or investigation.

More serious allegations, such as alleged criminal acts by police
employees, may be reported in writing by the supervisor for a more
detailed investigation by other members of the department such as
investigators of the internal affairs unit. Hopefully, however, the first-
line supervisor will become involved once again at the review and disposition end of the internal inquiry that involves any of his subordinates.

The experienced police supervisor knows that all sorts of people
complain about or at least question the logic of police actions for all
sorts of reasons, some good and some otherwise. The same experienced supervisor knows that complaints may range from the fifteen
year old unhappy because he got picked up for violating a curfew ordi-
nance to the wizened ex-con busted for armed robbery. He knows,
too, that the real reasons for this reporting can range from the innocent but puzzled individual, who truthfully believes he was wronged,

to the arrestee seeking revenge against the officer who caught him doing wrong.

One medium-sized police agency compiled an interesting set of citizen complaint statistics from a representative year of police operations. First, they broke down the complaints by source, age, and sex:

SOURCE OF ALLEGATION OF MISCONDUCT

Individuals	193
Organizations/Businesses	3
Government agencies	3
Internal (from within dept.)	7

AGE OF REPORTING PARTY		SEX OF REPORTING PARTY	
Under 14	0	Female	69
14–17	4	Male	127
18–25	31	Unknown	9
26–45	79		
46 and over	29		
Age unknown	67		

No one was too surprised when the results showed that those very active by sex and age group in criminal activities (borne out by other statistics) were also among the most likely to object to police actions.

Another set of figures revealed the kinds of police activities resulting in citizen complaints:

ACTIVITY BEING PERFORMED

Arrest	49	Follow-up investigation	22
Booking	2	Off-duty actions	4
Summons writing	23	Patrol duty	21
Court presentation	2	Telephone courtesy	5
Desk duty	1	Report taking	1
Dispatching	5	Traffic direction	1
Preliminary investigation	123	Other	19

In another sample year, the same police agency classified the duty assignments of the specific personnel complained against. Once more, there were no real surprises:

EMPLOYEE'S ASSIGNMENT

Patrol	592
Investigations	73
Intelligence	4
Support services	7
Inspectional services	1
Crime prevention	30

The police man or woman most frequently in contact with the public under a variety of stresses and related unfavorable conditions quite naturally bore the brunt of complainants' questions. This could be correlated with a table showing the rank or position in the agency of the employees who were complained upon:

POSITION OF EMPLOYEE

Officer	248
Sergeant	24
Lieutenant	0
Captain	0
Civilian	15

Even if the police agency finds that the majority of the complaints against its personnel are unwarranted, a considerable amount of effort must be directed at receiving, investigating, and otherwise processing the aggrieved party's questions or complaints. The first-line supervisor is certainly a part of all this.

The well-organized law enforcement agency will allow its first-line supervisors a good deal of discretion in handling minor complaints and inquiries regarding policy, procedure, or statute. Whether the situation is handled verbally with no written record made or whether some kind of form must be completed by the grievance processor varies from one agency to another. The old rule of thumb requiring the application of common sense and "an absolute minimum of paperwork to get the job done" certainly could be applied here.

The traffic-related question would be a good example of the inquiry handled with a minimum of fuss and red tape. Here the supervisor receives the complaint or question, either by telephone, e-mail or in person, and learns what he can from the reporting party. He may be able to answer a legal or procedural question immediately from his own knowledge of police tactics, rules, policies and laws. If not, he then makes independent inquiry into what happened. He, of course, lets the complainant know that he will get back in touch with an answer as soon as possible. The inquiry may require that he ask the employees involved about the incident. It may call for review of police reports, summonses, and other documents.

Whatever he must accomplish to answer the question, the supervisor does so as quickly as possible and gets back in touch with the party involved. The smart supervisor realizes that handling all such inquiries or complaints in a timely manner benefits everyone involved and helps the police agency's image of responsiveness, as well.

If his inquiry has revealed some fault on the part of an employee or the agency as a whole, the police leader sets the wheels in motion to remedy the problem. This may call for a counseling session with an employee or an overhaul of an antiquated procedure, but it must be accomplished if repeats of the same difficulty are to be avoided.

A sample of such a supervisor-handled inquiry should be of value. For illustrative purposes, an incident from a department that requires written records be kept of routine inquiries will be used. It should be kept in mind, however, that more informal handling of such incidents is also possible and may be preferable in many instances.

MEMO ON CITIZEN INQUIRY

PERSON CALLING: Ms. Josephine Small
ADDRESS: 10065 W. Eighth Avenue
TELEPHONE: 232-6009
DATE AND TIME OF INCIDENT: 2-20-09, 3 PM
DATE AND TIME OF COMPLAINT: 2-20-09, 4 PM
COMPLAINT OR INQUIRY: "Why was the police officer using his horn instead of his siren? He almost ran over me. . . ."

Ms. Small said that she was driving northbound on Garrison Street at First Avenue at about 30 mph when a police patrol car approached her from behind. She said the police car passed her on the left at about 45 mph, crossing a yellow double-stripe on the pavement to do so. She said that the officer, who had his car's red lights on, honked his horn as he passed her but did not use his siren. Ms. Small said she drove off the edge of the pavement and almost lost control of her car as she tried to get out of the way. She told this supervisor that "I thought cops were supposed to use their sirens when they were going to drive like crazy."

This supervisor learned from Ms. Small that Car #5 had been the one involved in this incident. This supervisor then contacted the driver of car #5–Patrol Officer Joe Leaman. He advised me that he was responding to a burglary-in-progress call near Third and Garrison. He said he was not using his siren as he did not want to scare away the burglars before he arrived. He did not remember Ms. Small's vehicle, but did recall that he was traveling about 45 mph in the area of Garrison and First, which he remembered did have a double-yellow stripe.

Patrol Officer Leaman was operating within the limitations set by departmental policies and procedures in approaching a burglary-in-progress scene without his siren. However, it is this supervisor's opinion that the speed at which he passed Ms. Small's car on a narrow roadway marked for "no passing" was risky under the existing conditions–moderate to heavy traffic and a wet pavement, as reported by Officer Leaman himself.

Officer Leaman was cautioned not to repeat such driving behavior, in lieu of more serious departmental action. He indicated that he understood and would be careful in the future.

This supervisor contacted Ms. Small by telephone and advised her of the results of this inquiry. She indicated that she understood why the officer was driving in that manner and had now "cooled off" some. She desired no further action.

Signed,
Georgia Goodman #1208
Sergeant

There are any number of inquiry or complaint situations that can and should be handled by the first-line supervisor. A partial listing of suggested topics to be handled by the line-level boss might include the following:

1. General questions on departmental policies
2. General questions on departmental procedures
3. Questions on police authority and responsibility
4. Questions on police tactics and practices
5. Questions on traffic law enforcement guidelines

6. Inquiries on handcuff use
7. Inquiries on booking and release procedures
8. Inquiries regarding use of force guidelines
9. Inquiries regarding search and seizure policies
10. Inquiries about seized evidence/property disposition.

There are, of course, many other areas of concern that can be quickly and accurately addressed by the police supervisor.

The point remains that some citizens will not be pleased with the researched response they receive from the supervisor, and they may indicate a desire to lodge their complaint farther up in the agency's chain of command. This is their right, and the supervisor faced with the persistent and still dissatisfied complainant should make the appropriate reference upstairs. It remains true, however, that the citizen unhappy with the timely reply received from the supervisor will very likely be just as displeased with the reply he receives later from higher up in the police organization. Often, the two responses will vary little in content.

More serious allegations of misconduct by police employees will require more in-depth investigation. Such investigations may, depending on departmental policy, be handled by the supervisor himself or by a special internal affairs unit. Other agencies may use still other methods by assigning the investigation to detectives, other supervisors, or managers.

As with the less serious inquiry, there are any number of subjects for complaint that would demand a deeper look at the facts. A listing of such topics requiring extensive investigation might include the following:

1. Complaints of police excessive force
2. Complaints of criminal acts by police employees
3. Complaints of immoral or unethical conduct by police
4. Complaints of false arrest
5. Complaints of rights violations and abuse.

Although all complaints of this nature would appear to be, at first glance, serious ones requiring careful and extensive investigation, the police supervisor also should exercise common sense in deciding upon how to proceed on the basis of what he has heard. He may want to include his own boss in the decision-making process. At the very least, his boss should be advised of the circumstances of the complaint of serious misconduct at the very earliest opportunity. *Remember:* supervisors and managers alike do not like surprises!

Common sense in making a decision on how to proceed should include an initial evaluation by the receiving supervisor of both the complaint and the complainant. The attitude, apparent sincerity, and general emotional stability of the complainant would be among the factors noted by the alert supervisor. It is highly unlikely, for instance, that anyone's best interests would be served by launching a full-blown investigation of the complaint alleging that officers transported the complainant to a spaceship and tapped his brain waves.

When the supervisor does become involved in an ongoing investigation of employee misconduct, the general requirements and guidelines surrounding any competent police investigation should apply here, too. Rights advisements will be necessary when criminal wrongdoing is suspected. In addition, the supervisor must remain especially conscious of his own attitude. He is an impartial fact-finder. He is not a prejudiced advocate for any party.

On occasion, the supervisor may find himself involved in conducting an investigation into a serious allegation of employee misconduct that involves alleged criminal activity. On such an assignment the police leader can rely on his usual skill for obtaining facts from victims, witnesses and assorted others who may have details to bring to bear on the case. It is in the supervisor's handling of the accused police employee that a different approach will be required. It all comes about because of a court case entitled *Garrity v. New Jersey.*

In *Garrity,* a representative of the Attorney General's Office interviewed several officers about their participation in an alleged ticket "fixing" scam. Prior to interview, the officers were told, in effect:

- That anything they said could be used against them in criminal proceedings.
- That they had the right to refuse to answer questions if doing so would incriminate them.
- That the Failure to answer the questions would subject them to being fired.

The officers were thus put in the position of either answering the questions and possibly being prosecuted or refusing to answer and being terminated from employment.

Several officers answered the questions and were subsequently convicted. The officers appealed their convictions on the grounds that they were coerced by threat of termination into answering the questions. The Supreme Court agreed that the information provided by the officers was indeed coerced under the threat of firing.

Since *Garrity,* public employers including police agencies have realized that self-incriminating statements obtained from employees who have been "ordered to talk" cannot subsequently be used against those employees in criminal proceedings. That is why an officer accused of misconduct that may also be a crime often will find himself the subject of two, separate investigations: one conducted by internal affairs investigators and a second carried out by criminal squad detectives. While the criminal detectives may share their information with internal affairs, the opposite does not hold true for information learned by internal affairs investigators from a "forced" interview with the employee.

What all of this means to the supervisor-turned-investigator is that he must proceed carefully to help assure that all interests, including those of the accused employee, are treated as protected. If what the supervisor knows about the incident or accusation includes even the slightest possibility that criminal conduct has occurred, he is obligated to give the employee what has come to be termed the *Garrity advisement.*

Most police agencies prefer to give an employee the Garrity advisement in writing and obtain the employee's signature that it has been received. The advisement is often provided on a preprinted form and may look something like this:

ADVISEMENT FOR ADMINISTRATIVE OR INTERNAL AFFAIRS INTERVIEWS PURSUANT TO THE GARRITY DECISION

You are being questioned regarding an official administrative investigation by the _____ Police Department. You will be asked questions specifically directed and narrowly related to the performance of your official

duties or fitness for office, and your knowledge of pertinent events.

If you answer truthfully, neither your statements nor any information or evidence which is gained by reason of such statements can be used against you in any subsequent criminal proceeding. However, these statements may be used against you in relation to a subsequent administrative personnel action.

If you answer untruthfully, your statements or any information or evidence which is gained by reason of such statements can be used against you in any subsequent criminal proceeding.

You are entitled to all the rights and privileges guaranteed by the laws and Constitution of this state and the Constitution of the United States, including the right not to be compelled to incriminate yourself. If you refuse to testify or answer questions relating to the performance of your official duties or fitness for duty, you will be subject to administrative personnel action which will result in your dismissal from the Police Department.

Interviewer_____   Date_____

Interviewer/Witness_____   Date_____

Employee _____   Date_____

When the need for *Garrity* arises, the smart first-line leader will seek the play-by-play guidance of his boss, his department legal advisor or attorney, and/or the Internal Affairs specialists in his organization. When *Garrity-related* issues are involved, it is worth slowing things down to be sure everything is done correctly. The welfare of the employee, the public and the law enforcement organization itself demand no less.

The supervisor must remain courteous and open while interviewing complainant and police employee alike. His job is to obtain information, not to blame, accuse, or convict anyone. As in any other sort of police investigation, the investigator who advertises a poor attitude may not be too successful in obtaining the information being sought.

The supervisor may wish to tape-record a lengthy or complex interview, in addition to taking detailed notes. This is just one more investigative technique, but the presence and purpose of the tape recorder should be explained to the interviewee whether he or she is a citizen or an employee. A fearful or mistrusting interviewee will not be a very informative source.

Some agencies replace or supplement the interview with the involved employee by requesting a letter or memorandum covering the issues in question. The employee thus provides a written record of his side of the story as he recalls it. He is thereby given a little better chance to organize his thoughts than he might have when responding orally to an interviewer's queries.

In the following example situation, a patrol sergeant has requested one of his officers to prepare such a written response to aid in the investigation of an arrestee's complaint of theft and general mistreatment by arresting officers. The officer, who had been called to assist another officer (who also was writing a memorandum to the supervisor), submitted an answering memorandum to his sergeant:

MEMORANDUM

TO: Herman Melrose, Sergeant
            Patrol Division
FROM: Joe Doakes, Patrol Officer
            Patrol Division
DATE: October 21, 2009
SUBJECT: Arrest of Mary Martin (Case Number: 09-98877)

On the afternoon of 10-20-09, reporting officer was called to Carr and Alameda Streets to assist Officer Blake in transporting an intoxicated and uncooperative female prisoner. Reporting officer spent the next two hours with the prisoner and Officer Blake, as the woman was transported to St. Anthony's Hospital for an examination and was then taken to Jefferson County Jail for incarceration.

Reporting officer stayed with the arrestee, Mary Martin, in the back seat of the patrol unit during these transports, as she was alternately kicking and thrashing about and had to be restrained so as not to hurt herself or damage the police car's windows.

While the arrestee was being transported, her purse was in the front seat of the patrol car. She had no personal property with her in the back seat, for safety reasons. At the hospital, the patrol car doors and windows were secured while officers literally carried the uncooperative subject inside. When officers arrived back at the car with the arrestee after about an hour in the emergency room, the car doors and windows were still secured. The arrestee's purse had not been molested.

The arrestee, still verbally abusive and resistive, was taken to the jail. Reporting officer carried arrestee's purse into the jail and turned it over to deputies there. This officer observed Detention Deputy Paula Smith inventory the prisoner's property, which included just over $22 in cash. The deputy counted the money in front of the arrestee, who then turned to this officer and Officer Blake and said, "You little crooks. I had over $500 in there." She then cursed everyone present, and repeated the statement.

At no time did this officer see more than $22 on or about arrestee Mary Martin.

It might be noted that upon being examined by the physician at St. Anthony's Hospital, arrestee was described by him as suffering from no more than "extreme alcohol intoxication."

Thus, the issues of the arrestee's money as well as her general treatment have been covered. With the memorandum from the initial arresting officer, the complainant's statement, and the information of any other witnesses, the investigation should be nearing completion.

When all the facts on a given incident are in, the supervisor must put this information together in a format that can be easily read and worked with by those in the chain of command who must review and act upon the findings. One useful format divides the presentation into several segments:

Specific Complaint(s)

Here the details of the complaint are stated. Sample complaints might be "Excessive Force" or "Improper Tactics."

Background Information

The situation leading up to and involving the complaint are noted here. Witnesses, complainants, and police employees involved would be listed in this section.

Investigation

The details of the investigation follow. Who was interviewed and what they said will be summarized. Complete statements, tape transcripts, and memorandums will be included elsewhere in the presentation, probably at the end.

Finding of Fact

The investigating supervisor's fact-based conclusions will go here. Whether the accusations are true or unfounded will be stated, based upon the investigative findings. If an answer cannot be found on a particular issue, this will be stated.

An allegation that cannot be proven must be declared to be unfounded. The police employee must receive at least the same presumption of innocence that is accorded the criminal defendant at trial.

Recommendations

If the supervisor is recommending discipline or corrective action, the suggestions should go into this section. Recommendations of commendations for personnel also should go here. Commendations for employees who have performed ethically and responsibly in the face of extreme provocation always should be emphasized.

Complainants and involved employees should receive prompt notification of the investigative findings. The supervisor might include his recommendations of how this is to take place: letter, telephone, or personal contact.

Attachments

Transcripts of taped interviews, copies of pertinent police reports, letters, and any other documents involved fall into this category. The section is something of a catchall for lengthy material that would slow down and otherwise complicate the review of the investigation. At the same time, it provides sources for reference if details are needed on a given issue.

Accomplishing necessary notifications of the results of the investigation also may involve the supervisor. Some departments want their supervisors to take care of such notifications orally–for employees and civilian complainants alike. Others want to retain a written record of the matter and wish to add to the file a written notification of the investigation's disposition as reported to those involved. Such memorandums or letters become a part of the file of the incident and its investigation.

A written notification of findings to the involved employee(s) also may be the job of the first-line supervisor. In some agencies, it might be written by the supervisor but signed by someone higher up in the chain of command. At any rate, such a notification is often prepared in the memorandum format:

MEMORANDUM

TO: Patrol Officer Sam Snoley
FROM: Chief Bob Boston
DATE: February 15, 2009
SUBJECT: Complaint of Arrestee Kenneth Kass

Mr. Kass alleged that officers were discourteous to him and did not perform properly while arresting him on February 1, 2009. You were one of the officers complained against by Mr. Kass.

The above complaint has been investigated and on the basis of available evidence has been classified as unfounded: the allegation is false or inaccurate.

The report of this investigation will be maintained in the confidential files of the Personnel Investigations Unit. The complaint will not appear in your personnel file.

The complaining party also must receive notification of the investigative findings. Using this same incident as an example, Mr. Kass might receive the following letter, once again prepared by the line supervisor for his own superiors' review and the chief's signature:

Mr. Kenneth Kass
601 Circle Street
Lakewood, CO 80228

On February 2, 2009, in a telephone conversation with Sergeant Joe

Smith, you alleged that officers of this department were discourteous and did not perform properly while arresting you the previous night. Specifically, you charged that you were humiliated by being handcuffed in your own home, that you were denied treatment for an injured foot and a migraine headache, and that the officers' actions prohibited you from telling your side of the story. I have had these allegations investigated and wish to convey the findings to you.

As you will recall, you were arrested at your home after your wife Betsy called this department saying that you were trying to kill her. When the officers arrived, they found your wife in the yard, hysterical, and in need of emergency medical aid. The circumstances, along with your wife's statements, quite properly led the officers to the decision to arrest you. When that decision was made, the decision to handcuff you was equally proper, inasmuch as you were being taken into custody for a violent crime, which was a felony.

You were, in fact, taken to Central Hospital for treatment of your alleged injury and headache. The hospital examination revealed no injuries, and the attending physician further advised that your requests for codeine and Valium® for an alleged headache should be denied.

You alleged that you were not allowed to tell your side of the story. Police reports reveal that the officers advised you of your rights and that you subsequently refused to say anything at all regarding the incident. This is your right to remain silent, but you can hardly expect the officers to continue to attempt to question or interview you after you have invoked it.

In short, Mr. Kass, the investigation shows that your allegations are without merit. The only conclusion to be had from the facts is that the officers did a commendable job in a disagreeable situation.

(signature)
Bob Boston
Chief of Police

Written or other notifications arising out of a complaint investigation that *did* find police misconduct would be somewhat different in the message delivered, but the format would remain about the same. In such a case, the employee notification prepared by the supervisor likely will include a reference to anticipated corrective action:

MEMORANDUM

TO: Sam Smith, Patrol Officer
               Patrol Division
FROM: Steve Shiffen, Sergeant
               Patrol Division
DATE: April 9, 2009
SUBJECT: Misconduct Complaint and Disciplinary Action

On April 1, 2009, a Mr. Joe Jones complained to this department that you utilized excessive force in affecting his arrest earlier that date. As a result, a thorough investigation of the complaint has been made. The investigation has determined that you did, in fact, utilize unnecessary and improper force in that you struck, with a closed fist, a prisoner in your custody who was handcuffed and was not then resisting. This is in direct violation of Departmental Policy B 6732.

You are to be suspended from duty, without pay, for one week, commencing on April 15, 2009. Your obligations and responsibilities to the department during this time will be explained to you at a later date.

You are further warned that the occurrence of a similar incident of excessive force by you in the future will result in stronger formal corrective action being taken, including but not limited to discharge from employment and the filing of criminal assault charges against you.

This department's discipline appeal procedure is explained on page 29 of the Department Manual. Your primary supervisor will answer any specific questions you might have regarding the procedure. He also can assist you in the filing of an appeal if you elect to do so.

The complainant also must receive notification of the results of the investigation. It is neither necessary nor desirable that the supervisor provide the complainant with specifics of corrective action taken with employees. He is, however, obligated to report accurately on the department's findings:

Mr. Joe Jones
309 Woodrow Avenue
Lakewood, CO 80228

On April 1, 2009, you alleged in a telephone conversation with Sergeant Steve Shiffen that an officer of this agency used excessive force in arresting you on the same date. You stated that you were struck unnecessarily during the arrest process.

It is the policy of this agency to investigate fully all allegations of misconduct by its employees. I have caused an investigation to be made of the circumstances surrounding your arrest and subsequent complaint.

An extensive inquiry conducted by this department revealed that officers responding to a drunk disturbance complaint at the Waterloo Bar on April 1, 2009 found you to be the source of the disturbance: you were intoxicated, loud, and had already engaged in a fight with another bar patron prior to the officers' arrival. The officers legally and properly arrested you for disorderly conduct.

Witness accounts revealed that you violently resisted the officers' attempts to handcuff you. After you were handcuffed, you spit in the face of one of the officers. It was at this point that an incident of improper conduct by an officer took place.

The police reports and your own statements indicate that you were uninjured during this incident. You required no medical attention or treatment.

Although your own unlawful and improper actions led to the unfortunate encounter of April 1, this department will not tolerate improper action by its personnel. Prompt disciplinary action has been taken with the officer responsible.

Thank you for bringing this matter to my attention.

(signature)
Bob Boston
Chief of Police

The supervisor probably will find few tasks less pleasant than writing notices of reprimand to his people and letters admitting police misconduct to arrestees and others. However unpleasant these tasks may be for him, they remain integral parts of his total job responsibilities. They must be faithfully executed if the police agency's effectiveness, reputation, and credibility are to be protected. If both employees and public are to be adequately and honestly served, the supervisor can do no less.

INTERNAL COMPLAINTS

The police supervisor also must remain sensitive to the problems and complaints of his fellow supervisors. He must stay equally attentive to the concerns of those in other units and sections of the law enforcement agency. If he is to expect others to act upon his own concerns, he must grant equal attention to their problems.

What sort of complaints and concerns should the supervisor expect from his peers? It is difficult to identify a specific set of gripes in advance, but some time-honored concerns appear to be consistently present. "Lack of communication" heads the list of causes for internal squabbling in many police agencies. Also known as the old "left hand doesn't know what the right is doing" syndrome, this problem, where prevalent, can result in a waste of resources and otherwise cause ineffective police operations. A simple example situation might be seen in the bad guy who is being followed around by officers of both the robbery and vice details of a large department, each unaware of the other's interest. Clearly, this is unacceptable for a number of reasons, officer safety foremost among them.

Many other very real situations find various elements of the police agency operating at apparent cross-purposes with one another. The best prevention for such a problem is constant and continuing direct communication among the line supervisors of the agency. Detective sergeants who meet with their patrol division peers regularly and sergeants from other departmental entities at least occasionally help avoid the dangers brought about by a lack of internal communication. The line supervisors of other departmental units are, of course, expected to do the same.

Communication-conscious police supervisors also encourage the officers under them to engage in a free exchange of information with police personnel elsewhere, within and without their department. In so doing, these supervisors may be avoiding unpleasant surprises and bad feelings at a later date.

The perception of unequal or prejudicial treatment of other employees of the department is another source of internal dissatisfaction and employee complaint. If the robbery detective thinks he is being sorely mistreated because he must carry an "issue" weapon while the undercover vice officer can carry a smaller firearm, internal grievances may well result, at least insofar as that detective is concerned. It is the job of the detective's supervisor to hear the complaint and ferret out the reasoning behind the varying treatment of otherwise equal employees. He then may be able to defuse his subordinate's beef by relating to him the departmental logic in the differences in weaponry: the vice officer needs a more easily concealed weapon, and the smaller weapon fulfills this requirement nicely.

While he should not engage in rumor-mongering himself any more than he tolerates it among his troops, the wise supervisor will keep his ears open for indications of real or perceived internal problems, especially those that involve his own unit, team, or section. He will then act to ascertain the validity of the information, identify the difficulty, and take action to resolve the issue within the limits of his authority.

EMPLOYEE GRIEVANCES

Police employees of today will not long tolerate the abuses and unfair practices that permeated many law enforcement agencies in an earlier age. This is as it should be. Police employees, not unlike workers in so many other fields, demand some kind of process by which their complaints of improper treatment can be heard and acted upon in an effective manner. This is a clearly reasonable expectation for the working man or woman.

The line supervisor plays a vital role in any grievance process or proceeding. It is at this level that the employee's problem should first be brought to official attention. It is likely that the perceived difficulty will have been brought to the supervisor's attention even before any formal redress is sought, if for no other reason than the supervisor's recognized ability to give a fair and informed "second opinion" to a troubled employee.

Even within those police agencies that have placed rigid, formal guidelines on their grievance procedures, the complaining employee's immediate supervisor is assigned an important role in the procedure. These agencies get the supervisor involved in two ways. First of all, he and the distraught employee are encouraged to resolve the issue informally between them whenever possible. Failing in this, the primary supervisor is generally the next step in the chain to whom the written, formal grievance is presented. The established procedure probably dictates a time limit within which the supervisor makes a written reply to the grievance. If the employee remains dissatisfied with the decision, he proceeds to the next level in the grievance chain, and a new set of time constraints goes into effect.

The emphasis is upon the supervisor's value in resolving the grievance as quickly and with as little disruption as possible. In doing so he can, of course, only make those offerings and concessions that his rank level allow him to make. At times, however, his attention to the problems of his employee may result in the employee achieving at the outset all he really wanted in the first place: the sincere, empathetic attention of a representative of management. The supervisor may not be able to change things for him, but he can appreciate his concerns.

The police leader will need to call upon all of his counselor's skills in hearing the grievance of his employee. He must listen attentively and listen well. He must be patient. He must permit the employee to talk freely, yet gently bring him back to the subject under discussion if he wanders afield. He must be able to give opinions without bias and deliver the facts without coloring them.

The police supervisor engaged at any stage of the grievance proceeding must remain mindful of his equal obligations to employees and management. He must avoid cheating or deceiving either, knowing that his credibility and continued effectiveness as a leader are hanging in the balance. He must walk a line of true objectivity, with the pitfalls of being labeled a "company man" or a "rabble rouser" on either side of this thinly stretched line.

As a recipient and processor of employee grievances, the supervisor must at all times preserve his reputation as a fair and just individual. Past feelings about individual employees, procedures, or policies must be put to the back of the mind in a sincere effort at impartial and honest action.

The supervisor also may become involved in a grievance proceeding by sitting on a departmental grievance or appeal board. The same guidance is appropriate here as served him well in his role as complaint recipient and processor. He must be thoroughly attentive to the facts presented him and must be impartial in any decisions he reaches as a result of hearing and analyzing the facts. He realizes that he best serves the employees and the organization by performing his job of "hearing officer" in such a fashion.

LABOR ISSUES

More and more today, employee associations, organizations, and unions are quite active. They are getting more numerous with larger memberships of employees and are forming in fields of work where a decade ago they were rare.

Any good working definition for the term *union* would note that such a word refers to a grouping or association of persons with some sort of a formal organizational structure and some specified reasons or purposes for existing. In the case of the police employees' labor union or association, those specified reasons and purposes naturally would revolve around the police organization and its treatment of its workers.

The term *labor,* so frequently connected with *union* as it is used in the manager/worker relationship, is equally easy to define. Generally, it may be used in reference to the work force or the group of employees whose actions most directly carry out the organization's goals and objectives. The police officer would certainly fall into such an employee grouping.

The police supervisor must be prepared to work in an agency where unions exist. Given the current trends in unionizing movements, there is no reason to believe that the department that has no union today might not have one tomorrow. This should not be a cause for alarm for the responsible supervisor. The stated purposes of police employee organizations usually relate to assuring fair and just treatment for their membership. The socially responsible police union does not try to take over the authority of management nor render the line supervisor helpless. Responsible union members are aware that destroying a police organization's effective management ultimately destroys the effectiveness of the organization itself.

The responsible police labor organization does not advocate anything that should be inherently distasteful to the police supervisor. The concerns and issues stirring the interest of police employee groups often fall into several, traditional categories, although not necessarily in the order of importance listed here:

1. Better overall working conditions and communication
2. Recognition and respect for employees
3. Some advisory role in management's decision making
4. Improved salary and benefits
5. Social benefits and increased officer solidarity; a sense of belonging to something worthwhile
6. No retribution for union activities
7. Fair disciplinary procedures

8. Fair hiring and promotional procedures
9. Recognition and respect for the union or association
10. Increased job security.

Many of the concerns expressed by the members of the police organization are little different from those voiced by union members in other lines of work. Good working conditions, fair pay, a say in how the organization is run, knowing what is going on and job security are topics dear to the hearts of all workers. They are also concerns shared by the supervisor in the police agency.

The police supervisor should not become a prominent fixture in the management/labor disagreement only after a problem has become full blown and has already resulted in bad feelings and poor police service. Ideally, the supervisor should be able to serve on a continuing basis as a relay between management and labor for their respective concerns. In such a way, the supervisor might be able to help defuse a potential problem by passing along strong feelings of either group and helping initiate corrective action while there is yet time. His serving in such an "early warning" capacity helps everyone.

What the association or union member wants does not pose a serious problem for the police supervisor, at least not often. The methods by which the union member attempts to achieve his aims and register his feelings may, on occasion, bring about a bit more cause for concern on the supervisor's part. "Job actions" such as planned enforcement slowdowns may result in officers taking enforcement action for only the most serious law violations. Enforcement slowdowns may affect a given target area, such as traffic law enforcement, or may cover a wide range of police enforcement activities, including the enforcement of the criminal statutes.

If continued over an extended time period, enforcement slowdowns may result in rising public concern that the criminal element will take note of reduced police activity. Consequently, citizen pressure for the police agency and its officers to settle their differences may be brought to bear. In some jurisdictions, "job actions" may be unlawful.

A variation of the enforcement slowdown may see the agency's officers engaging in a very selective approach to the work they will or will not do. While emergency calls for service will continue to be handled promptly, lower priority calls for routine service may be answered slowly, if at all.

The supervisor might be placed in the position of attempting to explain to citizens why their requests for service are being neglected. In such a situation, the supervisor may find that his reluctant subordinates are fast approaching insubordination, if not already arrived.

Exactly the opposite of the enforcement or work slowdown, the enforcement speedup may be an attempt to influence management's policies or stands by glutting the criminal justice system with a huge volume of officer-initiated enforcement work.

The police association member truthfully will state that he is doing nothing illegal or immoral here. He is enforcing the very letter of the law. He and his peers may be issuing summonses for petty violations of the law that would normally be overlooked: speeding 33 mph in a 30 mph zone, petty littering, license plate light burned out, etc. A drastic increase in police enforcement of minor ordinances carried out over an extended period of time is practically guaranteed to bring a stream of citizen protests to the chief's office.

Very much of this sort of activity damages the reputation of the employees' association as much as it does the credibility of the police agency. In the end, everyone loses.

While the actual strike or work stoppage by police officers is illegal in many locales, the mass sickout or "blue flu" epidemic is more widely utilized as a technique by which frustrated labor groups strive to get a point across. More than a few urban areas have felt the impact of the mass sickout style of job action in the past.

Results have varied widely: some jurisdictions afflicted by a police sickout have suffered almost immediate violence and disorder. More areas, however, have seen little or no increase in criminal activity, as supervisory and command personnel work the streets.

In any case, a loss of support for the police agency as well as for the protesting employee association has been the public's reaction in many such instances. Once again, both sides in the management/labor dispute have lost something worth saving, regardless of who might otherwise be said to "win" the confrontation. In such a sad state of affairs there can be no real winners. Everyone loses.

Another tactic occasionally relied on by the unhappy employee organization will call for the enforcement actions to be targeted or concentrated on a particular group of potential violators. County officials may suddenly find themselves the victims of increased surveillance of their driving habits. City vehicles may begin receiving an inordinate number of parking and "unsafe vehicle" citations. Downtown merchants may find that their customers' parking habits, which have been ignored for years, are receiving increased scrutiny from officers.

Once in a great while, the tool of mass resignations will be used by an organization or allied group of law enforcement personnel. One group of female support personnel walked off the job because of alleged sexual harassment by the chief of police; elsewhere, a group of officers quit because of a judge's excessively lenient handling of a violent local crook.

This technique is a dangerous one for the personnel involved. There is no guarantee that the local governing body will not announce a collective "good riddance" and start over with new employees. The agency's head loses, too: there, in full view of the public, is the thinly veiled accusation that he cannot control his own organization. His employment future there may begin to dim rather quickly. The public loses, too, as the quality of police service declines drastically. Depending on the outcome of the dispute, the cut in service may last for quite some time. Once again, everyone loses, especially the cops.

In all of these altercations between police employees and police management, the police supervisor is there, if uncomfortably so. As a part of both the managerial and work forces, his position is a unique one. He must continue to relay management's orders and translate them into effective police action. At the same time, he must remain attentive to the concerns and feelings of his troops, who may all be association or union members. In many agencies, the supervisor himself may be a member of the employees' association.

The police supervisor in the middle of a police labor dispute must, more than ever, remain mindful of his obligation to stay impartial and just in his dealings with superior and subordinate. He does not use his hard-earned rapport with his subordinates to spy on them for management. At the same time, he does not tolerate insubordination or neglect of duty. When improper police behavior occurs, he initiates appropriate investigative and corrective measures.

The supervisor may find his lot an even harder one if the dispute deteriorates to the point where he is called upon to verify officers' illness reports with visits to the homes of the "ailing" employees. He may find the need for great reserves of patience if he must endure the taunts and remarks of sidelined subordinates while he does their work in their stead.

The police supervisor faced with such an unpleasant situation cannot have too much ability to forget and forgive—he will need all that he can possibly muster. The conflict will pass. Long-nurtured grudges accomplish little. The supervisor stung by the less-than-kind comments or actions of fellow police officers might try to remain mindful of the frustrations and concerns that have brought them to this point. The situation and their reactions become more understandable even if no less painful when the police leader realizes that he may agree with some of their fears and demands.

Impartiality, patience, and an ability to take unhappy moments or acts with a grain of salt remain the watchwords for the police supervisor confronted with a fully blossomed labor protest. He must still lead. He must still control and direct. He must, in a few words, still be a supervisor. He continues to do his job, no matter what.

These demands do not preclude him from remaining an honest and caring advocate of his employees' feelings and worries. Representing their job welfare to management remains one of his most urgent duties.

As he represents his employees, the supervisor's own impartiality and fairness must stay above reproach. Such demands are not small ones for the man or woman who would lead others in an honorable profession. Then again, neither should the stature of the competent police leader be anything less than large.

SUMMARY

The police supervisor must hear and address grievances, appeals and complaints from a variety of sources. He must hear citizens' allegations of police misconduct and fairly investigate and follow up on them. He must receive employees' grievances against the police organization and its rules, regulations, policies, procedures and staff actions and attempt to resolve these, too.

As the one in the middle, the supervisor must work to maintain his integrity and neutrality as he gives testimony in a disciplinary, labor or appeal proceeding. It is all a part of his role as an impartial, patient and responsive complaint processor for other peoples' problems. It is a role vital to the well-being of the citizens, the employees and the management of the agency he serves.

POINTS TO REMEMBER

- The supervisor has a key role to play in receiving and investigating citizen and employee complaints.
- No complaint should be ruled out as "impossible" until at least a cursory examination of the facts has been completed.
- The supervisor must be familiar with the requirements of *Garrity*.
- The supervisor will follow his agency's format for written documentation of complaints and his response to them.
- The supervisor must maintain his professionalism and impartiality when handling employee grievances and union complaints.
- The ethical supervisor continues to do his job ethically and well while complaints and grievances of various kinds are being addressed.

Chapter Thirteen

SOME SPECIAL PROBLEMS

My boss is (choose one):

    a. an incompetent
    b. a crook
    c. a tyrant
    d. all of the above
    e. worse than any of the above.

What, if anything, should I do about it? A lot of books and articles have been written about supervision in general and, in a lesser number, police supervision in specific. Many things have been discussed in this gray sea of words, but little has been said of the police supervisor who feels he is faced by a question similar to the multiple-choice dilemma opening this chapter.

There are many more such perplexing questions and problems facing the professional police leader today. These matters are of a real and driving concern to him, as well they should be. They are talked about, sometimes in a semi-furtive manner, over coffee or in police cars with other police supervisors. They are the subject of many a late-night, bedroom discussion between the supervisor and someone near to him. At the same time, these sensitive issues are seldom addressed in the literature available on the topics of supervision and leadership in policing.

Any topic so obviously important to the police leader deserves all the light that informed discussion and argument can shed upon it. Inasmuch as police officers are (by training or nature) very curious and inquisitive creatures, it should surprise no one who knows anything at all about cops that the "cream of the crop" of police people—police supervisors—are highly thoughtful and imaginative people themselves.

When police supervisors get together with others like themselves—others with whom they feel they can talk freely—several traditional concerns seems to arise:

1. "What does this career hold in store for me? Isn't there something better somewhere?"
2. "My subordinates don't appreciate me and my boss doesn't understand me. Why do I continue to take such abuse?"
3. "The organization I'm a part of is not a very good one. It's ineffective at best. I don't see how it will ever change."
4. "My department is full of internal spying, back biting, and political intrigue. An honest, hard-working person doesn't stand a chance for advancement against the two-faced bootlicker. If I just had a job that would pay as well, I'd be gone tomorrow."

Frustration, resentment, perceived helplessness: all of these feelings are contained in such statements. The complaints may have been condensed, simplified, or even exaggerated for effect here. The feelings and fears represented by such statements are, however, very real among American police supervisors. Specific questions and complaints may vary in their terms and particulars from one place to another. However, the underlying discomfort and uncertainty remain the same.

Such supervisory questioning and concern are among the subjects that this chapter proposes to explore. It is hoped that the effort will help to reverse the trend of neglect that these topics have suffered in the past.

STRAIGHT TALK

It has been stated that the first-line police supervisor is something of a hybrid creation. He is not another cop on the street. Neither is he always welcomed to the top echelons of the management team. He is a part of each of these groups, but he is not wholly a member of either. The honest, conscientious supervisor is appreciated for what he is by upper management and street officers alike, but he is simply not considered an intimate part of either group.

The supervisor knows that, no matter how much rapport he builds with his people, there are always going to be those few things that they cannot bring themselves to tell him. No matter how much the majority of his people may trust him, his other role as a part of management will keep them from baring absolutely all in his presence.

He occasionally will have to discipline his subordinates or take other actions that they do not accept. Most of the time they will get over any resentment they may feel from his intervention, but occasionally, one or more of them may not. If it is extremely important to the supervisor that he be liked by everyone he works with, if he is terribly upset by resentment or bad feelings directed his way, he had best choose another line of work outside of supervision. In his role of police leader, he will never be consistently adored by everyone.

Neither can the supervisor expect to be admitted to the innermost circles of top management. His advice and counsel will be sought up to a point, the point being determined by any number of factors: his reputation and personality, the kind of department he works for, the personal attitudes of his bosses, and still other considerations.

If the police supervisor is seriously wounded by being essentially left out of the very highest policy decisions, even when he knows in his own heart that he has the right answer, then he is once again in the wrong endeavor. As a first-line supervisor, he cannot realistically expect to be held close to the bosom of top management. It generally will not happen and he must accept this fact.

A command staff member of a police agency once remarked that the further up the chain of command he advanced in rank, the smaller his circle of really close friends became. As a lieutenant, there were fewer persons with whom he had much in common than there were when he was a sergeant. If a shrinking group of on-the-job pals is troublesome to the police officer, he should think again about how much he really wants to climb the promotional ladder. Like so many other things in life, the attainment of higher rank offset by the loss of some close associations represents a trade-off that must be considered carefully.

The police leader who wakes up one day to find that he no longer sees his work as rewarding and fulfilling also may have a major career decision to make. Is there something better awaiting him elsewhere, perhaps in some other field of work? If so, where and what is it?

Most persons find themselves consumed with doubts about their past, present, and future at one point or another in life. Self-doubts are not unusual and, in themselves, are not particularly self-destructive. Allowed to persist too strongly and over too long a time, however, they can prove extremely vexing and distracting to the individual's current work and life. At their most extreme degree of persistence, they may drive the individual harboring them to "test the waters" of a new lifestyle or career, or to at least become so preoccupied with a desire to do so that his existing situation may suffer.

One experienced detective sergeant left his police department to invest his life savings and his family's happiness in a venture he had always wanted to try: dairy farming. After a couple of years of working sunrise to sunset, coupled with little financial reward, he made the decision to return to his old department to start over. Within another year or two, he had worked his way back to his old supervisory position.

A considerable amount of struggle and sacrifice was required as the ex-farmer labored towards regaining what he had lost in policing. He had something, however, that made the discomfort easier and the whole escapade worthwhile: rather than spend a lifetime doubting whether or not he had made the right career choice, he tried out the alternative role of farmer that he had always dreamed about. Finally, the disillusionment of the hard work and limited rewards brought him back to his other love: police work. He could now continue as a police supervisor, reasonably content with his place in life and no longer filled with doubts about his career choice. To him, the lesson had been worth it.

Probably not every supervisor with family and financial obligations can afford to try out a whole new career. More probably can do so than think they can. Still others can at least explore a dreamed-about career change. Information on job requirements, duties, benefits, and drawbacks are available from both written resources and personal contacts in every profession under the sun.

The interested supervisor may be able to resolve a good many of his doubts and questions without the necessity of leaving his current employment. He may, as a result, be able to form more fact-based opinions about the real desirability of a career and life-style change. The old "look before you leap" adage could prove invaluable to the marginally dissatisfied supervisor. Just how good is the organization that I belong to when it is compared to other agencies? While it is quite normal to lament the real or imagined shortcomings of one's job, things are not always as bad as they appear at a time when the employee's morale is low. The other agency probably has many problems of its own, as virtually all organizations do. Things on the other side of the proverbial fence may not be as green as they appear to the distant viewer. Just talking to some of those on the inside of the other organization may reveal a lot. It may also reveal some cracks and blemishes in an otherwise, outwardly lovely facade.

The dissatisfied but intelligent supervisor will avoid making momentous decisions—career related or otherwise—during moments of personal depression or unhappiness. Rather, he will take the time to bring objectivity and common sense into his deliberations. He knows that a major career change decision, once made and acted upon, is not easily undone or reversed.

The supervisor with more than his share of common sense will realize that the very bleak outlook of today may brighten considerably with the changing circumstances of tomorrow. He does not wait expectantly for the best of all possible worlds to hit him between the eyes. Neither does he see gloom and despair around every corner. He knows that holding either view would be totally unrealistic and self-defeating. He is not defeated easily.

Moods change, as do career outlooks. The wise supervisor is willing to wait long enough to see patterns and trends developing in his job. Maybe there are things he can do or changes he can make in himself that will influence what he sees going on in his career.

The intelligent police supervisor will do more than think about his job satisfaction and career options. He will engage in some realistic assessments of who he is, where he is, and where he would like to be someday. In this way can he hope to chart his own course towards job satisfaction.

ORGANIZATIONAL SURVIVAL

Police academies and training officers expend a lot of effort addressing the vital issue of field survival. Much less formalized effort is directed at teaching the new employee the rules of another sort of survival:

organizational survival. From his peers and from uncomfortable experiences, the employee gradually learns the rules of getting along in a bureaucracy, even if the bureaucracy is a relatively small one: he does not bait the sergeant; he does not park in the chief's parking place; he does not talk too loud or too long as a rookie; he does not let down a fellow officer.

The police organization also has its unwritten rules and informal codes of conduct for its supervisors. A good many of these informal rules and expectations find their origin in plain common sense and a generally shared desire to survive as a member of a police organization without undue hardship. As such, these informal but real guidelines help dictate the way the police supervisor does his job and relates to every other member of the organization.

The persistent theme running through all such expectations is again one of "let me do my job with a minimum of trouble and I'll do the same for you." There is nothing inherently wrong with this sort of logic, so long as it does not call for ignoring or covering improper conduct. The American character as a whole seems to have always demanded a minimum amount of outside interference as a prerequisite for getting things done right. The police supervisor of today may be following a tradition of sorts.

For the police leader, "leave me alone" may mean not talking about me behind my back. The supervisor who blasts his colleagues in their absence will probably get the same thing back in spades. Name calling and backbiting accomplish nothing other than the generation of internal strife and bad feelings. Avoiding such slander should be a cardinal rule for the ethical police boss.

The organizational survivor also knows better than to second-guess the decisions and actions of his peers. Probably no one in the police organization is held in more contempt by the street cop or street supervisor than is the deskbound Monday morning quarterback, regardless of his rank or position in the agency.

The truly sharp supervisor, deskbound or otherwise, realizes that frequently there is no way he or anyone else can accurately second-guess the actions/decisions of the man or woman on the scene at the time action had to be taken. To attempt to do so can bring him the contempt and ill will of the individual who had to make the decision without the benefit of remarkably clear hindsight.

The supervisor who earns a reputation as a vocal second-guesser will not find his future to be rosy in most police agencies. He may find that, as a result of his harassment of others, he has a ready-made audience anxiously awaiting his own foul-up, which will almost certainly take place sooner or later. He may then reap more grief than he dealt out previously.

The old "do unto others" advice may be pertinent to many aspects of good organizational survival skills. It is just common sense that the individual who treats others fairly and with genuine empathy receives the same treatment in turn, at least most of the time. There is no better advice for organizational survival in the contemporary police agency.

The organizational survivor does not jump the chain of command in his efforts to get a task accomplished, no matter how lofty the task or how noble his motives. Unless an emergency exists in which life or property are clearly in peril, the survival-wise supervisor does not correct or criticize the personnel of another supervisor. Instead, he makes his criticisms known to that supervisor at the earliest reasonable moment. The errant employee's boss can properly use his own knowledge of the situation and any necessary background information to formulate appropriate corrective measures.

When the situation at hand *does* require immediate intervention by a supervisor, that supervisor relates his actions and why they were necessary to the corrected employee's supervisor as soon as possible. He knows that getting there ahead of the employee's own explanation, which may be somewhat self-serving, does not hurt anything, either.

The wise supervisor remembers that an informed boss is generally a reasonably content leader, and he avoids keeping important facts from him. Bosses traditionally do not like secrets, at least not when they are the ones being excluded from the confidence.

Surviving the police organization means walking with care in several areas. One of those areas involves the reputation for moderate restraint (or lack of same) that the supervisor builds for himself. The leader who earns the label of a big mouth or rabble rouser will not go very far in the organization. Neither will the supervisor who develops the reputation of being a jellyfish who wants to agree to everything and please everybody. Some unfortunate police organizations have all of both types that they need. No others need apply.

The good leader does not agitate and foment just to see the smoke rise. If he has a worthwhile standard to bear, he first gets his facts in order. He then presents them in a calm, logical fashion. Reason is his weapon; emotion is not. He persuades and convinces others to come around to his viewpoint. He does not bully or bluster. Tantrum-throwers belong in kindergartens, not in police leadership posts.

No one can be all things to all people. The supervisor must take a stand for what he believes to be the correct, logical, and ethical course of action, whatever the topic of the dispute might be. In so doing, he cannot help but offend some while pleasing others. So be it. Performing one's supervisory duties in an honest fashion is not synonymous with competing in a popularity contest. At times, some must be offended for the long-term, overall benefit of everyone. This is just one more of life's realities that the new supervisor accepts when he dons the chevrons of his new status.

The short-sighted, egotistical, and probably ineffective supervisor devotes much of his energy to promoting internal feuds, holding grudges, and provoking disputes. The successful supervisor establishes contacts, makes friends and alliances, and works with others so that everyone can look good. The egomaniac who sees his recent promotion to detective sergeant as a good reason to look down upon his old patrol buddies is riding for a hard fall.

Few police supervisors have prospered by making enemies of wholesale numbers of their fellow supervisors. Cooperation, not constant controversy, is the key to getting things done. Getting many things done might can make many people look good.

The Big Boss who has to spend time making peace between two of his Little Bosses generally does not end up thinking too highly of either. In sum, good cooperation gets it done; needless, senseless, internal conflicts help no one, least of all the combatants. There are plenty of real crooks for the aggressive supervisor to tangle with. His peers do not deserve his aggression.

People in general and police officers in particular are diligent in their efforts at rumor-mongering. In truth, police people are basically curious individuals who like to hear a good tale. They also take considerable pleasure in relating that tale, embellished or otherwise, to others. Unfortunately, they do not always go to the trouble of confirming the truth of the matter before reporting it as fact.

False gossip, whether innocently or maliciously spread, has hurt most everyone involved in law enforcement for any length of time. This is a grand statement, but the experiences of the veteran police supervisor will bear out its truthfulness. Rumor-mongering may victimize an innocent officer on so minor a rap as having a "nutty" relative or a drunken mother-in-law. The rumor mill may hit him with an unfounded reputation for questionable honesty, traceable via a tortuous path back to an alleged incident that never happened.

The supervisor intent upon surviving in a healthy organization does more than challenge gossip originating from his subordinates. He also abides by a self-imposed rule of never engaging in rumor-carrying himself. In addition, he asks for the source of wayward tales he hears from his peers. Stories that are suddenly without a source or otherwise nebulous in origin have to be doubted very much.

In the end, no one benefits from rumors and gossip, least of all the parties named in them. The supervisor can protect others at the same time he helps himself by discouraging a climate in which character assassination can take place via rumor-mongering. This could be seen as yet another extension of the "do unto others" rule: you do not do it yourself and you require the same courtesy of others in the organization.

It has been claimed by critics of law enforcement that if police officers put as much energy into catching crooks as they did into gossiping and rumor-mongering, the current crime wave would dissipate. Right or wrong, the comment does emphasize the need for the supervisor to do what he can to stem the flow of disruptive and destructive tales within his own work unit. In so doing he may be helping to assure the good health of the police organization and his place in it. He is helping assure that he will be a survivor.

INTERNAL STRIFE

Election years can reveal some amazing if frightening scenarios in some of the police agencies where the head law enforcement officer is elected by the voters of the jurisdiction. If the top officer is elected every two years, the agency may see a year of relatively good police service, followed by a year of internal dissention and infighting as employees line up behind favorite candidates, declared or otherwise. It is not unusual to see a command staff officer running for election against his incumbent boss. Policing suffers as a result of the political jockeying for position. Following the election, law enforcement operations may continue to languish for awhile as internal rewards and retributions are handed out to supporters of the winning and losing candidates.

The preceding description of internal strife may sound both devastating and exaggerated. In the case of some police agencies today, the former is true, the latter is not. Such problems are not always found only in the small agency, either. Internal strife, in whatever form it arises in the police organization, is as destructive to employee morale as it is to the quality of service provided to the public.

A fact of life pertinent to virtually any group of people is that the members of that group are going to strive, maneuver, and otherwise engage in behavior designed to obtain for them some sort of advantage. This is normal and expected human interaction. When such actions and counteractions reach a point in number and intensity that the carrying out of goals and objectives of the group is hampered, then that group has a major problem. The term "group" as used here can certainly be said to include the law enforcement organization and its members.

Internal strife is a concern for every member of the police agency. As a recognized leader in the agency, the police supervisor is obligated to exercise his authority and influence to eliminate such difficulties whenever possible. For starters, he can help out by not participating in the internal game playing himself. Instead of actively currying favor with one power bloc or another within the organization, he can strive to deal fairly and cooperate equally well with all elements and individuals in the department. Instead of spending time and energy in lining up battles, he can concentrate his efforts on doing his own job as well as possible.

Instead of seeking the blessing of "in" groups within the organization, the supervisor can earn a good reputation by establishing his credentials as an intelligent and talented leader. Instead of participating in the choosing up of sides on issues, the supervisor more concerned with uniting than dividing the agency can work equally hard with *all* elements and persons.

The strife generated by internal bickering creates public doubts in the police agency's effectiveness if it is allowed to continue unabated. Continuing dissension cannot help but become fodder for conversation. A police organization that makes the news more often through internal convulsions than via crime prevention and suppression cannot hope to retain public confidence for long. The police supervisor will suffer along with the other members of the organization when that shortage of public faith surfaces.

Once again, the supervisor does what he can to reduce the damage caused by the encouragement of and participation in internal intrigue. He encourages his subordinates not to air their differences and arguments in the public forum. He follows the same advice himself. He recognizes that others will not respect him if he does not show respect for himself. He educates his people in this same line of thinking.

While he recognizes that there is no guaranteed formula for discouraging internal strife while encouraging organizational unity, the supervisor also relies upon a proven check list of things he can do to help:

1. He does not engage in the starting or passing of destructive rumors.
2. He does not second-guess his peers' decisions to others.
3. He does not ridicule his peers, subordinates, or superiors to others.
4. While he remains a member of an organization, he does not criticize and condemn it outside of the organization.
5. He treats his co-workers in the same way he would want to be treated by them.
6. He does not carry tales from one group to another or from one individual to another for the purpose of causing bad feelings. When he hears something derogatory from one of his peers regarding another of his co-workers, he refuses to serve as a conduit for animosity. He allows the message to die without being relayed.
7. He does not expend his energies in building hostile alliances within the organization. He treats everyone fairly and thus has nothing to fear from any individual or group within the agency.
8. He does not compromise his integrity by eliciting favors or special treatment from others when the payback may involve him in improper or illicit activities.
9. He does not allow his job and its distractions to become so all consuming that he misplaces the importance of his private life and responsibilities away from work.
10. He never replaces what he knows to be right with what appears

to be easier at the moment. He realizes that propriety and expediency are not always one and the same. His integrity and character are not for sale.

Most people (police officers included) do not enjoy strife between themselves and those with whom they share common beliefs, goals, and feelings. Sometimes it may initially appear that the easiest way to avoid dissension and unpleasantness is to go along with whatever emotion is holding sway at the moment. Generally, however, little good is accomplished by such a stand (or a lack of one). What is said to pacify one group or individual today may have to be quickly modified to fit an opposing idea tomorrow. Diplomacy is one thing; hypocrisy is quite another.

Perhaps a more reasonable course of action would be to avoid getting caught up in the choosing of sides in the first place. Neutrality in a destructive internal fight does not indicate weakness. It may instead be an island of reason and common sense in an otherwise stormy and unproductive atmosphere. The smart supervisor could do far worse than stay out of internal politics and intrigue, while insisting that his subordinates do the same.

CORRUPTION OR INCOMPETENCE?

A police supervisor can have a lot of reasons for not wanting to remain a part of a given police organization. He may be disillusioned with working conditions and job benefits. He may be unhappy with the clients he serves. He may be just plain burned out on a steady diet of other peoples' problems.

Then again, the supervisor may want to leave because he feels that the organization he is a part of is dishonest or hopelessly ineffective. He may have even come to see his bosses and peers as crooks or incompetents. In such an unhappy state of affairs, something surely has to happen.

Probably no law enforcement organization anywhere is as effective and well-run as its members would like for it to be. It is neither unusual nor inappropriate for police employees and supervisors to be dissatisfied to some extent with the *status quo.* That is a good sign of their own job interest, professionalism, and devotion to a calling they see as important.

Most of the time, problems with the operational efficiency of a given police organization can be accurately attributed to shortcomings in resources available, procedures, personnel skills, administrative functions, or supervisory leadership. Serious problems may be traced back to a combination of all of the shortcomings listed, and then some more.

Organizational incompetence is not something that the police supervisor has to accept as "just the way things are." An organization's inability to carry out successfully the role assigned to it is something that should do more than concern and upset the ethical police leader. It should also motivate him to do something about the state of affairs. It is easy to sit back and condemn one's own agency for its incompetence. It is something else again to give of one's own time and abilities to overcome that incompetence.

The supervisor who is dissatisfied with his agency's stature and accomplishments can work within his own sphere of influence to change attitudes and actions. If he perceives his agency as being at less than its maximum effectiveness due to community partnership problems tied to poor employee attitudes, he can work with his people in an attempt to change those attitudes. If he sees his department's field representatives as being inept in the handling of crime scene inquiries, he can call upon his own skills and those of other professionals in a training effort geared to improving officers' crime scene performance. Here again, he is doing what he can to eliminate incompetence from his workplace.

Whatever the supervisor *can* do in his own job position he *should* do in a calculated effort to help increase the competency of his organization and its members. If his peers do the same, the organization should be well on its way towards conquering its ineffectiveness. While nothing says that he must see himself as a cheerleader in his agency, neither is there anything that says he should not enlist his fellow leaders in the improvement effort. Shared skills and strengths can do wonders in improving police employees' job performance.

Unfortunately, there may be darker reasons behind an individual or agency appearing inefficient or ineffective. Although much suppressed and diminished from an earlier and uglier era, police corruption and misconduct still exist today. The police supervisor who believes that the last poisons of corruption have been totally rooted out of the police profession is living in a fantasy world.

Police corruption is not restricted to any particular part of the country nor to a comfortable home inside a major metropolitan police agency. It may be rampant in the tiny rural or medium-sized suburban department, while a nearby big city department remains quite clean.

Just defining what corruption really is may pose a problem for the police supervisor. At one agency, peer pressure and department policy may label as corruption the free cup of coffee or the half-priced meal for the uniformed cop. At another department, official concern about corruption may not be aroused at anything less than bribery, rape, and robbery committed by police employees. Hopefully, the latter agency is nearing extinction in America today.

It is common sense to say that the police supervisor cannot afford to participate in any questionable practice that could lead to legitimate cries of corruption or graft. More than this is expected of the police leader, however. It is not enough that he should refuse to participate in unlawful or improper practices himself. Neither can he stand idly by while other members of his organization exploit corruptive practices and influences. Action on his part is mandated. The question remaining for him is exactly what form the action should take.

The supervisor confronted by solid evidence of bribery, payoffs, protection rackets, purchased promotions, or other police abuses of the criminal justice system has several options available to him. Perhaps his easiest course of action is total inaction: he does nothing. He can vow that his own actions will be pure in character, and what others do is none of his business.

Such a philosophy obviously will not wash. The ethical leader who knows of the existence of corruption, regardless of the level at which it exists in the police organization, must do something constructive about it. He becomes touched by the corrupting influence himself if he tacitly acknowledges its existence yet refuses to act against it.

A head in the sand attitude is unacceptable conduct for the police professional. Making excuses for corruption ("the pay is bad," "nobody gets hurt by 'clean' money from a gambler," etc.) or hoping that there is a good explanation for strange happenings ("it was probably an honest mistake") accomplishes nothing. It fools no one.

Ignoring or trying to wish away police malpractice will not work. In the end, confrontation and upheaval will take place. The question for the supervisor to answer is which side of the fence he will be discovered on when the public revelation occurs.

An ethical response by the police supervisor is absolutely necessary. Nothing less will suffice.

Generally speaking, the only time that fleeing the agency would be an acceptable response to corruption would be after all possible efforts at fighting the blight had proven absolutely fruitless. Retreat before battle is seldom good practice. Only after he has worked at the problem from within and without the agency should the ethical supervisor abandon the field. To do otherwise would be to admit to the triumph of corruption over fair play all too easily.

If the supervisor has fought corruption in his agency by steering himself and his people away from it while bringing the problem to the attention of those in authority to eradicate it, then perhaps he can be excused for leaving if nothing changes or shows promise of changing. He should not give up too easily, nor should he pull back in the face of hostile opposition. In the end, however, no one can blame him if he gives his all to the cause with no result and then packs it in. Only after the supervisor has done his utmost to change an unacceptable situation and found it unchanging can he be excused for divorcing himself from an unacceptable organization.

There is no reason that the internal affairs procedures described earlier in this book cannot be utilized to ferret out, investigate, and adjudicate individual acts of employee corruption. Where these checks are in place and functional, the supervisor should have only to bring the alleged misbehavior to official attention to get the problem remedied. What happens, though, in the agency where internal monitoring machinery is either nonexistent or compromised?

The supervisor faced with an organization containing more than isolated incidences of corruption is in rough straits. He must search for the individual or individuals within his chain of command who will help him bring the monster to bay. If he does not find an interested and ethical individual as his immediate superior, then he must commit the otherwise unpardonable sin of jumping the chain to any link in it that will help him. He should be aware, of course, that at this point he has committed himself fully to his aim of exorcising corruption from his workplace. There is no turning back. Either he will be victorious in his honest quest or he likely will leave the organization, one way or another.

The supervisor instigating a corruption probe may find the reactions and attitudes of his fellow police employees to vary widely. Depending upon how isolated or pervasive the problem is, he may be widely acclaimed or thoroughly damned for his efforts. He may find the crusader's lot a lonely and uncomfortable one. Nonetheless, he must persist and allow the pieces to fall where they may.

Absolutely and finally failing in his attempts to dislodge corruptive practices in his organization, the supervisor is faced with disobeying yet one more cardinal rule of his calling. He may ultimately be forced to go outside his agency for help. Never an easy decision, it is one made as a last and desperate resort in the cause of law enforcement professionalism. The route chosen by the supervisor may range from the office of the district attorney to the state attorney general. It may involve him in a session with representatives of another law enforcement agency or governmental body. All the while the supervisor remembers, however, that his relationship with his job and his coworkers can never be exactly the same as before. At this point, he has taken a giant step and an irreversible one.

The supervisor lashing out at corrupt practices is by no means alone, however. Virtually no police agency in the land is devoid of ethical, professional police officers. The supervisor battling a bona fide case of police malpractice should seldom lack for moral support. The more professional the agency and its people, the stronger the support should be.

CURRENT ISSUES

Although the concerns may seem minor indeed when placed alongside the worries of a supervisor faced with corruption in his agency, staying up to date on the burning issues of the day is important for the successful police leader, too. The Americans with Disabilities Act, for instance, is important to all police managers for the effects it has on law enforcement hiring and retention practices. Fair treatment and reasonable accommodations for persons with handicaps are the just expectations of the ADA.

Sexual harassment issues are also a major concern for the police personnel manager today. By relying upon his good common sense and staying current on case law and accepted employee relations practices the alert supervisor can ensure that not even a hint of impropriety sneaks in to smear his associations with his subordinates, or their relations among themselves. If a problem does arise, his sensitivity to the issues involved will help assure that he is notified of the situation promptly so that he and the organization can deal with it at once. His "no tolerance" attitude on sexual harassment, communicated by words and actions to his subordinates, also can help assure that major difficulties do not arise in the first place.

The supervisor also will stay in touch with his agency's source of legal advice to ensure that he is aware of the tenets of the Fair Labor Standards Act that prohibits improper employer practices, such as assigning employees to work what amounts to overtime without appropriate compensation. (From the complaints brought to the attention of labor officials, it would appear that there are still a number of law enforcement agencies and supervisors who do not understand–or who deliberately choose to flout–these federal regulations.) An example of conduct prohibited by the FLSA might be seen in the frustrated patrol sergeant who *orders* a rookie officer to drive the jurisdiction in his personal car on his own time to learn the streets–all without compensation.

Diversity issues also will be of continuing interest to the ethical police supervisor. Fairness and an absence of bias are the guideposts of the competent supervisor's personal policy on diversity. Racial profiling–targeting members of certain races or ethnic groups for extra surveillance or enforcement–must never be tolerated by the police leader. Not only must he see to it that citizens and employees of all races, ethnic groups, genders and lifestyles are treated equally, he must also do his part to bring persons of diverse backgrounds and experiences into the law enforcement service. The police supervisor is, after all, an energetic recruiter of good people in addition to all his other responsibilities. He knows that where diversity is sought after and accepted it is much more difficult for intolerance to flourish. That, too, is a legitimate concern of the enlightened police leader.

Some have declared the oncoming generation of employees to be yet another "special problem" for today's police supervisor. Variously known as Generation Y, the Nexsters or simply the Next Generation, these young men and women following the much-ballyhooed Generation X into the workplace are not your grandfather's generation. They are probably quite dissimilar from the supervisors they will be encountering from the police academy onwards.

Generally well-educated and technologically competent, the members of this dangerously stereotyped group were born between the late 1970s and mid-1980s. As a group, they have been labeled as materialistic, socially conscious, and outspoken. If a member of this group feels wronged, his or her supervisor almost certainly will hear about it. Not overly impressed by rank or title, a Generation Y member likely will spout what is on his mind, or so the stereotyping goes.

If 'Nexsters are direct, the police supervisor may find directness his best bet for leading them effectively. The supervisor should approach the 'Nexster directly with no verbal beating around the bush. He should show him the same respect he shows all of his subordinates. He should, in fact, treat this employee in every aspect in *exactly* the same manner in which he treats his other people. Some of the members of this generation may look and sound a little different than the supervisor's other employees, but they are not strange beings to be handled as some kind of exotic freaks. Openness and honesty on the part of the leader likely will be returned in kind. It is also likely that the more "extreme" members of this generation probably have not chosen law enforcement for a career, thereby making it less likely that the police supervisor will have to deal with their foibles in the first place.

Like many other employees the police leader will supervise, Generation Y cops will appreciate being asked for their opinions. The smart supervisor will give them room and permission to solve a given problem for themselves. "Empowerment" is one of this generation's buzzwords, and the supervisor who wisely brings them into the problem-solving exercise may see good results. A word of caution: they may not arrive at the same solution he would devise, or get there via the same route he would take. Like many of his other employees, the members of this generation are often imaginative and not bashful about sharing their novel solutions to old problems. That's not so bad when the leader is confronted by a real problem looking for a real solution.

The members of the latest generation to reach working age offer at least as many opportunities and solutions as they do problems and challenges. The clever boss will draw on their assets even as he exercises patience and tolerance for their differences, perceived or real.

THE BOSS FROM HELL

Fortunate indeed is the employee who can say truthfully that he has never worked for a really bad boss. Unfortunately, such bad leaders are too plentiful in today's work world. Law enforcement is not immune to the hostile work environment that a really obnoxious leader can foment. Bad bosses come in a variety of types, shapes, sizes and genders. They range from the merely irritating to the dangerous and perhaps certifiable. Their bad behavior can be manifested in almost endless forms.

Some bad bosses take all the credit for work done by others. Some are quick to criticize and condemn for the slightest infraction, but have trouble praising even the most deserving conduct. Some of the worst bosses have no honor and simply lie, whether about employee performance or other things. Some lack the courage to do the right thing, or they show no indication that they know what the right thing is. Other bad bosses practice sexual discrimination or harassment, while yet others favor certain "pet" employees while constantly punishing a chosen "goat" on the team. Some others are just plain dishonest and even engage in criminal behavior.

Some bad bosses are bullies who enjoy making employees miserable. Some fail to set timelines or goals but then punish employees who do not reach these invisible targets. Others are loud and lace their orders with obscenities while omitting to practice even the most basic of human courtesies: an occasional "please" or "thank you." Still other bad bosses will never permit an employee to forget an error and instead repunish him for it over and over by bringing it up repeatedly. And some bad bosses are heavy-handed with discipline when simple advice or counseling would suffice to attain the desired change in behavior.

Bad bosses neither elicit nor accept constructive criticism from those they see as beneath them. While they figuratively rub their subordinates' faces in the dirt, they shamelessly kiss up to those above them. They appear to have no pride, and attempt to drive any pride or self-esteem out of their employees.

Some bad bosses may exhibit only one or two of these bad behaviors, and to varying degrees of seriousness. Others display most or all of them, with yet other negative traits and bad practices added to the toxic brew.

In the best of worlds, the law enforcement supervisor can fix his or her bad boss with just the right words from the heart spoken in a private but soul-searching exchange. That indeed may happen and it is certainly nothing short of wonderful when it does. In the real world, however, the supervisor with a bad boss adjusts and compensates for a bad superior rather that expecting him to change greatly. If he does change, that's all the better. If the situation remains static the survival-conscious supervisor will have minimized the obstruction to his own efforts at being a good leader. It can be done.

Some supervisors reduce the stress that a bad boss can cause by minimizing their contact with the offending individual. While that certainly can help, it still does not solve the problem. Others choose to confront the issue gently and (always) privately without putting the superior on the defensive. The encounter does not begin with accusations. It instead starts with a description of how the boss makes the supervisor feel when he attacks or belittles his subordinate. While it may not seem possible, some bad bosses truly do not know that they are bad bosses. ("That's just the way I am.") By addressing the issue in such a non-threatening manner, the subordinate supervisor may be able to get his point across without bringing down lightning on his own head. It might go like this: "Boss, I know you don't mean to hurt me, but when you respond to me that way it makes me feel pretty worthless and I know you don't mean to do that." The boss is left a way out if he chooses to take it: he may have been mistreating someone, but even the employee knows he didn't mean to do it. He can even apologize, if he feels up to it. If the problem recurs, the subordinate supervisor can repeat the performance in hopes of attaining eventual, long-term change in behavior. It will not work in every instance. But it will not fail every time, either. (Note: The supervisor who realizes he has been displaying "bad boss" behavior himself must know how to display gracious behavior to an offended subordinate!)

Generally, a problem that is not confronted will not get better, and may in fact worsen. The misbehavior of a bad boss is one such problem. Like a bad laceration, it requires treatment to get better. Ignored, it will fester. But there are some approaches to the bad boss problem that will make them a lot worse. Gossiping about the behavior won't help, and it may get back to the offender, thereby aggravating the problem. Neither is sending sniping messages to the boss's boss a very good idea. If the situation has deteriorated to the point that a direct sit-down with the boss's own boss is required, the difficulty might have passed the point of no return. Depending upon what the Big Boss is willing to do for the employee, the problem may get solved or it may get a lot worse. Terminally worse, that is, for the complaining supervisor. Talking to the Big Boss about one of his or her Little Bosses should be reserved as the nuclear option; there will be fallout from having done so. The supervisor with a knack for organizational survival will "go nuclear" only as a last resort.

As in so many other areas of the law enforcement supervisor's job, confronting a boss problem honestly and tactfully is most often the best way of addressing it. By providing the boss a chance to save face the supervisor may be able to achieve the desired change in behavior, or at least mitigate the dysfunctional practices of his superior. The "upward counseling'" session may have to take place more than once, but always in a quiet, private and unemotional manner. A shouting match will worsen the situation. So will threats to go to the boss's boss. If stiff resistance is encountered at a first meeting, it may be wise to take a break and try it again another time. But the effort is worth repeating. Too much is at stake to allow a bad boss to dilute the effectiveness of a good law enforcement leader.

SUMMARY

These are sobering thoughts. With luck, the average police supervisor may never have to work for a rotten boss or confront a serious incidence of police malpractice in a whole career of police supervision. With more and more people of high moral fiber and good common sense entering the police profession, the possibility of never encountering such malignancies increases steadily.

Nonetheless, the supervisor who would be thoroughly skilled in his calling and truly ready to handle any special problem that might come along readies himself for these, too. It is just another set of challenges to be capably addressed by the common sense supervisor.

POINTS TO REMEMBER

• An ethical supervisor will remain above the intrigue, back-biting

and internal drama that ensues at too many agencies.
- Organizational survival can prove just as much of a challenge as street survival in too many law enforcement organizations.
- Starting ill-advised wars with his peers and superiors will not endear a supervisor to his organization.
- If a supervisor believes his organization is so rife with internal strife and deep-rooted problems that he cannot change it, he owes himself a change in employment.
- Incompetence can be addressed; corruption or intentional malpractice can never be tolerated.
- His own ethics forbid a supervisor from participating in or covering up for dishonest or unethical behavior.
- The supervisor afflicted with a bad boss can only solve the problem by confronting the offending superior, but in a private and non-threatening manner that allows the boss to save face.
- Almost all of the "special problems" a supervisor will face can be fixed or mitigated.

Chapter Fourteen

THE POLICE LEADER'S ROLE IN
COMMUNITY POLICING

Community-oriented policing, or simply community policing, is the "preferred way of doing business" for American law enforcement in the twenty-first century, at least until the "Next Big Thing" comes along. Indeed, community policing in its many forms has become the catch phrase of police managers and politicians to the extent that it is the rare chief, sheriff or other law enforcement agency head who would admit that his or her department is NOT practicing community policing, whatever the phrase might mean. And just what *does* it mean?

WHAT IS IT?

Therein lies the problem. Today, what community policing means may depend on the identity of the one describing it. To one law enforcement manager, community policing may equate to police public relations, and nothing more. To the more enlightened leader it may refer to a whole changed outlook of law enforcement where local citizens work in partnership with "their" officers to solve crime or disorder problems of mutual concern to cops and community. Precisely what constitutes community policing thus varies from one police person and organization to the next. Nonetheless, there exists at least some common ground upon which a definition of community policing and the police supervisor's role in it can be built.

First of all, it should be emphasized that community policing is a philosophy or mindset for an entire law enforcement operation or organization. It is not a separate and distinct, specialized police unit. It requires a diversity of approaches ranging from vehicle patrol to foot beats; information-gathering to hard-nosed enforcement. It can be all of these things and a good deal more. It is NOT "police social work."

Community policing helps the members of a community feel and *be* safer by targeting both "hard" crime and nuisance offenses that breed disorder. The idea is to involve the police officers assigned to the area with the citizens living, working or playing there to identify problems and mutually develop solutions for them. This may require a single officer or a whole team of them to remain assigned to a specific geographic area and a specific problem long enough to develop personal ownership in the situation and the people affected by it. Often, community policing does not result in an overnight fix but rather requires patient, long-term treatment and observation.

Individual officers working in a community policing structure seek to be proactive as opposed to reactive in their approach to their duties. Where they can, they try to prevent a growing problem from escalating to the point where frequent police intervention is required.

Community policing in one form or another is practiced in a lot of American law enforcement agencies today. In many, community policing officers also work a regular beat or street assignment and respond to regular calls for police service. Most still perform traditional police duties like issuing traffic tickets, investigating crimes, writing reports and making arrests. Indeed, in some instances their community policing efforts may require that they write more tickets and make more arrests for targeted violations than would the regular beat cop.

Community policing requires problem solution on the part of the police professional. Problem solving is, of course, nothing new for police. But actively soliciting a community's help in identifying and then solving the difficulty IS, at least for many police officers and the agencies employing them. Community policing in its true form only exists where the community or some element of it *in addition to the police* participates in the problem identification, analysis and solution process.

In police agencies that have followed the trend to community policing, officers still solve traditional police problems that at a glance may have little or nothing to do with community-oriented policing. A simple example may be seen in the citizen forcibly taken into custody by police after going off his medication and becoming violent. The officers involved are merely doing something in addition to community policing tasks, such as working with citizens to clean up graffiti vandalism in a neighborhood. Police will always be reactive, too. The public's embrace of the 911 method of problem-solving will see to that.

PROBLEM SOLVING

In many cases, community policing officers follow a problem resolution formula in carrying out a given task. First they attempt to identify the problem or series of problems by breaking the situation down into its component parts. Next they try to identify the actors involved, either as suspects, victims or others touched by the situation. Then they solicit information and possible solutions from all those involved. Sometimes this includes interviews with the perceived troublemakers. With this information the officers devise a proposed solution to remove the problem or at least reduce its severity. The community is expected to contribute via concrete action towards the solution of the problem. Finally, the officers and the involved others assess the results of their actions. A different response or repeated efforts may be determined to be necessary. A long-term assessment may mean the whole problem solving process has to be repeated a month or a year down the road. And, of course, not all community policing efforts succeed or have the desired effects.

An example of a basic community policing effort can be seen in the experiences of a beat cop asked by citizens in a residential neighborhood to solve the problem of rowdy and sometimes destructive juveniles prowling a residential area located just off the town's "main drag" on weekend nights. Upon talking with the offending youngsters as well as the residents, the officer learns that the kids are coming through the area en route home after a nearby skateboarding rink closes. Most of the youngsters are too young to drive and have no other means of transportation, as local buses have stopped running by closing time at the rink. Utilizing the principles of problem solving contained in community policing, the beat cop meets with leaders of the neighborhood association and the operator of the skating facility and advises them of what she has learned. At the officer's urging, the two interests agree to share the cost of putting on an extra bus to make a few short runs late on Friday and Saturday nights. The next weekend, there are no complaints from the neighborhood. At least for the moment, the problem has been solved with the active (and even financial) aid of the community. The radio car officer has, for a time, stepped out of her traditional role of reacting to incidents to help her constituents solve their problem, and hers.

In determining just what community policing is, it may be helpful for the law enforcement supervisor to ascertain what it is NOT. Community policing is not, for example, intended to be another new public relations trick. Better police-community relations may, in fact, result from improved police service. Appearances are not the reason for going to community policing. Increased police effectiveness and efficiency is. Community policing is not intended to be warm and fuzzy or soft on criminals. In order to work well, community policing *does* require officers to do things that they might not otherwise think of as police tasks. (Example: lead residents in a neighborhood cleanup.) This they do *in addition* to their other, more traditional functions like putting crooks in jail. Generally speaking, community policing requires more, not less, work from interested officers. But the work should help save police effort in the long run by cutting repeat calls for service regarding the very same problems.

As noted, community policing does not necessarily require the creation of special units within the organization. To work best, community policing must be an agency-wide mindset or way of doing things that is practiced by patrol officers, detectives and support personnel alike. Uniformed officers are critical to the success of community policing and must be afforded the opportunity to participate regardless of where in the jurisdiction or the time of day that they work. Community policing is an all hands operation.

Done correctly, community policing is not anti-supervision or "no accountability" oriented, either. Officers involved in community policing require the wise counsel of an interested and intelligent supervisor at least as much as do their traditional policing peers. These officers still need advice, support, training, discipline and evaluation from a boss who knows the ropes. But often they work best when some of these things are delivered in a slightly modified way.

Even the most vocal advocates of community policing do not claim that the approach works every time and with every sort of problem. Most acknowledge the continuing need for cops who do traditional police tasks, too. They instead assert that community policing supplies one more versatile piece of equipment for law enforcement's tool box for addressing society's breakdowns.

THE SUPERVISOR'S ROLE

Advocates for community policing are in general agreement about something else. They note that it is the front-line supervisor who most often determines whether or not community policing will succeed. They point out that enthusiastic and sincere supervisory support make it difficult for the effort to fail, while indifference or hostility from the supervisory corps will make it hard for community policing to work, even if the police brass supports it.

Experts on community policing emphasize that ideas and efforts must originate with line-level officers and their first-line supervisors for the concept to work best. New projects and solutions for perceived problems should not come down from police executives who then assign a supervisor to find a front-line employee to tackle an issue and produce quick results. A lack of employee ownership in the process if not outright resentment could result from such an approach.

While there is general agreement that the first-line supervisor is a key to success in community-oriented policing, experience has demonstrated that he likely will have to alter slightly some long-held ways of doing things if he is to succeed as an effective leader in this new landscape where decentralized control and employee initiative are highly prized. In this new way of doing business supervisory flexibility and adaptability are particularly valuable assets.

Supervising effectively in a law enforcement agency that has switched to community policing may require that the supervisor modify somewhat the rigid controls that have long characterized the quasi-military way of directing and controlling subordinates. The older system relies upon a relatively inflexible set of rules that was developed long ago to counter the threats of police corruption and unproductive officers. The rules rely heavily on sanctions to punish those who stray from what is determined in black and white to be acceptable police behavior. In some departments, the production of numbers is encouraged while initiative and thinking for oneself are not as highly valued. Staying inside the lines is rewarded; innovation and risk taking are not. Yet encouraging officers to innovate and develop new responses to old problems is what community policing is about. Clearly some supervisory rethinking is required.

Under the old way of doing things in some departments, patrol officers are expected to stay in service available for radio calls, remain within the specific confines of a given geographic area and avoid unnecessary contact and conversation with residents and businesspersons. Initially, much of this was intended to help prevent unwanted familiarity between cops and citizens and the corruption or other trouble it might bring about. Officers were (and still may be) graded on response time, quickness in handling a call and returning to service, and quantifiable productivity.

Little of this works well in community policing, where patrol officers are encouraged to get out of their cars, mix and communicate with citizens and sometimes leave their area to follow up on resolving a problem. Community policing officers must, of necessity, get to know "their" people well to find out what is troubling them and how they can help solve the problem at hand. Productivity numbers are often not highly regarded as measures of officer success or failure. Quantity of enforcement will be considered along with other parts of an officer's work.

Community policing will force the traditional system supervisor to make some changes in what he monitors as well as in what he prizes in a subordinate. His expectations of his officers will undergo change, as well. He still will be thorough in the way he approaches his job; he simply will be somewhat less inclined to rely on a rigid set of bureaucratic expectations and prohibitions to tell him what to expect of his people.

Some things, of course, cannot change. Absolute integrity and the ability to qualify consistently with a handgun, for instance, will remain expectations whatever the style of policing being practiced. The same goes for the required skills of report writing and human relations abilities along with a few dozen other knowledge, skill and ability areas expected of today's police personnel. That remains true because officers working for the most community-oriented department imaginable still must be able to solve crimes and restore order in a crisis. And even the most community-oriented supervisor must be competent to oversee them as they carry out these basic, necessary functions.

To supervise effectively in an agency practicing community policing, a supervisor must be able to shift his attention away from numbers only and too-rigid rules and focus as well on his peoples' *knowledge* of their area, their citizens and the problems to be found there. With expanded leeway and trust extended to his subordinates the supervisor expects in turn that they will keep him briefed on their actions, problems, plans and whereabouts. Community policing does not reduce their accountability to their supervisor. It does mean that they may be given extra time away from handling calls to try and find ways to reduce repeat calls for police service for the same problems.

It is not unreasonable for a supervisor to let his people know that community policing puts added responsibilities on them to accompany the added freedoms. They must let him know immediately of any special problems or repercussions of their activities. They should make an honest effort to keep him from being surprised. In turn, he grants them room to work.

"Doing community policing here means you have an increased sense of trust from your sergeant," says one experienced patrol officer working on a problem on his beat.

"She'll still pull my leash if I get out of line. But the leash has gotten a lot longer so I can go out and do what I need to do to fix the problem. It works for me."

Supervisors can aid their community policing practitioners by helping them plan their efforts. The sharp supervisor can make suggestions as to possible resources to tap or courses of action to try. All the while, he does his best to label his contributions as suggestions that can be disregarded, not orders that must be obeyed. The supervisor who really understands how community policing works realizes that the best ideas for solutions most often come from the bottom up, not the other way around. He can help with a problem or project; he must not take it over. When a solution is successful in removing or mitigating a problem, he assures that the credit goes to the officer(s) who did the work. His own credit will come from their success.

Under the auspices of community policing, the supervisor gives the officer or officers interested in tackling the problem time away from other duties to gather information, analyze its meaning and then work with others to devise a workable solution. He is careful to see to it that the other officers taking up the slack and handling the calls have a chance to work, uninterrupted, on their own community policing efforts another time, if they so desire. He also remains mindful that there will always be a need for cops who just want to write tickets and put criminals in jail, too. He will assure that they are recognized and rewarded for their contributions. He knows that if he and his department fail to achieve fair treatment for both active practitioners and less active supporters of community policing, serious morale problems and agency divisiveness can occur. As always, *equality* in supervisory treatment of employees is the key.

The supervisor's own attitude towards community policing will go a long way in determining his officers' interest in it. Particularly where community policing has been newly installed in a department, there is evidence that supervisors who encourage, aid and reward employees who are looking for and solving problems will have most of their officers doing community policing. If the supervisor is lukewarm or clearly opposed to the concept, little community policing activity will be seen among his watching subordinates.

As might be expected, officers granted authority by their supervisors to use discretion and flexibility in their problem solving appear to be the most successful as community policing practitioners. Not infrequently, added trust and latitude result in additional success. At the same time, officers told by their supervisors simply to "go find and solve something" generally do not do as well. Clearly, continuing interest by the first-line supervisor is necessary if the community-oriented approach to solving problems is to work well.

The supervisors of many successful problem-solvers also stay involved in the evaluation or assessment phase of their peoples' work. Here they can give deserved recognition when things go well. Just as important, they can offer advice for needed changes in tactics or approach if things could be better.

Experience has shown that the most effective community policing supervisors welcome a novel approach to an old problem and are not quick to criticize a subordinate's proposed solution, however impractical or bizarre it may appear at first glance. These same, effective supervisors expect and generally get compliance with the rules and ethics accompanying good police work. Nevertheless, they are more concerned with solving problems with the community's help than they are with production numbers. Good community policing supervisors don't count beans; they DO number the solutions their people have achieved in combating the community's ills.

Likewise, good community policing leaders build trust and a positive attitude among their subordinates. They serve as reliable information channels and a buffer between line officers working on a real problem and the agency's brass hats who may on occasion want a moment by moment account of what is being done. They provide their officers with a reasonable degree of earned independence and allow them to "fail" successfully by learning from the experience without major repercussions. They give their officers the resources they need to work with the community on solving problems. They realize that time and supervisory support are perhaps the most valuable resources that they have at their disposal for aiding their employees.

SUMMARY

Supervision in a police agency practicing true community policing requires a partial break with the traditional style of law enforcement supervision. But supervision is not lacking. It is simply somewhat different in its approach and application. The effective community policing supervisor still guides, assists and evaluates his people and their work. But he also grants them additional independence, flexibility and authority to identify problems and secure the community's active assistance in solving them. In the final analysis, he emphasizes effectiveness over numbers; obvious results over old ways.

Community policing does not weaken supervision. It merely redirects some of its focus.

POINTS TO REMEMBER

- Community policing has different meanings in differing locales.
- The wise supervisor will understand his jurisdiction's definition and expectations of community policing.
- In its purest form, community-oriented policing calls for real partnerships with the customers of law enforcement services.
- Community policing does not do away with 911 responses or reactive modes of policing; it complements them.
- In community policing, the supervisor gives his employees additional flexibility to identify and solve the community's problems.
- Community policing does not mean less supervision; it calls for a

slightly altered style of supervision.
- In this style of policing leaders encourage their subordinates to innovate and imagine.
- Community policing allows its practitioners to learn from their failures without penalties.

Chapter Fifteen

THE POLICE LEADER'S ROLE
IN OFFICER SURVIVAL

Many long-time law enforcement supervisors can recall an era when the recruit academy included no "officer safety" or "officer survival" training. The novice cop of those days learned some basic laws and procedures, perhaps a few handcuffing techniques, something about which end of the gun the bullet came out of and then found himself out on the street with an "experienced" partner, who often as not turned out to be a grizzled old salt with little use for snot-nosed rookies. If the veteran knew something about officer safety, fine. If not, the rookie might soon find himself well over his head when facing his first dangerous situation, solo.

In the 1970s, officer survival as a separate and distinct topic of instruction began appearing in police academies and in-service schools on a relatively widespread basis. That change has escalated through the present time. It occurred after early officer safety experts like Pierce R. Brooks discovered that a central core of fatal errors was to blame for most police murders. It was only a step or two further to the development of experience-proven safety steps for keeping officers alive.

The errors that have resulted in police casualties have changed little over the years. The same careless mistakes that felled peace officers back when the U.S. marshals rode the dusty trails of the West are still killing cops in the twenty-first century. The major killers include the following:

1. Making false assumptions
2. Failure to watch a subject's hands
3. General carelessness and apathy

4. False, foolhardy courage ("cowboy policing")
5. Improper use (or no use) of backup help
6. Poor positioning or approach
7. Poor weapon retention practices
8. Lack of proficiency with equipment
9. Failing to wear body armor
10. Improper use of available cover
11. Improper handcuffing, including no handcuffing
12. Poor searches of subjects
13. Failure to remain constantly alert.

At the same time, the hard-earned and sometimes bloody experiences of a lot of law enforcement officers over many years have resulted in a reliable set of officer survival rules designed to keep a police man or woman from falling prey to one or more of the deadly mistakes. These steps to staying alive include:

1. First and foremost, always rely on your good common sense
2. Don't try to be a hero
3. Never stop learning your job; never become complacent
4. Do not underestimate your adversary
5. Never stop looking for one more threat or danger
6. Maintain proficiency with all the tools of your job
7. Stay in shape, both physically and mentally
8. Do not nap or daydream on the job
9. Watch your approach and positioning to a call or contact
10. Maintain a "reactionary gap" between you and your subject
11. Keep watching a subject's hands for threats
12. Use backup help wisely
13. Practice good weapon retention techniques
14. Watch yourself around all prisoners
15. Make no dangerous assumptions
16. Make the best use of available cover
17. Wear your body armor
18. Play imaginary threat scenarios through your mind; plan your responses
19. Remember to survive emotionally, too
20. Critique your officer safety practices; learn from your experiences.

Today's officer survival experts agree on one thing: the first-line supervisor has perhaps THE key role to play in helping officers stay safe on the job. It is the supervisor, they contend, who is most responsible for inspecting for unsafe practices, instilling proper safety techniques through training, and using correction and discipline to curtail unsafe behavior, where necessary. It is also the primary supervisor's role, many safety experts assert, to model proper safety and survival behavior for subordinates to emulate. As they see it, the police supervisor is clearly the most vital element in the overall officer survival picture.

Few veteran law enforcement supervisors would deny the vital role they play in ensuring the safety and ultimate survival of their frontline subordinates. Most would agree that they indeed have safety responsibilities in several different areas. Those areas will be explored next.

TRAINING RESPONSIBILITIES

A good supervisor assesses the training needs of his subordinates. This must be done on a continuing basis. In no single area of job knowledge is this continuing assessment more important than in the area of officer safety. A safety-savvy supervisor will assess the safety knowledge of his fresh-from-the-academy rookies by listening to them, questioning them and, most important of all, carefully observing their functioning on the street. Where they fall short he will show and counsel and correct them. He may personally demonstrate the right way to do a given task safely or assign that responsibility to a senior officer known for his or her safety know-how.

In some cases the supervisor may decide to assign personnel lacking the fine points of officer survival to attend a relevant in-service safety course either inside or outside the department. In this way he can take advantage of the safety expertise of others while freeing himself for additional supervisory tasks. Many excellent officer survival courses are available today, including some of those taught by the FBI and the International Association of Chiefs of Police. Firms such as Calibre Press® also put on some excellent survival seminars. In many areas, regional safety schools taught by current or retired police officers also are available. There are, unfortunately, some not-so-good schools out there, too. By maintaining close contact with the department's training unit as well as his own peers in other law enforcement agencies, the street supervisor should be able to stay current on training offerings while he sorts out the quality schools from the shaky ones.

Neither will the safety schooling needs of the veteran police employee be overlooked by the conscientious supervisor. Indeed, it is sometimes this officer who has developed the most dangerous bad habits. By observing the field work of this experienced but sometimes careless employee the sharp supervisor will be able to spot hazardous practices in time to correct them ahead of a disaster.

The supervisor's safety counseling task may, of course, become somewhat harder when it comes to dealing with the veteran employee who feels he or she has seen it all, done it all and knows it all. But the job is too vital not to accept. The supervisor may find his remedial training task easier here if he remembers to point out safety deficiencies in private and provide survival advice in a quiet and non-threatening manner. Little is learned when an overheated ego feels menaced, even through the best of supervisory intentions.

The supervisor's safety training job is an unending one. Training needs will change somewhat as new threats appear and new safety equipment and tactics are developed. The wise supervisor will stay abreast of changes in both threats and threat responses and brief his people accordingly. There is not a more important function in the list of supervisory duties and responsibilities.

INSPECTION RESPONSIBILITIES

Closely related to the supervisor's responsibility to train for safety is his obligation to inspect for it. That will require that he inspect his team's equipment including firearms, soft body armor, vehicles and other tools on a regular basis. But supervisors must do more than inspect for the presence, cleanliness and function of safety-related equipment. They also must require that the officer using the equipment can demonstrate proficiency with it. In other words, it is not enough that Patrolman X carries a clean sidearm. He must also demonstrate that he can hit what he aims it at on a consistent basis.

The supervisor's inspection duties extend well beyond equipment. He must observe how his people function in the real world of police work. This he cannot accomplish from his desk in the stationhouse. In spite of the burdens of managerial paperwork and related administrative duties, it is absolutely essential that the effective first-line supervisor spend much more time in the field than he does in the station. He must drop by unannounced on his officers' traffic stops, pedestrian contacts, report calls and arrest situations. He must carefully observe and assess real world tactics including approach, positioning, use of cover, use of backups, verbal techniques, conflict de-escalation and arrest and control mechanics, all from the standpoint of good survival practices. All of this the supervisor accomplishes without appearing to "hover" over his people ("I was close so I came by to see if you needed any help.")

With the information gained from his personal observations and inspection efforts, the supervisor can identify safety shortcomings in his troops and work with them to achieve the desired changes. In doing so he must be sure that his inspection and follow-up activities extend to veteran officers and not stop with the slick-sleeved rookie. As noted, it may indeed be harder for the police supervisor to recommend changes in behavior to the long-time employee who also may be a long-time friend. But the job must be done all the same if the supervisor is to discharge his safety related obligations to ALL of his employees.

EQUIPMENT RESPONSIBILITIES

Simply and directly put, it is the police supervisor's duty to see to it that his people have the best equipment the agency can provide for their difficult and often hazardous job. The smart supervisor stays current on what is available by keeping up with the ads and articles in the police professional journals. He also stays up to date by talking with his peers and the equipment buffs who are present in every law enforcement agency. Most important of all, he asks his subordinates for their ideas concerning equipment and tries to involve them in any field testing or evaluating of new tools being looked at by the department. He realizes that the views of the people who actually will use the equipment are virtually always the most relevant opinions of all.

On occasion the supervisor will be required to represent the equipment needs and interests of his people to his own bosses. When he does so he will do best if he goes armed with logical facts, figures and research as to HOW the new weapon, chemical spray, body armor, vehicle or whatever will benefit the agency and its employees. If increased safety is the only argument (and seldom will it be), it will suffice as the major consideration that it is. If other benefits like reduced exposure to lawsuits, increased officer efficiency and heightened officer morale can be expected as a result of the equipment purchase, then these must be cited, too. Helping police officers obtain what they reasonably need to do their jobs more safely is a major responsibility of an effective first-line leader.

INTERVENTION RESPONSIBILITIES

Who is responsible for detecting and dealing with the "cowboy cop"? Who is accountable for disciplining the "loose cannon" who refuses to change his or her irresponsible behavior on the street that all too often endangers the public as well as other officers? The answer to both queries, of course, is the same: the first-line supervisor.

Police managers quite logically expect that it is the first-line supervisor who first will pick up on unsafe practices by a line officer. Management also requires that same supervisor to work with the employee to solve the problem, whatever the required response.

In the best-possible scenario the unsafe police employee will respond voluntarily to the safety counseling of his or her supervisor. In many instances counseling, perhaps combined with safety refresher training and follow-up field inspections, will solve the difficulty. With the recalcitrant, arrogant or semi-insubordinate employee, negative discipline in the form of reprimands and/or suspensions may be required to get his or her attention. In this case a good supervisor will demonstrate the personal courage and administrative backbone required to get the unpleasant job accomplished quickly so that everyone involved can be safer.

The empathetic supervisor with an unresponsive safety "violator" in his work unit should keep one special truth in mind. Whether he works in a factory or a law enforcement agency, a first-line supervisor who shields a deliberately and chronically unsafe employee from correction does no one a favor. If a "cowboy" or "cowgirl" cop cannot be brought to mend their dangerously unsafe ways and work within the expectations of the law enforcement organization, for everyone's good they must be separated from the police service. What they will otherwise continue to do by way of direct action and poor example is too destructive to be permitted in a profession that demands safety as a watchword.

The first-line supervisor is responsible for the safe functioning of his work team. That responsibility includes applying punitive discipline when other measures fail to have the desired effect. That progressive discipline must be implemented even when it may culminate in a supervisory recommendation for employee termination. Safety is that important to the police organization, its people and the customers they all serve.

EMPLOYEES' EMOTIONAL SURVIVAL

The tragedy is not much lessened if an officer involved in a street shootout escapes his adversary's bullets only to fall victim to an emotional overload and mental breakdown later. But critical incidents do not represent the only threats to the mental well-being of the law enforcement officer. Cops also can be victimized by the pent-up stresses of everyday police work with its supply of mayhem and unpleasant people and situations. Stressed-out officers who abuse alcohol, drugs or their spouses can sometimes be the results of such unrelieved stress. A few of these officers cause serious harm to others; more harm themselves, perhaps fatally. Still others abandon law enforcement in search of a less emotionally-demanding career.

A good supervisor knows his people. He oftentimes senses changes in their day-to-day demeanor as well as job performance. He pays extra attention to the behavior of an officer who has recently gone through a traumatic incident or series of them, on or off the job. He lets his people know that it's alright to feel normal human emotions. He lets them know he is available to talk. He lets them know he can keep a confidence, where appropriate. And he lets them know he will do his best to get them whatever outside help (such as a police psychologist) that they may need following a crisis. All of this is part of the supervisor's officer safety duties, too.

EXPLAINING OFFICER SAFETY

The supervisor who expects his people to adhere to strict officer safety practices must back them up when citizens call to inquire why the officers acted in a certain manner during a police-public interaction.

The smart supervisor hears the puzzled or angry citizen out. He does not deflect fair criticism or cover up for excessive or uncalled for behavior by a subordinate. What he DOES do is explain the safety reasoning behind such standard survival practices as handcuffing, searching, use of backups, compliance holds and the display of police weapons.

If, after he gets his officer's side of the story, it appears to the supervisor that police overreaction or other misconduct has occurred, corrective action as well as an explanation and apology will be required. Fortunately, however, experience has shown that once supplied with a courteous, honest and logical explanation of legitimate police behavior in a potentially dangerous situation, the majority of puzzled or unhappy people are at least moderately content with the law enforcement response and wish no further action.

The supervisor also can discuss safety practices along the lines of "why cops do what they do" in his contacts with citizens groups, school classes and other public forums where he may be called upon to do a presentation or answer questions about law enforcement. Widely diverse groups love to hear about police work from someone who does it for a living. The officer safety aspect of that work is not an exception. It is here that the supervisor has an excellent opportunity to educate the public about the dangers and difficulties of the cop's job. Everyone can benefit from his efforts, not least of all the officers who work for him.

If police professionals are to earnestly implement the officer safety teachings of their supervisor, they must know that he will stand by them when they properly apply those teachings on the job. The supervisor must give them the confidence they need to act safely by explaining, as necessary, their legitimate street survival conduct.

THE SUPERVISOR AS ROLE MODEL

You must, above all, be a good role model.

It is something the novice police supervisor hears constantly as he prepares for his role as a leader. He continues to hear it throughout his leadership career. It's true, and in no area of his job is it more important than in the realm of officer safety.

The supervisor must model a good safety attitude if he is to expect the same from his team members. That means he never takes the quickest and easiest route to anything unless it happens to be the safest way to do it, as well. He refuses to get careless or lazy or display a less than totally alert attitude on duty. He knows that his people are watching and will mimic what they see.

The supervisor sets a good example by keeping himself and his equipment in top-notch shape. He also sets an example that he wants to be emulated when he follows without exception basic officer safety guidelines covering such activities as traffic stops, pedestrian contacts, building searches and arrests. If he does make an officer safety mistake, he admits it and later explains to his officer audience what he should have done instead. Honesty in safety practices, not unlike in other things, is worth a great deal in establishing the supervisor's credibility.

The survival-conscious supervisor develops a work team of safety-smart officers around him. The caring, conscientious police leader could hardly hope for more.

SUMMARY

In no area of his important job are the police supervisor's attitudes and actions more vital to his subordinates' welfare than in the area of officer safety. The effective supervisor helps his officers survive on the street by constantly assessing their safety-related practices and providing training and counseling where needed. He inspects his troops' safety equipment and ensures that they know how to use it well. He intervenes and, where necessary, disciplines when their officer safety practices are unacceptable. He helps with their emotional survival and explains their safety practices to others when questions arise. Most important of all, he serves as an excellent role model for good safety awareness and survival practices.

POINTS TO REMEMBER

- The supervisor must be aware of the most serious officer survival errors and know how to combat them.
- The safety-savvy supervisor teaches officer survival at every opportunity.
- The supervisor serves as an excellent role model for officer safety practices.
- The supervisor inspects and advocates for officer safety.
- The supervisor intervenes promptly when he detects unsafe practices by his subordinates.
- The supervisor ensures that his people have the best officer safety equipment and use it properly at all times.
- A good supervisor watches out for his employees' emotional survival, too.

Chapter Sixteen

THE POLICE LEADER AS
AGENCY SPOKESPERSON

It is not enough that the police supervisor has just handled successfully the tactical, procedural, and legal issues that he or she found
present on the scene of a major crime or other incident. There is yet
another challenge–or opportunity–that the alert supervisor should
expect to be there: the members of the news media. Today more than
ever in the highly competitive world of journalism, law enforcement
operations and law enforcement people are BIG news. Violent crime
interests the public. (As one cynical journalist stated, "If it bleeds, it
leads!") So does any hint of misconduct by an employee of a criminal
justice agency. As the individual wearing the stripes or bars on-scene
at a newsworthy event, the leader can count on drawing reporters and
photojournalists like ants at a picnic. How the police supervisor handles the situation will go a long distance towards determining how his
officers and his agency come across to the taxpaying public. It is then
up to the on-scene patrol sergeant, detective supervisor, specialized
enforcement team leader or internal affairs boss to show a potentially
huge media audience the best face of the law enforcement organization. But precisely how is it done?

There is no good reason why a law enforcement supervisor who
does not hesitate to lead his or her troops into a darkened building
seeking a hidden criminal should quake at the sight of a camera,
microphone, or notepad in the hands of an aggressive reporter. The
sharp police leader can survive the media circus, even when he is in
the center ring. All that is required is an ample supply of common
sense, an ingrained habit of telling the truth, a willingness to treat others as he would want to be treated himself, and adherence to a few

293

basic guidelines for feeding the news hounds without getting bitten. It all starts with thorough, careful preparation.

GET THE FACTS STRAIGHT

The law enforcement supervisor would not attempt to write a police report or employee performance appraisal without first getting the facts, double checking them for accuracy and organizing them for presentation. He should do no less when he is gathering the information he will require to respond to the questions he might expect from an on-scene member of the media. In gathering the data needed to respond to a media grilling, the supervisor should expect to be questioned on at least the basic "5 W's and an H" ingrained in reporters from journalism school onwards:

WHO–Who was the victim? Who was the offender? Who was hurt or killed? Who were the involved officers? Who else was involved?

WHAT–What happened here? What may happen next? What are the police doing about it?

WHEN–What was the time and date of the crime or incident? When did other, related key events take place, such as arrests, searches, pronouncements at the hospital?

WHERE–What was the location of the main event? How about the location of related events, such as arrests or searches?

WHY–Is there a motive that the police are willing to talk about? Why did the accident occur? Why did law enforcement respond as it did?

HOW–What was the crime committed? How did the accident happen? How did law enforcement solve the crime and make the arrest?

Each of these queries can have any number of follow-up questions attached. At the same time, the supervisor may have good reason for not answering some of them at all, such as to protect an investigative key (example: type of injuries on the victim). In addition, the supervisor's agency almost certainly has guidelines for what can and cannot be released to the press, both now and later. It is absolutely vital that the front-line leader be conversant with his department's rules on media relations as well as information release and follow them to the letter.

Accuracy of the information to be released must be a major concern of the law enforcement supervisor. From the news-gatherer's point of view, the only thing worse than getting no information at all from the on-scene law enforcement representative is getting inaccurate information that will require correction or clarification in print or on the air later on. The supervisor can forestall the embarrassment and bad feelings almost certain to emanate from releasing such erroneous information by assuring that he has his facts straight in the first place. He will go to the best on-scene source for his data. That likely will be the investigating officer or detective in charge of the case. It could be a written report. The supervisor will double-check names and addresses for accuracy. If criminal charges are involved, he will be sure they are relayed accurately to the media.

In releasing information to the press, the supervisor turned spokesperson will avoid guessing, speculating or passing along *anything* he does not know for certain to be true. It's all too easy for rumor to get reported as fact by the media; it's vital that law enforcement not be the source for such incorrect information. It is best that the supervisor avoid giving opinions, even if asked, and stick strictly to what is factual. Virtually every veteran law enforcement officer has voiced opinions to his colleagues or others about how or why something happened, only to discover later that his conclusions were not even close to the truth. In front of a media audience is not the place to guess, editorialize or condemn.

ANTICIPATE AND PRACTICE

Naturally the police leader will want to know what he is likely to be asked before an interview, whether "live," taped or on paper, takes place. One way to determine which facts he needs to know is to place himself in the reporter's shoes. What would *he* want to know if the roles were reversed? Some queries are fairly easy to anticipate. (Some version of *who* and *what* will almost always be important.) If, for example, the supervisor is reporting on a major motor vehicle accident, he can count on being asked about names of the drivers and injured, how bad the injuries are, where the injured were taken, what caused the accident, and what charges are anticipated. As is almost always the case, some questions he will not be able to answer. He sometimes will have to refer his questioner elsewhere, such as to hospital officials or the victims' relatives for the nature of the injuries and the condition of the injured. If a property crime is the focus of the story, the supervisor can anticipate questions about how the crime was perpetrated, dollar loss in taken or damaged property and suspect information, if any. If the incident involved a shootout between cops and criminals, questions will arise about the identities of the shooters, how many shots were fired, who and what was hit, and why the shooting occurred, for starters. Once more, some questions cannot and should not be answered at this stage of the investigation. As always, the supervisor must be aware of his agency's policies regarding the release of such data. He must take care not to say too much, even in the face of very insistent and somewhat agitated journalists. ("But Anytown PD down the road ALWAYS releases the info we're asking for!") For all practical purposes, once information is in the hands of the press it cannot be recalled. Citing to news media representatives his agency's guidelines for what can and cannot be released may take at least a little of the pressure off his back.

It is perfectly acceptable to *ask* a newsperson what he or she plans to ask so as to be ready with the answers when the interview gets underway. At the same time, the supervisor should remain aware that it is unlikely a reporter will tell him in advance *every* question he will ask. This is not necessarily deceptiveness on the part of the reporter; the interview may simply have developed in directions that called for additional queries. The sharp supervisor will be ready for unexpected twists and turns as the questioning progresses. If he truly does not know the answer to a particular question, it is certainly acceptable to say so. If he knows the answer but cannot reveal it, that's okay, too, but he owes the questioner the courtesy of explaining *why* he cannot release that particular bit of information.

But before the police leader steps in front of notepads, microphones, and cameras, he should make an effort to *practice* what he is going to say and how he is going to say it. If there is time, it is a good idea to actually do a "rehearsal" in which another officer asks the questions and the supervisor practices responding. This obviously should take place out of public view. If a real-life rehearsal is impractical, the novice spokesperson may have to be content with running the questions and his planned answers through his mind and repeating his responses to himself, out loud or mentally, several times. Even a couple of minutes spent practicing what he wants to say will help the police leader by boosting his self-confidence with the knowledge that he is prepared when the grilling begins for real.

WHAT TO SAY

The written media relations policies and procedures with which the police supervisor should be intimate will provide the on-scene boss with direction on what to say and what to avoid talking about. If, for whatever reason, the supervisor is unaware of those guidelines or if his agency simply does not have any, the following general guidelines may prove helpful:

- DO furnish a general overview of the crime or incident, including times, places, and crimes involved.
- DO obey local or state guidelines governing the release of sensitive information, such as the identity of sex crime or child abuse victims.
- DO identify yourself and provide a telephone number where you can be reached, if necessary.
- DO provide the name of a follow-up contact person, such as the department's public information officer, unless you will continue to be the contact throughout.
- DON'T release the names of deceased persons until next of kin have been notified.
- DON'T release the amount of monetary loss in a property crime.
- DON'T give out information that may become an investigative key, such as the type of weapon used in a homicide.
- DON'T express opinions about motives involved or the guilt or innocence of anyone.
- DON'T comment on evidence, such as confessions, admissions, the presence of fingerprints, etc.

Whatever you say, make certain that you tell the truth. Say nothing at all as opposed to lying to the media. Credibility is everything to a police leader, in press matters the same as in everything else he says or does. Half-truths and lying by omission are just as dangerous for the law enforcement leader. A reputation for truthfulness, once lost, is very difficult for the individual or his agency to rebuild. Meanwhile, it is unlikely that the supervisor's boss is going to be too happy if he or she has a lot of explaining and apologizing to do because a subordinate lied to a reporter.

The media as well as the public in general hold law enforcement personnel to a particularly high standard for integrity and truthfulness. Veteran reporter Mike Wallace of *60 Minutes* fame has this advice for the law enforcement person facing a media blitz: "Credibility in an interviewee comes from openness, a willingness to take questions, the understanding that most reporters are simply trying to do the job they are paid for. Some police interviewees seem reluctant to believe that."

Another veteran reporter has an additional piece of good advice for the law enforcement interviewee: "We'll forgive you for not knowing. But we won't forgive *or* forget if you lie to us."

The advice is excellent. The police leader serving as the press officer of the moment does not have to know everything. He is not obligated to answer every question thrown at him. But the answers he does choose to give must be truthful and contain no inaccurate information, intentionally inserted or otherwise. That's what credibility means.

What to say and do during an on-scene media encounter includes more than the on the air presentation. It is also important that the supervisor remains calm and in control during his encounter with a reporter or photojournalist and respond with patience and courtesy even if the other party demonstrates neither. It is vital that the police leader stays polite and professional in the face of persistent probing. A competent journalist knows that there are places on a crime or incident scene that he will not be allowed to go, but he's obligated to try and go there, anyway. He also knows that there are likely questions that the supervisor cannot or will not answer. Nevertheless, he is obliged to ask. During this whole game of thrust and parry the media-savvy law enforcement leader must call upon all of the self-control he has developed over a career in policing in order to remain courteous, keep smiling and convey an honest and earned image for professionalism for both himself and his organization.

A veteran editor of a major American newspaper tells the tale of his encounter as a young cub reporter with the chief of a small town police department many years ago. Unhappy with what the reporter had truthfully written about a major snafu perpetrated by his department, the police administrator literally tossed the offending newsman down a flight of stairs. The reporter survived the encounter. The officer's career did, too. Today, it is unlikely that any American police leader could survive a duplicate performance.

DOING IT ON TELEVISION

Today, Americans form many of their beliefs about law enforcement and law enforcement officers from what they see on television. The police agency of the twenty-first century can ill afford to come across looking anything other than competent and professional to a critical viewing audience. That is simply today's reality. It is equally real that today's police leader cannot afford to look like a boob on the tube.

Television can expose an interviewee's shortcomings like no other medium. Sloppy appearance, mumbling, stumbling speech, and a less than professional demeanor can come back to haunt the law enforcement supervisor facing one or a battery of cameras. Fortunately, even a modest effort aimed at preparation for a television interview, live or taped, can help assure that the law enforcement leader represents himself and his agency in the highest traditions of the police service. It all starts with a few, basic guidelines for an effective response in the presence of the Big Eye:

- Do not be overly concerned about having a bit of camera fright. Even veteran television journalists have confessed to a few pre-broadcast butterflies. This can help keep you sharp and focused. Take a few deep breaths and go ahead.
- As noted previously, assemble your facts ahead of time, double-check them for accuracy, and practice, at least mentally, what you plan to say in response to the questions you anticipate.
- Take a few seconds to check your appearance before you go on camera, even if the best assistance you can hope for is the rearview mirror in your police car. Comb your hair, get rid of your gum, check your teeth for last hour's pizza dinner and straighten your tie and uniform.
- Avoid noisy or otherwise distracting mannerisms during the inter-

view. Turn off your portable radio, pager, and cell phone. Don't nervously jingle your coins, keys, or anything else. Keep your hands out of your pockets.

- During an on-camera interview, look at the person asking the questions, not the camera lens. Direct your responses to him or her.
- Keep your statements and responses short and concise. Remember that a local newscast may devote 15 seconds or less to your answers.
- Be sure you understand the question before you answer. Ask for a repeat or clarification if necessary, even if the interview is live. You don't want to end up answering something you were not asked. What you have to say is important, so it is vital that the viewing audience gets it right.
- Never get visibly angry with an interviewer, even if you feel he is deliberately misrepresenting the facts or attempting to lead you somewhere you do not want to go. Simply restate the facts, if need be, and keep your cool.
- Treat all microphones and cameras in your presence as "live" at all times. On occasion, interviewees have mistakenly believed the interview was over (or not yet started) and that they were having a private chat with the interviewer, only to discover their unguarded words broadcast later.
- If it is a taped interview and you discover that you have made serious misstatements or stumbled badly in your speech, ask the interviewer if it is possible to do it over. The television interviewer also has a stake in producing a professional-looking product.

TRAPS TO AVOID

While the smart law enforcement supervisor will take pains to avoid an unnecessary confrontation with a representative of the press, he is also responsible to his own agency for preventing media excesses and other misbehavior at the scene. Three restrictions on news-gathering activities are reasonable and are easily explained to any member of the press questioning their propriety:

First, the media cannot be permitted to destroy evidence or otherwise contaminate a scene. Police crime scene tape and barriers apply to news media reps just as they do the rest of the public. Although virtually all news-gatherers know this, some will push for special privileges, anyway. They must be denied entry with a courteous explanation. At the same time, a member of the press corps cannot be denied access to an area open to other members of the public. Carrying a camera or notepad may not give one special privileges, but it should not deny freedoms accorded others, either.

Second, the media cannot be allowed to obstruct or interfere with police operations on-scene. Saying something the cops do not like is not a crime; physically getting in their way may be. That's why permitting reporters and photojournalists inside the barrier tape is unacceptable. Another example of the media interfering with a police operation may be seen in a scenario in which news camera lights spoil the night vision of tactical team members and reveal their location to a barricaded criminal. The offending journalist must be told immediately, politely and firmly to desist. Taking a member of the press into physical custody for interference at an incident scene should remain a last option for the police supervisor, after warnings and other measures have failed. But it remains an option nonetheless.

Third, members of the media must not be allowed or assisted to break the law. Reporters do not get a special pass on law violations because they are accompanying the police or reporting on a crime or accident. An example may be seen in the cameraperson who enters private property along with officers in order to document their doings. Unless the property owner has given his consent, this action could be construed as trespassing. Once again, a firm warning to the media people to cease their illegal behavior is the supervisor's first option with arrest being the last resort for repeated or flagrant disregard of police orders. Any time a member of the press is arrested or charged, of course, the wise supervisor makes sure his own chain of command is promptly made aware of the dustup.

A good rule of thumb for the police leader enforcing media restrictions on-scene is this common sense piece of advice: Have a good reason for what you do. Unless you can identify a tangible reason why the media should not be allowed to do something, it is probably alright to allow them to proceed. An example here might be seen in the supervisor whose sense of propriety tells him that a photojournalist should not be allowed to take pictures of a mangled dead body lying in a public place. Unfortunately, the law is not with him on this one. If the photographer and his employer have so little sense of decency as to publish or broadcast such a gruesome scene, it will be up to the public, not the police, to condemn them. As long as the picture-taker is in a place where he lawfully has a right to be, he should be permitted to continue with his bad taste performance.

Other traps to avoid include the tricks that certain journalists sometimes pull on their interview subjects. These tricks and their antidotes include the following:

The dead air ploy. In this one, the interviewer simply remains silent and stares intently at his subject when the person has finished his answer. A series of pregnant pauses could go on for some time. The interviewer's hope is that his subject will eventually fill the uncomfortable silence by talking some more, perhaps saying something he had never intended. The solution? The police supervisor should remain silent and return his interviewer's gaze. Nothing else has to be said. After a few volleys of this game, the interviewer may get the picture and desist.

The convoluted questioner. Whether they do it accidentally or not, some interviewers have a knack for asking complex, multipart questions that are so lengthy the interviewee may be clueless as to exactly what he is answering. The smart supervisor will ask clarifying questions if he is unsure what he is being asked to answer. He also can laughingly tell his questioner that he's a little confused by the lengthy query and will repeat each part of the question before he answers it just to be sure everyone is on the same page.

The misinterpreter. This character may begin the interview by stating factually incorrect information, or he may paraphrase the supervisor's answer incorrectly or with a different meaning than its speaker intended. Whatever the case, the law enforcement leader must stop everything and politely correct his conversation partner. A good street cop is accustomed to taking control of a situation or conversation under less than perfect circumstances. It is perfectly acceptable to take control of a media interview, too, but quietly and with a good-sized dollop of courtesy thrown in for good measure. It must be done to prevent the media audience from being left with incorrect facts and impressions.

The interrupter. This individual may or may not intend to be tricky, but he is rude. A few journalists have the nasty habit of interrupting their subject with opinions of their own or yet another question before the interviewee has finished talking. They may not be hesitant to smother the interviewee's version of events with one of their own. The police supervisor faced with interruptions to what he is trying to say must keep talking, raising his voice slightly if need be, until he is finished with what he initially intended to say. While it sounds (and is) rude to have two people talking at once, this is one exception to the mandate for absolute courtesy to the media. The polite interviewee who clams up every time his tormentor begins spouting may find at the end of the interview that he never had a chance to place his important message in front of his audience.

Going "off the record." A street-smart reporter may ask the police leader questions that he states are "off the record," or "on background only." The leader who elects to respond is playing a potentially dangerous game. Anything an interviewee says to a reporter, off the record or not, is fair game for publication or broadcast. The reporter who elects to use it may be breaking the rules of fair play, but he is not breaking the law. If what the supervisor has to say is particularly "juicy" and amounts to something that the competing news organizations do not have, he should not be surprised to see his "confidential" tidbit leading off the ten o'clock news broadcast. The obvious defense to off the record dangers is not to play the game at all.

The good news is that most journalists are honest sorts who are just trying to do a difficult job as best they can, not unlike the police professional. For those few who do break the rules and push the limits, a police supervisor who is willing and able to enforce reasonable guidelines in an even-handed and courteous manner should be able to keep media relations on an even keel. That is yet another of his important duties as a leader.

WRITING A NEWS RELEASE

Most law enforcement agencies have a standard form utilized for information to be released to the news media. It includes the basics of what happened, at least to the extent that can be made public at the time. Most agencies likewise have procedural guidelines covering what can and cannot go into the release. If the department has a PIO or press officer, oftentimes that individual will prepare press releases to be faxed or otherwise disseminated to the media outlets. But if the agency does not have a PIO or the PIO is unavailable, the law enforcement supervisor may be called upon to write a press summary of what happened.

The police supervisor should find doing a news release no more difficult than completing the other writing assignments he handles on a regular basis. By following a few guidelines as well as the dictates of his good common sense, he can produce a document that both satisfies the needs of the media and serves the interests of the law enforcement agency. Here are a few suggestions for doing it the right way:

Include the "5 W's and an H." Those, of course, are who, what, when, where, why and how. They are the same elements that should be covered in good police reports. For the purposes of the news release, at times the "why" may be self-obvious or omitted altogether. Motive may not be something investigators want to get into at this point. The writer of the release should get the approval of the involved investigator before covering the "why" aspect of the case. The news release should not contain the amount of detail that goes into a complete police report. It is only intended as a quick summary of the most vital points concerning the crime or other incident that can be released at the time.

Keep it short. The release should be kept to a single, double-spaced page or less. The facts should go in descending order of importance. Sentences and paragraphs should be short, concise, and to the point.

Type it, if feasible. It is vital that reporters get the information right, so it is important that they be able to read the release easily. The information should be keyboarded on one side of an eight and one-half by eleven sheet of white paper. If typing is out of the question, the writer should block print neatly.

Avoid jargon and legalese. The supervisor should remain mindful that he is writing for the general public, not an audience of cops. He should omit "police speak," including acronyms, abbreviations, and terms not necessarily known to the public. "Perps" and "pinches" do not belong in news releases. Times and dates should be written in civilian, not military, fashion.

It must be right. The release writer must check and double-check his facts for accuracy before they go into a news release. After the release is completed, it must be proofread carefully for factual, typographical or grammatical errors. The release represents the agency and the individual who produced it, so it must be right. It is especially important to check names and addresses for accuracy. A lot of grief can follow if the drug raid is reported as occurring at 405 West Maple when it actually happened at 405 East Maple. Charges filed or pending also must be reported accurately.

Avoid giving opinions. A news release is not the place for the writer to editorialize on the guilt or character of any of the participants. News releases should not refer to "brave" officers or "guilty" offenders. The news release should report exactly what happened in a clear and straightforward manner. It is then up to the reader of the document to use his intelligence to form his own opinions.

Give it authority and credibility. Reporters who read the news release will want to attribute it to a source. This gives the information they will print or broadcast authority and believability. It also will help cover their backsides if the information turns out to be in error. The writer of the release should include his or her name, rank or title and agency. A telephone number for follow-up questions also should be provided.

Get required approvals. The agency's guidelines for the release of information to the press must be followed to the letter in preparation of the news release. If in serious doubt about whether or not to release a specific piece of information, the smart supervisor will decline to release it. It always can be released later. The supervisor also should know if his or her boss's signoff is required before the release goes out. A news release once placed into the public domain is virtually impossible to recall.

Do not overuse it. The supervisor should be certain that the event he is writing about really merits news release treatment. Agencies that generate blizzards of news releases, often for minor happenings, eventually find that most of their releases get ignored by the media. The agency's written guidelines may help the supervisor decide if a news release is warranted. Also, if there has been little or no press interest expressed in an incident, a news release may not be necessary at the moment.

Timeliness is vital. Most news organizations feel that, to be of interest to their audience, police news is best savored fresh. A news release prepared a week after a great arrest may draw little or no interest from the press. Today's public depends more and more on the Internet for news and accompanying video clips. The "get it now" nature of Internet news assures that stale stories are quickly deleted from the Net's pages. If the supervisor wants his or her people to get deserved credit for excellent work, the news release should be prepared and disseminated as shortly after the event as practical.

SUMMARY

The public gets most of its information about law enforcement officers and law enforcement operations from Internet news, television, radio, and the print media. Clearly it is in the best interest of the supervisor, his employer, and the policing profession that all information reaching the public is accurate and, whenever possible, presents law enforcement and its people in a positive light. That does not obligate the ethical law enforcement leader to lick anyone's boots or otherwise "kiss up" to the press. It DOES mean that the police supervisor who deals competently, honestly, and fairly with the media on the scene of a crime or other interest-generating incident makes it more likely that his agency will be well-treated when the news hits the airwaves or the morning headlines.

The intelligent leader prepares carefully for his "fifteen seconds" in the media spotlight. He gets his facts straight, plans, and practices what he wants to say ahead of time and then says it–clearly, concisely, and briefly. He follows his department's rules for what he can and cannot release, but everything he does say is the truth. He aids the media's representatives in every way he legitimately can, but he does not permit them to run rampant or otherwise interfere with a crime scene or police operation.

Any police supervisor can contribute to good news media relations for his department when he is on the spot and on the news. All it takes is the application of attention to detail, good judgment, common sense, and an absolute devotion to telling the truth. Chances are, each of those key tools is already in the toolbox of the competent law enforcement leader.

POINTS TO REMEMBER

• Who, what, when, where, why and how are the pieces of information that a reporter seeks from the law enforcement spokesperson.

- The supervisor must know his agency's media policies well so that he is aware of what he can and cannot release to a reporter.
- Intentionally providing false information to the media is an improper practice.
- Practicing for an interview with a reporter helps calm the jitters while the spokesperson organizes what he wants to say and avoid saying.
- Once it has been said the reporter has no legal obligation not to use it.
- All microphones and cameras present should be considered live at all times.
- Going "off the record" with a reporter is very risky.
- Media representatives must not be allowed to obstruct law enforcement operations, contaminate evidence or break the law.
- Reporters use a number of tricks to get more out of the spokesperson than he intended to say.
- News releases should be brief, clear, accurate, timely and devoid of the opinions of the writer.
- Internet news should not be overlooked for its value to law enforcement and public alike.

Chapter Seventeen

THE POLICE LEADER'S ROLE IN EXCEPTIONAL CUSTOMER SERVICE

Every police supervisor has been confronted in his or her private life with exceptionally poor customer service. It may have been delivered by a snotty clerk in a retail store, a twenty-something airhead at an airline ticket counter or a "I'm a civil servant don't bother me" drone in the offices of a government bureaucracy. However and wherever it happened, there is a pretty good chance that the chagrined police supervisor remembers the episode chapter and verse. What's more, he or she has probably told more than a few other people about the lousy experience.

It might come as a surprise that all too many citizens–the customers of any law enforcement agency–have some of the same kind of tales to tell *about their experiences with law enforcement personnel.* Indeed, all too many citizens view law enforcement people as just another species of bureaucrat whose goal seems to be making life as difficult for everyone else as possible. That may be hard to swallow for the law enforcement leader who *knows* how hard his or her people work, often under extremely trying conditions. But it's true. And if that same law enforcement leader will be honest, he almost certainly will remember instances in which he has personally observed less-than-helpful service from police personnel. If he's really honest with himself, he will admit he has been personally guilty of such conduct. In the urgency and pressure of police work, it simply happens sometimes.

But does it really *have* to be that way?

The answer is no. Even in the pressing business of the police job, certain niceties are worth doing for more than the reason that it's the right thing to do. Treating people as one would want to be treated himself is also worth the effort because it can make the job easier for the police practitioner. That's the real message that the leader needs to get across to his subordinates. The information provided in this chapter will help him deliver that message.

WHAT DO THEY WANT?

There is no denying that law enforcement officers sometimes have to deal with jerks. There is not a more honest way to say it. At the same time, it is also true that most of the people contacted by a law enforcement officer are NOT jerks. Many of them are simply people with a question or a problem in search of an answer or a solution. Some of them are confused. And more than a few may be lacking in the basic courtesies themselves, at least during their current moment of crisis.

While some of the people contacted by the police employee, either in person or over the telephone, may seek some specific action, at least as many others may want only to vent to an empathetic ear. Frequently, these individuals are not crooks. Even if they ARE part of the problem, experience has demonstrated that the police employee who employs some basic customer service skills in responding to these people will find them easier to handle. Patience and tact clearly must be components of the police employee's customer service tool bag.

Huge, private sector corporations as well as tiny, mom and pop operations enjoying a deserved reputation for great customer service require that their employees buy into several key guidelines for handling customers:

- Customers are individuals with names and feelings.
- Customers are very important to us.
- Customers are the reason we have a job.
- Customers are not interruptions to our work; they ARE our work.
- The most vital thing we do is take care of our customers.

The reality is, of course, that a cop who has just encountered a "customer" who has cursed, attacked, and spat on him is probably not in a customer service frame of mind. He is likely to think of a number of things to call the individual who has just abused him, but "customer" is probably not among them. The fact remains, however, that the majority of people he meets on the job do not respond to him in that fashion. Some are quite friendly and cooperative. Most are, at worst, "neutral" in their reaction to police authority. The officer, like the agency he works for, truly does have customers who are seeking some kind of service.

Not unlike the off-duty police person, the citizen seeks some specific things when interacting with a service provider. Whether he is dealing with the counter guy at the fast food establishment or a civil servant who happens to be wearing a police uniform, the average citizen expects several things from that exchange:

Reliability: "You can count on me."
Responsiveness: "I'm familiar with that kind of situation and we'll handle it."
Reassurance: "The worst is over. It's going to be alright."
Empathy: "I think I know how you're feeling."
Results: "Here's what we're going to do."

The citizen-customer who feels shorted in any of these expectations probably will be feeling no differently than the police supervisor who has just been short-changed for service at the local big box store. The citizen, not unlike the supervisor, will have bad feelings for the entity from which the perceived poor service originated. Citizen and officer alike will not be hesitant to tell others about the bad experience.

In addition to what he wants, there is also a list of things that the average customer does *not* want to hear from a service provider, whether that provider is a cop or a clerk. Those spoken phrases include the following:

"You should have called earlier." (As likely as not, the individual probably already wishes he had).

"That's impossible." (Internal affairs investigators eventually learn not to use that statement. Unless the citizen is reporting that the cops are really disguised Moon Men who tried to remove his organs, whatever it is probably isn't TOTALLY beyond the realm of possibility).

"That's department policy." (The supervisor might recall how pleased that response makes him when he gets it from a haughty retail clerk or self-important bank manager. A bit more explanation might help soften the blow.)

"You will have to. . . ." (That one is about as welcome as the immediately preceding comment. There probably is a better way of saying essentially the same thing.)

"I can't help you." (Alright, but would you at least TRY, or perhaps you could refer me to someone who MIGHT be able to do something).

There are almost certainly better ways to deliver these same messages, but with less of a perceived "I don't really care" attitude on the part of the employee delivering the news. Sometimes all a citizen-customer is looking for is a patient, empathetic ear and a willingness from someone to at least TRY to help. That attitude, clearly transmitted by a police employee who means it, can make a world of difference in the impression made on that individual by the employee and his or her agency. It will be an impression carried long past the actual interaction between service seeker and service provider.

WHAT THEY DON'T WANT

Customers of law enforcement organizations are not unlike law enforcement agency employees when it comes to what they do NOT want to encounter in their interaction with a service provider. On a national scale, the things that really fire the jets of unhappy customers are fairly consistent from one part of the country to the next. Frequently heard customer complaints include:

- Slow (or no) service.
- Rudeness; discourtesy.
- "Can't do" attitude shown by the employee.
- "Nobody listened to me."
- Attitude of "indifference."

As the police leader will recall from his or her own experiences as a service recipient, even the perception of the existence of any of these problems is practically guaranteed to result in a frustrated, disgruntled customer.

Reality dictates, of course, that not everyone will be happy no matter how much customer service he receives. Even so, there are a number of common sense steps that any law enforcement practitioner can take to increase the number of customers who leave with a favorable impression of the agency in spite of the fact that they did not get exactly what they wanted or expected. All of these steps require an honest expression of concern and a sincere willingness to at least TRY to help on the part of the employee involved. This approach is sometimes referred to as the Golden Rule of Customer Service. It amounts to little more than the way in which the service provider would want to be treated if the tables were turned. It is absolutely applicable to the daily challenges faced by the law enforcement officer or civilian police employee.

Nothing works every time. Nevertheless, there are some basic "tricks of the trade" any police employee can apply to leave a citizen-customer with positive feelings about his or her encounter with law enforcement. The supervisor can outline them for his or her subordinates as quick and simple means for increasing customer satisfaction. They include:

Treat people as individuals and use their name. Personalizing service to an individual with a face and a name can sometimes make that individual easier to handle. Even a criminal has a name. "Difficult" people who are called by name sometimes become more reasonable. However, some older citizens regard today's "instant familiarity" as rude. The wise service provider will get that individual's permission before calling him or her by a first name.

Be a very good listener. The urge to cut off a long-winded speaker is strong. Listening patiently, however, may help an officer get the information he needs to resolve a problem or accurately answer a question, thereby preventing a return call to the same individual. Making eye contact, nodding empathetically from time to time and maintaining open body posture all can help the law enforcement person keep an individual talking. At the same time, it is reasonable to steer a wandering talker back to the subject. "We need to stick to the present problem right now. . . ."

Allow him (or her) to save face, if possible. Face-saving is important for just about everyone. If a police customer has made an error, rubbing his nose in it probably will not make things go any smoother for the employee handling the problem. While the police person may not agree with the individual's viewpoint, allowing him to say what he has to say without a putdown just might make him easier to deal with. No one likes to be embarrassed, especially in front of others.

Build trust. That is obviously an easier task to accomplish with some individuals than it is with others. In good customer service, it is at least worth the effort. A law enforcement service provider who displays courtesy, sincerity, reliability, and credibility has put a great deal of effort into trust building with a police customer. It is also helpful for an employee to express appreciation, where appropriate. While a desk officer may not be exactly ecstatic that a complainant has just brought him his ninth car vandalism report of the shift, that same complainant just might have a piece of information that will lead to the clearance of all of those crimes. Even if that ninth reporting party can't help solve the criminal mischief episode, he likely will remember the officer's attitude, for better or worse, as indicative of all employees of the agency. Doing it the right way really IS worthwhile, for more than one good reason.

HOW CAN THEY BE REACHED?

The importance of excellent communication skills for the police leader has already been discussed. It is also true that exceptional customer service flows from employees who display excellent communication skills. Many police employees are excellent communicators. Some of the best display similar traits in dealing with the customer service challenges of the job. The sharp supervisor will "mine" their abilities to be passed along to other police people who might need a little work in the communication skills department. For example, excellent police communicators smile, when appropriate. They make good eye contact with those they are talking with and display an open posture as opposed to the crossed arms and sour expression of someone who has already made up his mind, or who does not want to be there in the first place. Good communicators avoid cop talk (police slang) and utilize vocabulary appropriate to their audience. They tell the truth and take nothing for granted when it comes to reaching understanding with their audience. They stress what they CAN do to help the citizen-customer. They nod their head affirmatively from time to time, not necessarily to indicate agreement but to tell the speaker he or she is being understood and to keep talking.

As any veteran peace officer will attest, perhaps the most difficult customer to address is the angry individual. Whether he is shouting in person or heating up the telephone wires, this difficult individual can strain the customer service skills of the most saintly civil servant. Once again, however, there exist a number of time-proven techniques that can be used to help calm an angry complainant. Also once again, none is guaranteed to work every time. Each is nonetheless worth trying in an honest effort to improve communication and get to the central issue of solving the problem at hand. These "chill out" tactics include:

- Try not to take the verbal barrage personally. That is a lot easier said than accomplished. But it's also true that the angry individual may be reacting to the situation rather than the police employee he is haranguing. The smart employee will endeavor not to make it a contest of wills.
- Be a good listener. The value in letting them vent is that they may be a lot easier to deal with once they have exhausted their supply of venom. Some angry people just want someone to listen to them. Once they're done, at least some of them are easier to handle.
- Try to demonstrate empathy with their situation, insofar as is reasonable under the circumstances. While it never ceases to amaze law enforcement officers just how badly some people can complicate their own lives, many people truly are victims and deserve an empathetic ear. Empathy, of course, is not synonymous with sympathy. By empathizing, an employee is simply indicating that he or she understands WHY the individual is upset.
- Obviously, any law enforcement officer must defend himself if attacked. Absent a physical assault, however, meeting verbal aggression with more aggression probably will accomplish little good. Yelling or cursing back at even the most obnoxious individual is beneath the dignity (and the ethical expectations) of a law enforcement professional.
- To the extent possible, ignore insulting comments and exaggerated statements. It is sometimes helpful to restate the speaker's claim, but in less volatile words. Once again, the police employee's very practical aim is to get past the bombast so the real issue can be addressed.

- Here is an effective response that at times will disarm the most antagonistic complainer: agree with him. If the agency or one of its members actually HAS made a mistake, it is entirely permissible to admit the error. Even more important, it is equally acceptable to offer an apology where one is appropriate. It is not unusual for a law enforcement supervisor to be the one hearing a complaint from a disgruntled citizen. Any experienced supervisor will attest to the value of an expressed apology, even if he or she believes one is only remotely in order. That same veteran supervisor is likely to have more than a few stories of irate complainants and complaints that literally went away following a voiced "I'm sorry." Too many police employees are much too afraid of being sued to admit error when error has been made. Yet this honest response is highly effective when the agency has done less than a flawless job. For most citizens, it is a refreshing and totally unexpected response from a public servant. It works.

- It is acceptable to confront inaccurate statements made by a complainant ("it took you guys an hour to get there"), but the intelligent police person will do so as gently as possible ("it was actually ten minutes, sir, but I know it felt like an hour"). An individual who has just had his face rubbed in his error, particularly in front of other people, is an individual who is unlikely to be easy to work with for the police person doing the rubbing. The wiser course of action is to allow him to save face while still getting the correct facts.

- In defusing an unhappy customer it is often helpful to try and reach agreement on SOMETHING, even if it is no more than concurring that it's a beautiful day. Reaching agreement on even a minor point can sometimes lead to additional agreements on other, more important things as the conversation continues. It is almost always worth a try.

GOOD CALL OR BAD?

Telephone manners, or a lack thereof, are often a very good indicator of the overall health of customer service in a business or government agency. Unfortunately, some callers to the public sector are convinced before they even make the connection that the government employee is going to be abrasive, rude and/or just plain unhelpful on the phone. If the agency being called is part of the criminal justice system, it is just possible that the citizen-caller's expectation for unhelpful discourtesy is even stronger.

Most people, police leaders included, have had the experience of being "serviced" over the telephone by an employee who clearly does not give a damn. Likely, they have communicated this state of mind and attitude as much through their tone of voice as through what they actually had to say. When it comes to customer service, these frontline employees have just made it clear that customer service is the last thing they intend to provide. Often, the caller is made to feel unwelcome, a bother and, perhaps, not too bright.

It is true that some of the callers to law enforcement organizations make serving them courteously more than a little difficult. At the same time, exposure to some basic telephone courtesy can make these callers easier to handle and the whole exchange more pleasant for cop and citizen alike. A few "telephone tricks of the trade" for police employees include the following:

- It may be difficult, but when you are on the telephone try really hard to sound pleasant and upbeat. It can set the tone for the whole conversation.
- Include your name in your telephone greeting. No one likes talking to an anonymous voice at the other end of the line. Again, personalizing the response could set the tone for what follows.
- Be articulate and try not to talk too fast, even though you ARE very busy. You have not saved any time if you have to repeat yourself.
- Minimize interruptions to the extent possible. Avoid carrying on a separate conversation with a colleague when you are on the telephone.
- Avoid abandoning a caller on "eternal hold." No one really likes to listen to elevator music, the local rock station, or even a taped crime prevention message all that much. If there is going to be a delay in getting back to the caller, at least break in and tell him so. You have saved neither time nor effort if a "parked" caller hangs up and calls back because he thinks he has been forgotten or disconnected.
- Consider asking the caller in a courteous manner if he under-

stands what he has been told. Ask if he has any further questions. A caller who calls right back because he is unsure about what he has been told only costs more time and effort. It makes good sense to handle the problem completely the first time.

SUMMARY

Good customer service contains heaping measures of basic courtesy and plain common sense. It really is common in good organizations, law enforcement organizations included. It is not a mysterious or unattainable commodity. In the final analysis, good customer service amounts to little more than a version of the Golden Rule: TREAT OTHERS AS YOU WOULD LIKE TO BE TREATED YOUR-SELF.

The police leader who demands exceptional customer service from his subordinates role models it himself in all of his contacts with his organization's internal as well as external customers. He rewards employees displaying it and he corrects and trains them when he finds it lacking. Information provided in this chapter can be provided to his employees by the leader interested in improving the customer service they provide. It is in this way that he helps assure that law enforcement gets better and his citizen-customers get served in the manner they deserve.

That is, after all, what truly exceptional customer service is about.

POINTS TO REMEMBER

- Many citizens *expect* to receive poor customer service from government employees.
- Law enforcement has customers, too. They are the reason the supervisor has a job.
- Exceptional customer service can pay off in dividends for the agency as well as the person receiving the service.
- Customers want reliability, courtesy, responsiveness, trust, reassurance, empathy and results from their interaction with law enforcement.
- Customers do not want slow service, rudeness, a "can't do" atti-

tude, indifference or someone who won't listen to their story.

- Customers of law enforcement should be listened to carefully, treated as individuals and allowed to save face where possible.
- Angry people test the best supervisor's patience but require his best efforts at restoring calm.
- The supervisor must teach his or her employees to avoid telephone discourtesies.
- The best, single exceptional customer service guideline is to treat customers like you would want to be treated yourself.

Chapter Eighteen

WHERE DO I GO FROM HERE?

G etting there can be half the fun. That old saw can be applied to the law enforcement leader's quest for advancement in his profession.

The law enforcement practitioner who has mastered the huge leap from front-line officer to first-line supervisor already has a major accomplishment under his or her belt. Many successful law enforcement leaders have reported that the next steps are easier. For the supervisor happy to continue in his present, vital role for the rest of his career, no criticism is warranted. All agencies need plenty of competent first-line leaders. But for the man or woman thinking about climbing higher, this chapter will provide sound advice on how to do it.

For the supervisor planning to advance his career to a higher rank, an analysis of the current situation is in order. For one thing, how mobile does he want his career to be? Is he limited to his current employer, is he willing to look externally for advancement or is he willing to do both? He will call on his best judgment and common sense as he sizes things up. He also will need to keep his timeframe in mind. A supervisor nearing the end of his working life likely will have fewer options than will a 25-year-old sergeant.

PLANNING FOR THE FUTURE

The career-planning supervisor will examine carefully the possibilities for advancement in his current agency. A small department that promotes a lieutenant every ten years or so will not offer the advancement opportunities of an agency that promotes several times a year. If the supervisor is seeking a fast track to promotion, he may have to face the challenges of starting over at a new, bigger department.

The smart supervisor also will include his or her significant others in the career planning. If the spouse and/or kids vehemently oppose a long-distance move, the supervisor's choices may be limited. Advancement at work is always a poor tradeoff for disrupted peace on the home front. Leadership career planning always should start with an open and honest discussion at home concerning the changes, good and bad, that promotion will bring. A good leader is not selfish at work. He should not be at home, either.

Constructing a career plan should not preclude the willingness to overreach a bit. There is nothing wrong with a new sergeant in a fifty officer department planning to be chief of the agency one day. Similar scenarios certainly have come to pass many times before. There is also a lot of truth in the old saying "fly for the top of the tree and you're sure to grab at least one of the middle branches." Today's novice sergeant may never make it to chief. Very few do. But he may be quite content to serve as captain one day in the department he really loves. He might not have gotten there had he not set his sights on the top job.

At the same time, the career planner should keep his goals realistic. Today's sergeant at a Nebraska police department of eight sworn personnel is unlikely ever to be chief of the Los Angeles, California Police Department. But if he is bright and willing to work hard, he certainly may head his own agency or a considerably larger one someday. The point is, *today* is the time to start planning and working to get there.

Preparation for a future career does indeed start now. Experience, training and formal education all will contribute to the campaign. Determining where one wants to go and how to get there is a big part of the task, as well. The supervisor needs a more specific goal in mind than "getting as far as I can as quickly as I can." He also needs to have some idea of the timeframe he is thinking about. It is good to be optimistic. It's advisable to be *realistic,* too. The supervisor who plans to advance in rank every two years is probably in for a disappointment in most law enforcement organizations.

Realistic career planning is not selfish. The police supervisor regularly engages in planning in his job as a leader. The only difference is that his career planning is being done for personal benefit as well as for his employer. Career plans may change radically or a little over the span of someone's work life. During that time the supervisor may start down the path to one career ("I want to be an FBI agent when I get my degree") only to find one that he likes better ("I can do my lieutenant's job") during the trip. As noted, sometimes the journey can be as much fun as reaching the destination!

It is also true that career plans are individualized. No one else's career plan will be an exact fit for the law enforcement supervisor. Planning a career is not unlike planning any other long journey: mileposts can help the traveler get there. The first might be finishing that college degree. The second may be competing for lieutenant. The next might be getting an advanced degree in preparation for tackling the captain's promotional process five years down the road. And so on. The idea is to construct a thoughtful plan for what should happen next throughout a long and continuously upward career progression. There doubtlessly will be dead ends and detours, but the trip should continue in the same general direction.

Career planning will take some of the supervisor's personal time and emotional energy, but the effort will be worth it. Planning for the future is an important part of life. Considering the amount of time that today's professional spends at work, failing to plan adequately for that part of the future is an unpardonable sin. The supervisor who only recognizes his error in failing to plan out his career when he is twenty or thirty years farther down the road of life may be more than a little bitter about his lack of attention. By planning now he can avoid that disappointment later when it may be too late to fix the problem.

The supervisor intent on career advancement should be mentally and emotionally prepared *not* to get the prize on the first try. Few well-known homerun hitters blasted the ball out of the park on their very first time at bat. Many promotional candidates do not win the sought-after position the first time out, either. The successful ones are prepared to try again and again, if necessary. Most find that the experience helps them get ready for the next attempt by taking the mystery out of the process. They also get better at handling promotional questions or exercises that they are not seeing for the first time.

Changing one's goals along the career path is acceptable. Being intimidated by the task ahead is not. Surprises and setbacks will occur, as will unexpected opportunities. Obstacles and side trips are inevitable, too. One sergeant was hot on the trail for an upcoming promotion to lieutenant when the department engaged in a downsizing brought about by budget shortfalls. On the other side of the coin, another first-line leader at a small agency was facing years without any planned promotions when an outside career opportunity caused a relatively new commander to depart. The sharp supervisor interested in career advancement always will remain flexible enough to handle the good and bad surprises of the job.

For the supervisor, there should be no guilt attached to wanting more. Moving a qualified leader up the chain of command is how organizations get better. It must be done in order to keep the organization healthy. Fresh eyes and ideas in the middle and upper levels of management are needed to keep the agency's outlook fresh. Indeed, the talented first-line leader who repeatedly refuses to go for advancement may be cheating the organization that employs him. He may truly be a terrific first-line leader of law enforcers. The argument can be made, however, that he would be doing his department even more good by training additional terrific first-line leaders as their boss and role model. He can only do that by moving up.

A good supervisor is not selfish. He recognizes that by advancing his own career he may pull talented and deserving people along with him. If he heads an agency or some branch of it in the future, he may have the opportunity to help prepare these deserving others for their own leadership roles. In addition, by the act of moving up the supervisor likely will open a position under him for a talented up and comer to assume. The law enforcement organization has thereby bettered itself—twice!

The ethical supervisor will not sell his soul in the name of advancement, however. He wants to climb, but he will do it by the rules. He will not resort to shortcuts, trickery, foul play or cheating. The first-line leader who wants to get ahead is good-natured and helpful to his subordinates, peers and bosses. But he does not "brown nose" or pander to get there. Most people, police leaders included, can see through the fakery of a bootlicker. In a good organization, that individual will not get ahead. Loyalty is expected. Enthusiasm is wonderful. Competence is absolutely required. But insincere cheerleading and hero worship of one's boss are death to career advancement in a quality law enforcement organization. Hard work and talent will get the upwardly mobile supervisor where he wants to go. There are no shortcuts for the ethical leader.

TOUCHING ALL THE BASES

The supervisor intent on planning intelligently for the future will be willing to invest some time in researching the possibilities. Unless he has some sort of ogre or other dysfunctional personality as his own superior, the first-line leader might start by seeking his boss's advice on career goals. It is likely that the boss already has trod at least some of the path that the supervisor is thinking about following. He or she may be able to share some personal insights on the right and wrong ways to make the journey. The boss also may be willing to relate some experiences illustrating pitfalls to avoid along the way.

Most leaders are willing to discuss their own up-through-the-ranks experiences with interested subordinates, if for no other reason than it gives them an opportunity to talk about their favorite subject: themselves. Even if he does not accept at face value everything the boss has to say, the supervisor can learn a lot by asking questions and listening carefully to the responses. On occasion, he may decide he wants to take exactly the opposite route to career advancement that the boss followed. But he would not be in a position to make that decision if he did not first ask and listen.

Since a competent law enforcement supervisor is already a pretty good judge of people, he should be able to detect the rare boss who really doesn't want to be bothered with helping a career-minded subordinate. Thus alerted, the supervisor can address his career-oriented queries elsewhere. It remains true that the majority of police leaders will be only too happy to help. The supervisor simply needs to ferret out a "good fit" for himself who is willing to assist.

THE RIGHT AND WRONG WAYS

Just as there are many things the supervisor intent on climbing the advancement ladder must do, there are a number of career killers he must avoid. One of the first requirements for a supervisor who desires a job with greater responsibilities is to see to it that he is doing an excellent job of handling his current tasks. Bosses know that most of the time what a person is doing now is a good indicator of what he will do in the future. As a consequence, they are unlikely to promote someone who is careless, complacent or just plain lazy with his current responsibilities. The supervisor who wants to get noticed for the future will do his best now. That may sound like leadership propaganda, but it is the truth.

The supervisor intent on organizational advancement will avoid coming to management's attention for the *wrong* reasons. He will never criticize his organization or its leaders in public. That is a cardinal rule. He will not run with a group of rabble-rousers, gripers and malcontents. He won't affect an "angry young rebel" personality or be seen as a chronic whiner. His knack for organizational survival also will tell him not to ally himself with a mentor seen as a "problem" in the organization. The last thing he wants is to be seen as a problem child himself. The top leaders of the organization are looking for people to make their lives easier, not more difficult. A subordinate supervisor identified as trouble is unlikely to be promoted. In fact, he may find it increasingly difficult to keep his current rank.

Everyone makes mistakes. That reality is a part of the increasingly complicated profession of law enforcement. The advancement-minded supervisor will admit mistakes, do what he can to fix or mitigate them and then move on without losing his positive outlook. Bosses often watch how a subordinate handles adversity, including negative discipline meted out by the employer. A subordinate leader who takes a temporary setback in stride without losing his upbeat outlook or his work ethic may be marked for advancement even ahead of the employee who never messed up at all but risked little in going by the book. In good organizations, initiative is valued even when it occasionally results in a misstep. Good leaders recognize that the best intentions sometimes result in unintended consequences. They realize that *they* make mistakes, too.

The first-line leader already knows the importance of role modeling the behavior he expects of his subordinates. His bosses know the value of setting a good example, too. He will be scrutinized for any indications of poor character or lapses of good judgment in his personal or professional life. Sometimes an interview for a top law enforcement management position will include this question: "Is there anything in your background that, if it came to light, would cause embarrassment for you and this organization?" The top management wannabe must live his life in such a way that he can respond with a quick "no" to that query.

If the position being sought is of widespread public or organizational interest, it is possible that competitors for the position, other employees, the union or the news media will examine the promotional applicant's personal and professional background for flaws. That may not be fair, but it is one of life's realities. The important thing is that the dirt search is an unsuccessful one. The hard-working, ethical law enforcement supervisor should have nothing to worry about.

There are any number of things today's corporal or sergeant can do on the fast track to become tomorrow's lieutenant, commander or captain. Department-sponsored leadership classes can be helpful and also display the employee's interest in advancement. Continuing education classes at community colleges and universities also can prove useful as well as showcase the student's intentions. The same holds true for outside, advanced classes in leadership sponsored by such organizations as the Police Executive Research Forum and the International Association of Chiefs of Police. Course offerings from PERF and the IACP can be found on the two organizations' web sites.

Good police organizations are interested in preparing the next generation's leaders. Sometimes all one has to do is ask to be sent to advanced leadership training. More than a few law enforcement CEOs have complained about their employees' perceived lack of interest in training that does not include technical skills or officer survival on the agenda. Interest shown by the upwardly-mobile employee should get noticed.

The supervisor with his sights set on career advancement will be aware of the educational requirements of the position he is seeking. More and more agencies are requiring a college degree for leadership positions. Even more are likely to do so in the future. They also require that leaders must be able to communicate effectively, especially using the written word. College training can contribute greatly to that ability.

The supervisor intent on organizational advancement also will take every opportunity to do oral presentations in front of diverse groups. He knows he will get more competent with practice, and with increased competence comes increased comfort. Volunteering to appear in front of news media representatives can build confidence in his speaking abilities, too. The promotion-bound leader will volunteer for those "meet the press" moments rather than avoid them. Once again, practice makes for a more polished presenter who is more likely to get noticed for the *right* reasons.

While it may run contrary to everything the supervisor learned as a street cop, *volunteering* to handle tasks that will make his boss's life a little easier is a great way to get noticed. Many of law enforcement's top leaders admit to being "suckers" for enthusiasm displayed by their subordinates. It tells them that this is somebody who is excited about the job and will get things done. This is an employee they are likely to watch for future possibilities. The sharp promotional candidate knows this and will seek projects to handle and problems to solve for the boss. His willingness to take on challenges that he does not *have* to face sets him apart as an enthusiastic, energetic problem-solver likely to get noticed. If the problem or project he has just taken on makes his boss's life better, he has just reaped the proverbial double-whammy of positive strokes!

Writing assignments that he can assign to a subordinate with the knowledge that they will get done correctly and on time tend to warm a boss's heart. The same holds true for well-done budgeting and grant-writing tasks. The key, of course, is that the jobs are done well and do not have to be corrected.

It is absolutely necessary that the supervisor interested in career advancement let his bosses know of his interest. They may have career advice that will prove extremely helpful. Finding a coach and mentor also can help to advance a career. The best law enforcement leaders sincerely *want* to help prepare the next generation of leaders who eventually will replace them. They have an interest in securing the organization's future and want to leave it in good hands. They know that selecting and preparing their replacements will help accomplish that goal.

The supervisor's best approach for securing a teacher and mentor is also the easiest and most honest one. He will approach the chosen individual, express his interest in advancement and ask for guidance. Good leaders are willing, even anxious, to help. The rare, retired on-the-job leader generally will communicate his lack of interest by words or demeanor which the alert supervisor will detect. The supervisor can then move on to the next possibility while maintaining a courteous relationship with his initial contact. The smart supervisor does not burn bridges that can be salvaged.

In talking with an experienced law enforcement leader who is also a mentor, the supervisor can learn a lot about that individual's route to his present post. How did he get there? What did he (or she) do and avoid doing? What painful lessons did he pick up along the journey that an attentive listener can avoid having to learn the hard way?

A good mentor also can provide a respectful, interested supervisor with the political lay of the land of the organization to which they both belong. What are the behind the scenes relationships? What are the cardinal sins in the eyes of the agency's leaders? What is the quickest way to find oneself in career Hell? On rare occasions, what the listener learns may convince him that he really does not *want* to advance, at least not in that agency. (That realization will present him with yet another career decision to make.) Much more often, however, the information learned from his mentor will aid him in better preparing for advancement. In the meantime, the interest and respect he has accorded the mentor likely will have the added benefit of placing that individual in his camp for the future.

There is no reason, of course, that the supervisor interested in advancing his career should limit himself to the teachings of one individual, no matter how highly-valued that person's advice may be. It is a good idea to seek the counsel and experiences of others who already have traveled the route that the supervisor wants to go. All of these people can provide information. Some may proffer examples of practices to avoid. The observant supervisor can learn something from each one. The individual who listens more than he talks can assemble priceless data that will help him immeasurably on his climb.

The thinking lawman or woman doubtlessly has put a great deal of effort into planning where he or she wants to be at the end of a badge-toting career. This same individual may have given less attention to where he wants to be during the rest of an increasingly lengthy lifespan. Thanks to medicine's advances, second and even third careers are within reach for many today.

Career planning for the law enforcement leader of the twenty-first century should include planning for life beyond the badge. While some law enforcement retirees have found great satisfaction in teaching and consulting in the criminal justice arena, others have experienced equally satisfying lives in fields totally unrelated to the work they did for twenty-five years or more.

The good news is that today's law enforcement retirees have more good choices than ever about what to do with their remaining years. One thing is certain, however. There is solid evidence that keeping one's mind active and focused often helps keep the brain healthy late into life. By remaining active both mentally and physically, today's contributing police supervisor will be tomorrow's contributing police retiree.

GOING ALL THE WAY

Whether they will admit it or not, most law enforcement officers believe that they could run the organization that they are a part of better than the individual who presently is doing so. Perhaps it has to do with their "take charge" personality type. Maybe it has something to do with the cynical view of life that some possess. Whatever the case, more than a few cops would like to be the Big Boss one day. Most will never make a serious effort to get there. But for many who have the ability as well as the desire, the goal is within reach, if not at their own agency then at another, perhaps smaller one.

The vast majority of American law enforcement agencies employ 25 officers or fewer. There are thousands of small- and medium-sized law enforcement agencies in the United States. So, there are potentially a lot of top leadership jobs out there for the person willing to relocate. Large states such as Texas and California have many hundreds of law enforcement agencies, each of which requires a leader. On any given day a number of law enforcement CEO jobs at the local level are advertised as "open" in those two states alone. Many others likewise need filled across the nation. For the upwardly-mobile law enforcement supervisor willing to move and go through the peace officer licensing process outside his home state, the possibilities are numerous.

Each law enforcement leader must decide for himself if the position of head of a police organization is really what he is seeking. Almost without exception he can anticipate more prestige along with a better salary accompanying the CEO position. What he can also expect is longer hours and a lot more work. He will be even more in the public eye than he was as a first-line leader. He may face less physical danger; he will encounter more of the political variety. He probably will not enjoy the protection of civil service or a union contract. Indeed, some have compared the chief's or sheriff's job security with that of a professional sports team coach: he is only as good as his most recent season. He can lose his job over something a member of his agency did (or didn't do) in spite of having no connection to the incident himself. In other words, the supervisor can count on losing some job security as the price for advancing to the peak of the organizational pyramid.

At the same time, the potential rewards can be great for the supervisor seeking the top rung on the ladder. For the man or woman harboring the desire to change an organization for the better while helping society as a whole, there is no better opportunity to do so than as the person in charge of a law enforcement entity. Here his or her ideas can be put into play for better or worse. Here lies the chance to make a difference.

All of this is within reach for many law enforcement supervisors. Getting there may require movement outside of one's current organization as well as one's comfort zone, but the opportunity is present. Career planning will be required, as will hard work. But the goal is within reach for many. The first step is for the supervisor to decide *now* that is where he wants to go. The subsequent steps are milestones for the journey.

The supervisor interested in becoming the head of a law enforcement agency must be willing to devote a lot of personal time to the effort. He will need to stay up with current events in the geographic area that he is interested in. The news can tell him when a top job is open—or about to be—and why. Professional journals such as the IACP's *The Police Chief* carry CEO position announcements from around the nation. For the supervisor focused on a particular state or region, oftentimes municipal, county and state organizations maintain web sites describing current top job openings. For example, the Texas Municipal League maintains a web site that lists top cop jobs available statewide. In addition, the web sites of professional organizations like the International Association of Chiefs of Police and the Police Executive Research Forum often list open executive positions for law enforcement agencies around the country.

Leaders interested in being the top dog one day also stay plugged into local and area networks of police leaders who are in the know about top leadership jobs. (They know because some of *them* are looking, too.) Chiefs' associations often permit memberships for leaders who are not yet CEOs themselves.

Executive search consultants are good people to know for the individual wishing to lead an agency one day. The wise police supervisor will keep an up-to-date resume on file with some of these people and make telephone or e-mail contact with them periodically. The best executive search consultants pride themselves on their "stable" of top-notch chief executive candidates. An industrious supervisor interested in a chief executive's job will be in that file.

There are publications available that will help the candidate for a law enforcement top leadership post get ready for the competition—and what comes after he wins all the marbles. Two excellent books, *Command Performance* and *Managing for Success: A Police Chief's Survival Guide* are available from the Police Executive Research Forum. Each should be in the serious competitor's personal library.

The law enforcement supervisor on the way up cannot afford to be bashful or falsely modest. He needs to be aggressive without being obnoxious; persistent without becoming a pest. He knows that desirable positions will not come looking for him. It is up to him to seek and win them.

The importance of a good resume cannot be stressed too much. The resume and its accompanying letter of introduction often will determine whether or not the candidate gets an interview with the hiring authority. Resume reviewers can be ruthless. Many will quickly discard a resume that looks messy or is otherwise difficult to read. For example, documents with small or hard to read type often get tossed. If there are a large number of applicants, reviewers may scan rather than read for details. They will not give applicants the benefit of the doubt. All by itself, a poorly prepared resume will stop the position seeker from progressing to the next stage of the chief hiring process.

There are many good publications and helpful web sites dealing with the preparation of an effective resume. Law enforcement professional groups often publish information on resume preparation, too. Additionally, there are several common sense guidelines that the supervisor can rely on in assembling a resume that stands out—for the right reasons:

- Twelve point type is best.
- Arial, New Roman or a very similar type face is easiest to read.
- Omit photos and personal information such as hobbies, number of children.
- Cite the most recent work experience and work back in chronological order.

- Do not overuse the word "I."
- Never use a generic resume; tailor it to the desired executive position.
- Try to keep it to a maximum of three pages.
- Do not use a lot of graphics or artwork.
- Proof, proof and proof again for spelling errors and other mistakes.
- Tell the truth and do not exaggerate accomplishments.
- Be sure that personal contact information is provided and is correct.

From his experience in gaining supervisory rank, the chief executive applicant is already knowledgeable about the interview or oral board process. Still, brushing up on those skills via some practice will strengthen the applicant's chances. It also is a good idea to do enough research to determine the current issues in the agency and community doing the hiring. Thus prepared, the candidate can craft his presentation to include what he would do to address those problems. His responses will be more effective because he has had the opportunity to consider and plan them in advance.

Likewise, the exceptionally well-prepared candidate will have planned and practiced what he will say if given the chance to make a closing statement at the conclusion of the interview. He may want to use this brief time to reemphasize the three or four main things he wants the interviewers to remember about him after he has left the room. Again, he will devise his closing statement to fit the local situation and the positive role he will play in addressing it. For instance, the supervisor applying for the CEO slot in an agency recently besieged by serious employee misconduct might touch on these key points:

1. My personal integrity is absolutely above reproach.
2. I will hold myself and my people strictly accountable for our actions.
3. You will see specific, positive changes in the department within 30 days if you hire me.

Since the individuals doing the hiring are seeking a leader that will make their own lives easier, these words will cheer their organizational hearts. The supervisor who wins the job now needs only to make the words come true. For the law enforcement leader who already has proven himself in his rise from front-line service provider, getting it done again will become reality!

SUMMARY

The law enforcement supervisor's career planning begins today and should continue throughout a long work life. Periodic reassessment and redirection may be required, but planning must continue all the same. Challenges and even opposition are likely to be encountered en route, but the effective supervisor is a stranger to neither. He should not underestimate his own abilities in seeking advancement. By making contacts, gathering information and seeking advice from reliable sources he will close the gap between himself and his next career advancement post. By avoiding personal and career mistakes he will continue to prepare himself for the next higher step on the career ladder.

The upward-climbing supervisor will hone his communication and leadership skills throughout a career. He will volunteer for greater responsibilities and prepare himself to assume his boss's job one day. He will not underestimate the possibilities or his own abilities. For many leaders, winning the position of head of the organization is not beyond reach.

POINTS TO REMEMBER

- Career planning for the supervisor begins today and continues for the rest of his or her working life.
- Targets and goals may change over the length of a career.
- Planning for the future requires hard work, including the willingness to continue one's education.
- Serious errors in personal or professional life can derail a career plan, but many missteps can be overcome.
- Finding the right mentor can boost the supervisor's opportunities for career advancement.
- Volunteering for extra assignments can help the supervisor glean the added experience he needs for advancement.

- Assuming he wants the job, becoming head of a law enforcement agency is not beyond the reasonable expectations of the industrious career planner.

INDEX

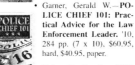
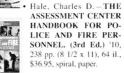

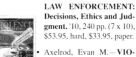
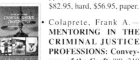